DATE DUE

Ethics, the Heart of Leadership

Second Edition

Edited by Joanne B. Ciulla

Foreword by James MacGregor Burns

Westport, Connecticut
London

Library of Congress Cataloging-in-Publication Data

Ethics, the heart of leadership / edited by Joanne B. Ciulla ; foreword by
   James MacGregor Burns.—2nd ed.
      p. cm.
   Includes bibliographical references and index.
   ISBN 0–275–98248–3 (alk. paper)—ISBN 0–275–98252–1 ((pbk) : alk. paper)
   1. Business ethics. 2. Leadership—moral and ethical aspects. I. Ciulla,
   Joanne B.
   HF5387.E875 2004
   174'.4—dc22   2004009602

British Library Cataloguing in Publication Data is available.

Library of Congress Catalog Card Number: 2004009602
ISBN: 0–275–98248–3
      0–275–98252–1 (pbk.)

First published in 2004

Praeger Publishers, 88 Post Road West, Westport, CT 06881
An imprint of Greenwood Publishing Group, Inc.
www.praeger.com

Printed in the United States of America

The paper used in this book complies with the
Permanent Paper Standard issued by the National
Information Standards Organization (Z39.48-1984).

10 9 8 7 6 5 4

For James MacGregor Burns

Contents

Foreword

If you're teaching a class in leadership and wish to start up a lively discussion, try posing that old chestnut of a question: "Was Adolf Hitler a leader?" The last time I tried this, in an honors course at the University of Maryland, a woman student vehemently answered "YES"—bad as he was, she said, he mirrored the hopes and hates of the German people, he won elections, and he fulfilled his promises by changing Germany along the lines his followers wanted—how could he not be called a leader? She had the class all but convinced and almost me. Almost.

It was not, of course, that she was in any way pro-Hitler, who stands as the most universally detested man in history. The problem was not confusion about Hitler but about the true nature of leadership. One of the many virtues of this excellent collection is Joanne Ciulla's confrontation at the outset of the question, what constitutes a good leader? This central question raises further questions about ethical and moral leadership. The problem is that in this book, and in many others on leadership, the richness and heterogeneity of the field of leadership have led to great confusion about the difference between ethical and moral leadership; some use the terms interchangeably, in this volume and elsewhere.

I discern three types of leadership values: *ethical* virtues—"old-fashioned character tests" such as sobriety, chastity, abstention, kindness, altruism, and other "Ten Commandments" rules of personal conduct; *ethical* values such as honesty, integrity, trustworthiness, reliability, reciprocity, accountability; and *moral* values such as order (or security), liberty, equality, justice, community (meaning brotherhood and sister-hood, replacing the traditional term *fraternity*).

Each of these types of leadership values has implications for styles and strategies of leadership itself. *Status-quo* leaders, presiding over relatively stable communities, are dependent on ethical virtues, rules of personal behavior, such as kindness and altruism, that make for harmo-nious communal relationships. *Ethical values* are crucially important to transactional leaders, whether in politics or education or other fields, who must depend on partners, competitors, clients, and others to live up to promises and understandings, as they themselves must. Respon-sibility and accountability are the tests here. *Moral values* lie at the heart of transforming leadership, which seeks fundamental changes in soci-ety, such as the enhancement of individual liberty and the expansion of justice and of equality of opportunity.

Wouldn't it be lovely, in this fragmented world, if all these three sets of values, and hence all these forms of leadership, could exist in happy harmony? Alas, it cannot be. The more that a community embraces *ethical* virtues of mutual helpfulness, the more it is likely to come into conflict with the ethical virtues of other communities—for example, in business practices, or in religious dogma and behavior. *Ethical* values, too, tend to be culture-based and hence diverse. One society's honesty is another society's incivility; one society's reciprocity is another society's corruption.

Consider the question of manipulation—"managing" other persons' motives—which is so crucial to transactional leadership. Over three de-cades ago, in the April 1965 issue of *Journal of Social Issues*, Herbert Kelman, recognizing increasing concern over ethical problems in the study of behavioral change, saw a basic dilemma: "On the one hand, for those of us who hold the enhancement of man's freedom of choice to be a funda-mental value, any manipulations of the behavior of others constitutes a violation of their essential humanity. . . . On the other hand, effective behavior change inevitably involves some degree of manipulation and control, and at least an implicit imposition of the change agent's values on the client or the person he is influencing." In short, a dilemma.

Of my three sets of values I would guess that ethical values are most diverse among cultures. While ethical virtues have had far more rele-vance to modern market societies than to Third or Fourth World "tra-ditional" cultures, transactional leadership values may become more universal as markets and privatization become more global. What about *moral* values? One might assume, in this ideologically torn world, with its fierce religious and secular conflicts, that moral values might be the most multifarious of all.

I believe, however, that the people of the world, even under diverse leaders, have been—slowly, gropingly, tortuously—shaping and rank-ordering sets of supreme principles. I believe the Enlightenment values of liberty, equality, and fraternity (community) are still evocative and controlling for vast numbers of people in the Western world at least. I believe that life, liberty, and the pursuit of happiness not only dominate the American "mass mind" but that of most other societies in the West. Despite numerous violations of its terms, the UN's "Universal Declaration of Human Rights" continues as a moral standard for most nations of the world.

Moral values are not only standards by which we measure our character, our transactions, our policies and programs. They may also contain enormously evocative and revitalizing ideas, for which men and women fight and die. Hence they can serve as transforming forces. But much depends on a crucial step—to translate ideals into action, promises into outcomes, "to walk the talk." Joanne Ciulla wrote me: "You have to make a lot of assumptions to make a value *do* something. You have to assume that because people value something they act accordingly, but we know this isn't the case. Value articulations of ethics often leave the door open for hypocrisy. Many people sincerely value truth, but often lie. People can also tell the truth, but not value it" (Correspondence, March 1997). The test lies in *outcomes*—real, intended, and durable change.

And what is the relationship of all these values to *vision*? We think of vision as an overarching, evocative, energizing, moralizing force, ranging from broad, almost architectural plans for a new industry, say, to an inspirational, spiritual, perhaps morally righteous evocation of future hopes and expectations for a new political movement. Visions are often projected by charismatic leaders, calling for mass mobilization and action over the long run on many fronts, perhaps even for a revolution. To the extent that vision is transformational—that is, calls for real change—must it not embody supreme values in some kind of hierarchy? Otherwise would not vision be a kind of loose cannon, lurching back and forth as the visionary leaders follow their own guiding stars?

Another question posed by visionary leadership is the balance of cognitive and affective forces in change decisions. That visionary leadership embraces much that is spiritual and even emotional its proponents do not deny—they assert it. They like to point to Thomas Jefferson's famed dialogue between "the Head and the Heart" as proof that even a great Enlightenment rationalist understood the place of sentiment in the affairs of state, as well as the affairs of people.

So was Adolf Hitler a leader, measured by those three levels of values? He was a terrible mis-leader: personally cruel and vindictive, politically duplicitous and treacherous, ideologically vicious and annihilative in his aims. A leader of change? Yes, he left Germany a smoking devastated land. My student may have Hitler—I'll take Gandhi, Mandela, and King.

James MacGregor Burns

Acknowledgments

The first edition of this book emerged from the Kellogg Leadership Studies Project (KLSP), which was initiated by the Center for Political Leadership and Participation at the University of Maryland, College Park, and a special issue of the *Business Ethics Quarterly*. The essays by Al Gini, Bob Solomon, and my essay "Leadership and the Problem of Bogus Empowerment" came out of the focus group that I convened for this project on ethics and leadership. These papers were initially published in a set of working papers by the KLSP. I am grateful to the Kellogg Foundation for its support of the KLSP. The articles by Edwin P. Hollander and Michael Keeley and my article, "Leadership Ethics: Mapping the Territory," were first published in *The Business Ethics Quarterly* (Vol. 5, No. 1, January 1995). My thanks to David C. Smith, who edited this extraordinary issue on ethics and leadership.

There are three new additions to the collection. Terry L. Price's piece is from an article that he wrote for a special issue on ethics and leadership that I edited for *The Leadership and Organization Development Journal* (4/21/2000). I am grateful to the editor, Susan Cartwright, for giving me the opportunity to pull together the work of such talented scholars. The other new articles in this edition, by Bernard M. Bass and Paul Steidlmeier and by Bruce J. Avolio and Edwin E. Locke, are from *The Leadership Quarterly*.

I also want to thank all contributors to this volume. It was an honor and a pleasure to work with them. I am grateful to my husband, René Kanters, who helped prepare the manuscript; Cassie King for editorial assistance; and my editor for the first edition, Alan Sturmer. A special thanks goes to Praeger editor Hilary Claggett for suggesting a second edition and the editor for this book, Nick Philipson.

I am indebted to my friend and colleague James MacGregor Burns for rethinking his foreword to the book and for the many years of conversation and correspondence that we have had on ethics and leadership. While we don't always agree on things, we both share the passionate belief that ethics are at the heart of leadership.

Introduction

Some people become leaders because they develop or possess certain talents and dispositions, charisma, or passions, or because of their wealth, military might, job title, or family name. Others lead because they possess great minds and ideas or they tell compelling stories. And then there are those who stumble into leadership because of the times they live in or the circumstances in which they find themselves. No matter how people become leaders, no one is a leader without willing followers. Managers and generals may act like playground bullies and use their power and rank to force their will on people, but this is coercion, not leadership. Leadership is not a person or a position. It is a complex moral relationship between people, based on trust, obligation, commitment, emotion, and a shared vision of the good. Ethics is about how we distinguish between right and wrong, or good and evil in relation to the actions, volitions, and character of human beings. Ethics lie at the heart of all human relationships and hence at the heart of the relationship between leaders and followers. The essays in this volume explore the ethical complexities of leadership.

I dedicated this book to James MacGregor Burns because his theory of transforming leadership rests on the ongoing moral relationship of leaders and followers. In his book, *Leadership,* Burns describes transforming leadership as a relationship in which leaders and followers morally elevate each other. Leadership for Burns is about change and sharing common purpose and values. The transforming leader helps people change for the better and empowers them to improve their lives and the lives of others.

In the foreword to this book, Burns laments that the authors in this volume do not make a crisp distinction between ethical and moral leadership, and that they fail to use the terms consistently. If you look up the words, you will see that ethics is defined as morals and morals as ethics. In ancient times the Romans translated the Greek word *ethikos* into the Latin word *morale*. In the foreword Burns' definitions of *ethical virtues*, *ethical values*, and *moral values* differ from the way other writers in this book define them; but rather than quibble over terms, let us look at what he means. For Burns, the values of moral leadership are those of the Enlightenment—liberty, equality, and community. This is a big-picture view of the ultimate ends of leadership. Most authors in this book probably believe in these ideals, just as they would agree that leaders should be honest, fair, and just. Nevertheless, in ethics, as with many other things, the devil is in the details. The essays in this book probe the details of the many aspects of ethics and leadership.

In the beginning, I said no one is a leader without willing followers. Most people agree that coercion is not leadership, but what is coercion and what is a willing follower? How do we draw the moral line between free will and subtle forms of manipulation, deception, and the pressure that group norms place on the individual? Similarly, few would argue with Burns' idea that the leadership relationship should be one that morally elevates both parties, but again, the details matter. Elevate from what to what? Who determines which moral values are better and what are the criteria for better values? What if people don't want to be elevated, or what if they incorrectly understand the common good? Authors in this collection treat these questions in different ways.

The essays in this book touch on three very general facets of ethics and leadership.

1. The ethics of the means: What do leaders use to motivate followers to obtain their goals? What is the moral relationship between leaders and followers?
2. The ethics of person: What are leaders' personal ethics? Are they motivated by self-interest or altruism?
3. The ethics of the ends: What is the ethical value of a leader's accomplishments? Did his/her actions serve the greatest good? What is the greatest good? Who is and isn't part of the greatest good?

These may all seem like obvious questions until you consider cases in which a leader is ethical in some of these areas but not others. For example, some leaders may be personally ethical but use unethical means to achieve ethical ends; other leaders may be personally unethical, but use ethical means to achieve ethical ends, etc. This raises the question: Do leaders have to be ethical in all three areas to be ethical? Some might argue that the only thing that matters is what the leader accomplishes. Others might argue that the means and ends are ethically important, but the personal morality of a leader is not.

The chapters in this book look at ethics through different lenses. Four of the contributors are philosophers, four are distinguished leadership scholars with backgrounds in industrial and organizational psychology, and two are management scholars. Burns and all of the contributors in this book cast their ideas about ethics in slightly different terms.

Part one of the book provides two overviews of ethics and leadership, one from the perspective of leadership studies and one from business ethics. In the first chapter, I argue that a greater understanding of ethics will improve our understanding of leadership. Debates about the definition of leadership are really debates over what researchers think constitutes good leadership. The word *good* refers to both ethics and effectiveness. Some things have changed since I first wrote this chapter. There is more research on ethics and leadership today and, as illustrated by the other new additions to this book, leadership scholars have begun to pay more attention to ethics. Al Gini's essay explores the intersection of business ethics and leadership studies. He offers an excellent profile of the issues and literature in both fields. Gini emphasizes the role that "the witness of moral leadership" plays in improving the standards of business and everyday life.

Part two is about the relationship between leaders and followers. Noted leadership scholar Edwin P. Hollander takes us into the psychological and moral depths of leadership. He describes the leader-follower relationship as a unified interdependent relationship held together by loyalty and trust, and rooted in the leader's commitment to principles of justice, equity, responsibility, and accountability in the exercise of authority and power. Hollander examines the moral hazards of leaders who feel the need to maintain power and distance and become detached from how followers feel about them and their actions. He says that this pattern can be especially damaging to teamwork when leaders continue to receive disproportionate rewards despite their poor performance, especially when coupled with organizational downsizing and layoffs.

My chapter on "bogus empowerment" is about honesty and the distribution of power in the leader-follower relationship. Burns' theory of transforming leadership emphasizes the importance of morally improving followers so that they can lead themselves. This is a very good idea, but what does it really mean to give followers power? And why is it so difficult for leaders to give people power? In the chapter I examine the failure of empowerment schemes in the workplace and argue that empowerment that attempts to change workers without changing leaders, and empowerment aimed at making people feel good but not at giving them resources and real discretion, are bogus. Authentic empowerment requires honesty and a full understanding of how the redistribution of power changes the leader-follower relationship.

Robert C. Solomon's chapter analyzes the role of emotions in the leader-follower relationship. He begins by exploding what he calls the myth of charisma. According to Solomon, charisma is not a quality of a leader's character, nor is it an essential element of leadership. He believes it is a general and "vacuous" way of talking about the complex emotional relationship of leaders to followers that is empty of moral content. He argues that trust is the emotional core of the leader-follower relationship and that we can better understand this relationship by looking at how the leaders and the led give trust to others.

The next part of this book is new. It describes the moral behavior of leaders. In it, Bruce J. Avolio and Edwin E. Locke debate whether a leader has to be altruistic to be ethical. Avolio makes the case that leaders who are altruistic are ethical, and they are successful *because* they are altruistic. Locke, a professor and senior writer for the Ayn Rand Institute, argues that altruistic leaders are unethical and that ethical leaders should be self-interested. Terry L. Price's article takes a different view of leaders' ethics and intentions. He believes that the moral behavior of leaders goes beyond the motives of altruism and self-interest. He says that the moral failures of leaders are usually cognitive. According to Price, leaders consciously act in unethical ways because power and position lead them to believe that they are not bound by the requirements of morality. His paper examines the intellectual challenges of leadership that make leaders susceptible to ethical failure.

The last part of the book is about the conflicts between leaders and groups of followers over what constitutes the common good. Popular media, communitarian writers, and recent management literature suggest that communities and organizations are rife with social interest groups who pursue their own selfish interests without regard for the common good. Burns and other scholars believe transformational leadership offers a solution to this problem because it refocuses people's attention on higher goals and collective interests. Michael Keeley thinks this is a dangerous solution, one that James Madison and the Constitutional Convention of 1787 sought to thwart. Using examples from the organizational literature as well as history, Keeley argues that it is better to accommodate factions and individual interests by building them into the leader-follower relationship. For Keeley, a system of checks and balances is morally better than transforming people so that they share the same higher collective goals. In his essay, Keeley explains the implications of this approach for leadership in organizations and political theory. In another new addition to the book, Bernard M. Bass and Paul Steidlmeier defend transformational leadership from Keeley and other critics. This is an important essay because in it, Bass changes one feature of his theory on transformational leadership. In his earlier work, Bass' theory was morally neutral. Transformational leaders could be good or evil. In this chapter, Bass and Steidlmeier argue that only ethical leaders are authentic transformational leaders. Self-aggrandizing and immoral leaders are pseudo-transformational leaders. By the end of Bass and Steidlmeier's chapter, the differences between Bass' transformational theory and Burns' transforming leadership theory seem significantly narrower than they were in the past. The argument that only ethical leaders are really transformational raises a whole new set of questions. Once again, the devil is in the details.

What is clear from this book is that the morality of leadership depends on the particulars of the relationship between people. It matters who the leaders and followers are and how well they understand and feel about themselves and each other. It depends on whether leaders and followers are honest and trustworthy, and most importantly what they do and what they value. Behind all of these things are broad philosophic questions such as: What is the common good? Do people have free will? How should we treat one another? These are eternal questions that have kept generations of leaders and thinkers up late at night. This book probes what the answers to these questions mean for today's leaders. They offer the reader hands-on insights into the ethical dynamics that make the heart of leadership tick.

Part I

The Scope of the Issues

Leadership Ethics: Mapping the Territory

Joanne B. Ciulla

We live in a world where leaders are often morally disappointing. Meticulous biographers sometimes diminish the image of great leaders such as Martin Luther King, Jr., and George Washington by probing their ethical shortcomings. It's difficult to have heroes in a world where every wart and wrinkle of a person's life are public. Ironically, the increase in information that we have about leaders has increased the confusion over the ethics of leadership. The more defective our leaders, the greater our longing to have highly ethical leaders. The ethical issues of leadership not only are found in public debates but lie simmering below the surface of the existing leadership literature.

Most scholars and practitioners who write about leadership genuflect at the altar of ethics and speak with hushed reverence about its importance to leadership. Somewhere in almost any book devoted to the subject, one finds either a few sentences, paragraphs, pages, or even a chapter on how integrity and strong ethical values are crucial to leadership. Yet, given the central role of ethics in the practice of leadership, it's remarkable that there has been little in the way of sustained and systematic treatment of the subject by scholars. A literature search of 1800 article abstracts from psychology, business, religion, philosophy, anthropology, sociology, and political science yielded only a handful of articles that offered any in-depth discussion of ethics and leadership.

Articles on ethics and leadership are either about a particular kind of leadership (i.e., business leadership or political leadership) or a particular problem or aspect of leadership, or they are laudatory articles about the importance of honesty and integrity in leadership. There are also a number of studies that measure the moral development of managers.[1] The state of research on leadership ethics is similar to the state of business ethics 20 years ago. For the most part, the discussion of ethics in the leadership literature is fragmented; there is little reference to other works on the subject, and one gets the sense that most authors write as if they were starting from scratch.

In this chapter, I map the place of ethics in the study of leadership. I argue that ethics is located in the heart of leadership studies and not in an appendage. This chapter consists of three parts. The first part discusses the treatment of ethics within existing research in leadership studies. In the second part, I look at some discussions concerning the definition of leadership and locate the place of ethics in those discussions. In the third part, I examine two normative leadership theories and use them to illustrate how more rigorous work in the area of leadership ethics will give us a more complete understanding of leadership itself.

Throughout the chapter, I use the term *leadership ethics* to refer to the study of the ethical issues related to leadership and the ethics of leadership. The study of ethics generally consists of the examination of right, wrong, good, evil, virtue, duty, obligation, rights, justice, fairness, etc. in human relationships with each other and other living things. Leadership studies, either directly or indirectly, try to understand what leadership is and how and why the leader-follower relationship works (i.e., What is a leader and what does it mean to exercise leadership? How do leaders lead? What do leaders do? Why do people follow?).[2] Since leadership entails distinctive kinds of human relationships with distinctive sets of moral problems, I thought it appropriate to refer to the subject as *leadership ethics*; however, my main reason for using the term is that it is less awkward than using expressions such as *leadership and ethics*.

TREATMENT OF ETHICS IN LEADERSHIP STUDIES

Ethics without Effort

Ethics is one of those subjects that people rightfully feel they know about from experience. Most people think of ethics as practical knowledge, not theoretical knowledge. One problem in applied ethics is that scholars from other fields sometimes feel that their practical knowledge and common sense (and exemplary moral character) are adequate for a discussion of ethics in their area of research. Their research is sometimes good, sometimes awful, but without some background in ethics, it is simply not very informative. Philosophical writings on ethics are frequently (and sometimes understandably) ignored or rejected because they appear obtuse and irrelevant to people writing about ethics in their own area of research or practice.[3]

What is striking about leadership studies is not the absence of philosophic writings on ethics, but the fact that authors expend so little energy on researching ethics from any discipline. To some extent this is even true of Joseph Rost's book, *Leadership in the Twenty-First Century*, which contains one of the better critiques of the field of leadership studies. I will frequently comment on Rost's book in this chapter because it is an important new contribution to the field. It is extensively researched and contains a terrific 24-page bibliography. However, the chapter on ethics stands out because of its paucity of references. After a very quick run through utilitarian, deontic, relativistic, and contractarian ethics, Rost concludes that "None of the ethical systems is particularly valuable in helping leaders and followers make decisions about the ethics of the changes they intend for an organization or society."[4] He condemns all ethical theories as useless, using only two books, James Rachels' *The Elements of Moral Philosophy* and Mark Pastin's book, *The Hard Problems of Management*.[5,6]

Scholars who either reject or ignore writings on ethics usually end up either reinventing fairly standard philosophic distinctions and ethical theories, or doing without them and proceeding higgledy-piggledy with their discussion. Rost concludes his chapter on ethics: "Clearly, the systems of ethical thought people have used in the past and that are still in use are inadequate to the task of making moral judgments about the content of leadership."[7] Citing the work of Robert Bellah et al., William Sullivan, and Alasdair MacIntyre, Rost proposes "a new language of civic virtue to discuss and make moral evaluations of the changes they [leaders] intend."[8] (He fails to notice that the language of civic virtue is quite old.) After dismissing ethical theory, Rost goes on to say that out of this new language there will "evolve a new ethical framework of leadership content, a system of ethical thought applied to the content of leadership, that actually works."[9] Rost does not really tell us what will take the place of all the theories that he has dismissed, but rather he assures us that a new system of ethics will emerge. At least Rost pays some attention to the literature in ethics; however, he spends most of his time throwing it out and then runs out of steam when it comes to offering anything concrete in regard to leadership, except for some form of communitarianism.

Another more significant example of the paucity of research energy expended on ethics is *Bass & Stogdill's Handbook of Leadership*, hailed by reviewers as "the most complete work on leadership" and "encyclopedic."[10] This is considered the source book on the study of leadership. The text is 914 pages and contains a 162-page bibliography. There are 37 chapters, none of which treat the question of ethics in leadership. If you look ethics up in the index, five pages are listed. Page 569 contains a brief discussion of different work ethics, page 723 is a reference to the gender differences in values, and page 831 refers to a question raised about whether sensitivity training is unethical. The reader has to reach a subsection of the last chapter called "Leadership in the Twenty-First Century" before there is a two page exposition on ethics. What we are treated to on the first page of the handbook is a meager grabbag of empirical studies and one fleeting reference to the James MacGregor Burns argument that transformational leaders foster moral virtue.[11]

The empirical studies include a 1988 Harris poll of 1031 office workers that revealed 89 percent of employees thought it was important for managers to be honest, upright and so on; J. Weber's study of 37 managers that led to the conclusion that managers reasoned to conform to majority opinion rather than universal rules;[12] and Kuhnert and Lewis' discussion of how transformational leaders develop and move up Kohlberg's scale from concern for personal goals to higher levels of values and obligations.[13] Final references are to a study of seven mainland Chinese factories, hospitals, and agencies, which included, among many other questions, survey questions on the character function of leadership and moral character.[14] The last part of this subsection on ethics contains a paragraph describing how professional associations such as the American Psychological Association set standards of ethical behavior.

The second section on ethics, "A Model for Ethical Analysis," sounds more promising. Bass, the author, defines ethics as a "creative searching for human fulfillment and choosing it as good and beautiful." He goes on to argue that professional ethics focuses too much on negative vices and not on the good things. Bass' definition of ethics and sole reference on ethics in this section is taken from *The Paradox of Poverty: A Reappraisal of Economic Development Policy* by Paul Steidlmeier.[15] The model for ethical analysis that it suggests "determines the connection between moral reasoning and moral behavior and how each depends on the issue involved."[16] After reading these two pages, one gets little information about ethics and leadership.[17] Most remarkable about this section of the book is that it offers little insight into what the questions are in this area. It is not surprising that the standard reference work on leadership does not carry much information on ethics, in part because not much research is available.[18] Nonetheless, for all of the research that went into this book, Bass seems to wing it when it comes to talking about ethics.[19]

Leadership and the Rosetta Stone

As Rost points out in his book, one of the problems with leadership studies is that most of the work has been done from one discipline and a large part of the research rests on what he calls the industrial para-digm, which views leadership as good management.[20] (Bass and Stogdill are both management scholars.) Rost also criticizes the field for overemphasis on things that are peripheral to leadership such as traits, group facilitation, effectiveness, or the content of leadership, which includes the things that leaders must know to be effective.[21] This is clearly the case if you look at the contents of Bass and Stogdill. The largest section in the book is on the personal attributes of leaders.

Marta Calas and Linda Smircich also offer a provocative critique of the field that indirectly helps to explain why there has been little work on ethics in leadership studies. Along with Rost, they point out the positivist slant in much of the leadership research (particularly research on leadership in psychology and business). According to Calas and Smircich, the "saga" of leadership researchers is to find the Rosetta stone of leadership and break its codes. They argue that since the research community believes that society puts a premium on science, researchers' attempts to break the Rosetta stone have to be "scientific." Hence the "scientists" keep breaking leadership into smaller and smaller pieces until the main code has been lost and can't be put together.[22] This fragmentation accounts for one of the reasons why Rost urges us to focus the essence of leadership, and it also explains why there is so little work on ethics and leadership. Ethical analysis generally requires a broad perspective on a practice. For example, in business, ethical considerations of a problem often go hand in hand with taking a long-term view of a problem and the long-term interests of an organization.

Calas and Smircich also observe that the leadership literature seems irrelevant to practitioners, whereas researchers don't feel like they are getting anywhere—nobody seems happy. They believe that leadership researchers are frustrated because they are trying to do science, but they know they aren't doing good science. The researchers are also trying to do narrative, but the narrative is more concerned with sustaining the community of researchers than helping explicate leadership. Calas and Smircich, like Rost, point to the necessity of a multidisciplinary ap-proach to leadership. All three scholars emphasize the importance of narratives such as case studies, mythology, and biography in under-standing leadership.

It is interesting to note that the two most respected and quoted figures in leadership studies, John W. Gardner and James MacGregor Burns, both take a somewhat multidisciplinary approach to the subject. John W. Gardner's book, *On Leadership,* is a simple and readable outline of the basic issues in leadership studies. Gardner writes as a practitioner. He has held many distinguished posts in the government and in busi-ness and has taught at Stanford. He offers a good commonsense discussion of ethics and leadership in his chapter "The Moral Dimension." The phrase, "the moral dimension of leadership," is now frequently used in the leadership literature. The conceptualization of morality as a *dimension* of leadership, rather than a part or element, is significant in that it implies that it is another way of seeing the whole of leadership rather than simply investigating a part of it.[23]

Gardner's chapter on ethics is a thoughtful piece that uses examples from several disciplines. It is often quoted because Gardner is a talented wordsmith; he uses engaging examples, and he offers wisdom that comes from experience. Gardner lines up the usual suspects of evil leadership, such as Hitler and the Ku Klux Klan, and peppers his discussion with a diverse set of examples from history and politics. For the most part, his discussion of ethics is hortatory. He says that we should hope that "our leaders will keep alive values that are not so easy to embed in laws—our caring for others, about honor and integrity, about tolerance and mutual respect, and about human fulfillment within a framework of values."[24] Gardner offers some good advice on ethics, but that's about all.

James MacGregor Burns' book, *Leadership,* is considered by many to be the best book to date on leadership. Burns, a political scientist, historian, and biographer, is probably the most referenced author in leadership studies. Burns' theory of transforming leadership is built around a set of moral commitments. I will discuss Burns' work later in this chapter because his work is central to my contention that ethics is at the heart of leadership.

In this section I have discussed some representative examples of the ways in which ethics has been treated in the leadership literature. Most of what is considered leadership literature comes from the social sciences of psychology, business, and political science. The scarcity of work done on leadership in the humanities is another reason why there is little done on ethics. Burns, the most quoted scholar in the field, takes a multidisciplinary approach to leadership. However, it is not the number of disciplines that makes Burns's work compelling, it is the fact that he tries to understand leadership as a whole and not as a combination of small fragments.

Paradigm, Shifting Paradigm, or Shifty Paradigm?

For an investigation into leadership ethics to be meaningful and useful, it must to be embedded in the study of leadership. Again, it is worthwhile to make an analogy to business ethics. If courses and research on business ethics ignore existing business research and practice, then the subject of ethics would become a mere appendage, a nice but not a crucial addition to a business school curriculum and our knowledge about business. Research and teaching in areas like business ethics and leadership ethics should aim not only at making business people and leaders more ethical, but at reconceptualizing the way that we think about the theory and practice of business and leadership. This is why both areas of applied ethics have to embed themselves into their respective fields.[25]

There are two ways to understand the current state of leadership studies using Thomas Kuhn's analysis in *The Structure of Scientific Revolutions*. Given the criticisms of the field, one might argue that there exists a paradigm of leadership studies, based primarily on the work done in business and psychology.[26] Kuhn says that one way you can tell if a paradigm has been established is if scientists enhance their reputations by writing journal articles that are "addressed only to professional colleagues, the men whose knowledge of a shared paradigm can be assumed. . ." Before the establishment of a paradigm, writing a textbook would be prestigious, because you would be making a new contribution to the field.[27, 28] Using Kuhn's criteria, there is evidence for the existence of a paradigm of leadership studies. The evidence is Bass and Stogdill's handbook (now in its third edition), various symposia on leadership,[29] the kinds of leadership articles that are accepted to journals, and the literature that is cross-referenced in these journals.

According to Kuhn, when a paradigm is established and researchers engage in "normal science," there is little discussion of rules or definitions because they become internalized by researchers working in that paradigm. Kuhn says, "lack of a standard interpretation or of an agreed reduction to rules will not prevent a paradigm from guiding research."[30] He points out that over time, the meaning of important terms can shift along with theories, which seems to be what has happened in leadership studies. Kuhn believes that scientific progress would be impeded if the meaning of terms were overly rigid.

Rost criticizes some research in leadership studies because researchers don't define leadership. But as Kuhn points out, this sort of definition is not really necessary if researchers are working in a paradigm, because definitions are internalized and unarticulated. Rost's second charge is that researchers all have different definitions of leadership and that the field cannot progress unless there is a shared definition of leadership.[31] If Rost is correct and researchers have radically different definitions of leadership (meaning that leadership denotes radically different things), then either there never was a well-formed paradigm (so leadership studies is in a preparadigm phase), or there exists a paradigm, and that paradigm is shifting. In both cases, there would be considerable debate over definitions. However, if there is a paradigm of sorts and researchers are still arguing over definitions, then there is a third alternative. There is a paradigm of leadership studies but it is a shifty one. By that I mean, scholars don't really trust this paradigm, but they nonetheless stick to it and keep doing research in the same old ways.[32]

LOCATING ETHICS

What Do the Definitions Really Tell Us?

Leadership scholars have spent a large amount of time and trouble worrying about the definition of leadership. Rost analyzes 221 definitions to make his point that there is not a common definition of leadership. What Rost does not make clear is what he means by a definition. Sometimes he sounds as if a definition supplies necessary and sufficient conditions for identifying leadership. He says: "Neither scholars nor the practitioners have been able to define leadership with precision, accuracy, and conciseness so that people are able to label it correctly when they see it happening or when they engage in it."[33] He goes on to say that the various publications and the media all use leadership to mean different things that have little to do with what leadership really is.[34] In places Rost uses the word *definition* as if it were a theory or perhaps a paradigm. He says that a shared definition implies that there is a "school" of leadership. When the definition changes, there is a "paradigm shift."[35]

Rost's claim that what leadership studies needs is a common definition of leadership is off the mark for two reasons. One would be hard-pressed to find a group of sociologists or historians who shared the exact same definition of sociology or history. It is also not clear that the various definitions that Rost examines are that different in terms of what they denote. I selected the following definitions from Rost's book on the basis of what Rost says are definitions most representative of each particular era. We need to look at these definitions and ask: Are these definitions so different that there is no family resemblance between them? (i.e., Would researchers be talking about different things?)[36] What do these definitions tell us about different periods of history? What do these definitions tell us about the place of ethics in leadership studies?

1920s	[Leadership is] the ability to impress the will of the leader on those led and induce obedience, respect, loyalty, and cooperation.[37]
1930s	Leadership is a process in which the activities of many are organized to move in a specific direction by one.[38]
1940s	Leadership is the result of an ability to persuade or direct men, apart from the prestige or power that comes from office or external circumstance.[39]

1950s   [Leadership is what leaders do in groups.] The leader's au-
          thority is spontaneously accorded him by his fellow group
          members.[40]

1960s   [Leadership is] acts by a person, which influence other per-
          sons in a shared direction.[41]

1970s   Leadership is defined in terms of discretionary influence.
          Discretionary influence refers to those leader behaviors
          under control of the leader, which he may vary from individ-
          ual to individual.[42]

1980s   Regardless of the complexities involved in the study of lead-
          ership, its meaning is relatively simple. Leadership means to
          inspire others to undertake some form of purposeful action
          as determined by the leader.[43]

1990s   Leadership is an influence relationship between leaders and
          followers who intend real changes that reflect their mutual
          purposes.[44]

If we look at the sample of definitions from different periods, we see
that the problem of definition is not that scholars have different meanings of leadership. Leadership does not denote radically different
things for different scholars. One can detect a family resemblance
between the different definitions. All of them talk about leadership as
some kind of process, act, or influence that in some way gets people to
do something. A roomful of people, each holding one of these definitions, would understand each other.

The definitions differ in their connotation, particularly in terms of
their implications for the leader-follower relationship. In other words,
how leaders get people to do things (impress, organize, persuade, influence, and inspire) and *how* what is to be done is decided (forced
obedience or voluntary consent, determined by the leader, and as a
reflection of mutual purposes) have normative implications. Perhaps
what Rost is really talking about is not definitions, but theories about
how people lead (or how people should lead) and the relationship of
leaders and those who are led. His critique of particular definitions is
really a critique of the way they do or don't describe the underlying
moral commitments of the leader-follower relationship.[45]

If the preceding definitions imply that leadership is some sort of
relationship between leaders and followers in which something happens or gets done, then the next question is: How should we describe
this relationship? For people who embrace the values of a democratic
society such as freedom, personal autonomy, and equality, the most
morally unattractive definitions are those that appear to be coercive,
manipulative, and dictatorial. Rost clearly dislikes the theories from the
1920s, 1970s, and 1980s, not because they are inaccurate, but because he

rejects the authoritarian values inherent in them.[46] Nonetheless, theories from these decades may be quite accurate descriptions of the way some corporate and world leaders behaved back then and today.

The most morally attractive definitions hail from the 1940s, 1950s, 1960s, and Rost's own definition of the 1990s. They imply a noncoercive participatory and democratic relationship between leaders and followers. There are two morally attractive elements of these theories. First, rather than *induce*, these leaders *influence*, which implies that leaders recognize the autonomy of followers. Rost's definition uses the word influence, which carries an implication that there is some degree of voluntary compliance on the part of followers. In his chapter on ethics, Rost says: "The leadership process is ethical if the people in the relationship (the leaders and followers) *freely* agree that the intended changes fairly reflect their mutual purposes."[47] For Rost, consensus is an important part of what makes leadership leadership, and it does so because free choice is morally pleasing. The second morally attractive part of these definitions is that they imply recognition of the beliefs, values, and needs of the followers. Followers are the leader's partners in shaping the goals and purposes of a group or organization.

The morally attractive definitions also speak to a distinction frequently made between leadership and headship (or positional leadership). Holding a formal leadership position or position of power does not necessarily mean that a person exercises leadership. Furthermore, you do not have to hold a formal position to exercise leadership. Leaders can wield force or authority using only their position and the resources and power that come with it.[48] This is an important distinction, but it does not get us out of "the Hitler problem," that is, how do you answer the question, "Is Hitler a leader?" Under the morally unattractive definitions he is a leader, perhaps even a great leader, albeit an immoral one. Ron Heifetz argues that under the great man and trait theories of leadership, you can put Hitler, Lincoln, and Gandhi in the same category because the underlying value of the theory is that leadership is influence over history.[49] However, under the morally attractive theories, Hitler is not a leader at all. He's a bully or tyrant or simply the head of Germany.

To muddy the waters even further, according to one of Warren Bennis' and Burt Nanus' characterizations of leadership—"The manager does things right and the leader does the right thing"—one could argue that Hitler is neither unethical nor a leader; he is a manager.[50] Bennis and Nanus are among those management writers who talk as if all leaders are wonderful and all managers morally flabby drones. However, what appears to be behind this in Bennis and Nanus' work is the idea that leaders are supposed to be morally a head above everyone else.[51]

So what does this all mean? It looks like we are back to the problem of definition. The first and obvious meaning is that definitions of leadership have normative implications (the old, "there is no such thing as a value-free social science"). Leadership scholars such as Bennis and Nanus are sloppy about the language they use to describe and prescribe. While it is true that researchers have to be clear about when they are describing and when they are prescribing, the crisp fact/value distinction will not in itself improve our understanding of leadership.

Leadership scholars who worry about constructing the ultimate definition of leadership are asking the wrong question, but inadvertently trying to answer the right question. As we have seen from the examination of definitions, the ultimate question in leadership studies is not "What *is* the definition of leadership?" The ultimate point of studying leadership is "What is *good* leadership?" The use of the word *good* here has two senses; morally good and technically good or effective. These two senses form a logical conjunction. In other words, for the statement "She is a good leader" to be true, it must be true that she is effective and she is ethical.[52] The question of what constitutes a good leader lies at the heart of the public debate on leadership. We want our leaders to be good in both ways. It's easy to judge if they are effective, but more difficult to judge if they are ethical because there is some confusion over what factors are relevant to making this kind of assessment.

Ethics and Effectiveness

The problem with the existing leadership research is that few studies investigate both senses of good and when they do, they usually do not fully explore the moral implications of their research questions or their results. The research on leadership effectiveness touches indirectly on the problem of explicitly articulating the normative implications of descriptive research. The Ohio and Michigan studies both measured leadership effectiveness in terms of how leaders treated subordinates and how they got the job done. The Ohio studies measured leadership effectiveness in terms of consideration, the degree to which leaders act in a friendly and supportive manner, and initiating structure, or the way that leaders structure their own role and the role of subordinates in order to obtain group goals.[53] The Michigan studies measured leaders on the basis of task orientation and relationship orientation.[54] These two studies generated a number of other research programs and theories, including the situational leadership theory of Hersey and Blanchard, which looks at effectiveness in terms of how leaders adapt their leadership style to the requirements of a situation. Some situations require a task orientation, others a relationship orientation.[55]

Implicit in all of these theories and research programs is an ethical question. Are leaders more effective when they are nice to people, or are leaders more effective when they use certain techniques for structuring and ordering tasks?[56] One would hope that the answer is both, but that answer is not conclusive in the studies that have taken place over the last three decades. According to Gary Yukl, the only consistent findings that have come from this research is that considerate leaders usually have more satisfied followers.[57] The interesting question is, What if this sort of research shows that you don't have to be kind and considerate of other people to run a country or a profitable organization? Would scholars and practitioners draw an *ought* from the *is* of this research?[58] It's hard to tell when researchers are not explicit about their ethical commitments. The point is that no matter how much empirical information we get from the "scientific" study of leadership, it will always be inadequate if we neglect the moral implications. The reason why leadership scholarship has not progressed very far is that most of the research focuses on explaining leadership, not understanding it.[59]

The discussion of definition locates where some of the ethical problems are in leadership studies. As we have seen, ethical commitments are central to how scholars define leadership and shape their research. Leadership scholars do not need to have one definition of leadership to understand each other; they just need to be clear about the values and normative assumptions that lie behind the way that they go about researching leadership.[60] By doing so, we have a better chance of understanding the relationship between what leadership is and what we think leadership ought to be.[61] This state of affairs would represent a marked shift in the existing Bass/Stogdill-type paradigm (and maybe finally put to rest the pretensions of value-free social science).

THE NORMATIVE THEORIES

Transforming Leadership

So far we have located the place of leadership ethics in definitions and in some of the empirical research on leadership. Now we look at two normative leadership theories.

James MacGregor Burns' theory of transforming leadership is compelling because it rests on a set of moral assumptions about the relationship between leaders and followers.[62] Burns' theory is clearly a prescriptive one about the nature of morally *good* leadership. Drawing from Abraham Maslow's work on needs, Milton Rokeach's research on values development, and research on moral development from Lawrence Kohlberg, Jean Piaget, Erik Erickson, and Alfred Adler, Burns argues that leaders have to operate at higher need and value levels than those of followers.[63] A leader's role is to exploit tension and conflict within people's value systems and play the role of raising people's consciousness.[64]

In Burns' account, transforming leaders have very strong values. They do not water down their values and moral ideals by consensus, but rather they elevate people by using conflict to engage followers and help them reassess their own values and needs. This is an area where Burns differs from Rost. Burns writes that "despite his [Rost's] intense and impressive concern about the role of values, ethics and morality in transforming leadership, he underestimates the crucial importance of these variables." Burns goes on to say, "Rost leans towards, or at least is tempted by, consensus procedures and goals that I believe erode such leadership."[65]

The moral questions that drive Burns' theory of transforming leadership come from his work as a biographer and historian.[66] When biographers or historians study a leader, they struggle with the question of how to judge or keep from judging their subject. Throughout his book, Burns uses examples of a number of incidents where questionable means, such as lying and deception, are used to achieve honorable ends or where the private life of a politician is morally questionable.[67] If you analyze the numerous historical examples in Burns' book you find that two pressing moral questions shape his leadership theory. The first is the morality of means and ends (and this also includes the moral use of power) and the second is the tension between the public and private morality of a leader. His theory of transforming leadership is an attempt to characterize good leadership by accounting for both of these questions.

Burns' distinction between transforming and transactional leadership and modal and end-values offers a way to think about the question, "What is a good leader?" in terms of the relationship to followers and the means and ends of actions. Transactional leadership rests on the values found in the means of an act. These are called modal values and include responsibility, fairness, honesty, and promise-keeping, among others. Transactional leadership helps leaders and followers reach their own goals by supplying lower level wants and needs so that they can move up to higher needs. Transforming leadership is concerned with end-values, such as liberty, justice, and equality. Transforming leaders raise their followers up through various stages of morality and need.[68] They turn their followers into leaders and the leader becomes a moral agent.

As a historian, Burns is very concerned with the ends of actions and the change that they initiate. In terms of his ethical theory, at times he appears to be a consequentialist, despite his acknowledgment that, "insufficient attention to means can corrupt the ends."[69] However, because Burns does not really offer a systematic theory of ethics in the way that a philosopher might, he is difficult to categorize. Consider, for example, Burns' two answers to the Hitler question. In the first part of the book, he says quite simply that once Hitler gained power and crushed all opposition, he was no longer a leader. He was a tyrant.[70] Later in the book, he offers three criteria for judging how Hitler would fare before "the bar of history." Burns says that Hitler would probably argue that he was a transforming leader who spoke for the true values of the German people and elevated them to a higher destiny. First, he would be tested by modal values of honor and integrity or the extent to which he advanced or thwarted the standards of good conduct in humankind. Second, he would be judged by the end-values of equality and justice. Last, he would be judged on the impact that he had on the well-being of the people he touched.[71] According to Burns, Hitler would fail all three tests. Burns doesn't consider Hitler a leader or a transforming leader because of the means that he used, the ends that he achieved, and the impact of Hitler as a moral agent on his followers during the process of his leadership.[72]

By looking at leadership as a process and not a set of individual acts, Burns' theory of good leadership is difficult to pigeonhole into one ethical theory and warrants closer analysis. The most attractive part of Burns' theory is the idea that a leader elevates his or her followers and makes them leaders. Near the end of his book, Burns reintroduces this idea with an anecdote about why President Johnson did not run in 1968. Burns tells us: "Perhaps he did not comprehend that the people he had led—as a result in part of the impact of his leadership—had created their own fresh leadership, which was now outrunning his." All of the people that Johnson helped—the sick, the blacks and the poor—now had their own leadership. Burns says: "Leadership begat leadership and hardly recognized its offspring. Followers had become leaders."[73]

Burns' theory has inspired a number of descriptive studies on transformational and leadership. For example, Bernard Bass studies transformational leadership in terms of the impact of leaders on their followers. In sharp contrast to Burns, Bass removes Burns' condition that leaders have to appeal to higher order needs and values. Bass was originally willing to call Hitler a transformational leader, but in his work in the late 1990s he argues that unethical leaders like Hitler are not authentic transformational leaders but rather pseudo-transformational leaders.[74] A number of other researchers are writing about transformational leadership, including Judith Rosner, who uses transformational leadership as a means for understanding how women lead.[75]

The other area of research related to transformational leadership is charismatic leadership. Charismatic leaders, according to Jay Conger, "hold certain keys to transformational processes within organizations."[76] Bass believes that charismatic leadership is a necessary ingredient of transformational leadership.[77] Research on charismatic leadership opens up a wide range of ethical questions because of the powerful emotional and moral impact that charismatic leaders have on followers.[78] Charismatic leadership can be the best and the worst kind of leadership, depending on whether you are looking at a Gandhi or a Charles Manson.[79] Leadership ethics clearly finds a place in this literature where the moral problems are near the surface, but not explicitly explored.

Servant Leadership

The second example of a normative theory of leadership is servant leadership. Robert K. Greenleaf's book, *Servant Leadership: A Journey into the Nature of Legitimate Power and Greatness,* presents a view of how leaders ought to be. However, the best way to understand servant leadership is to read *Journey to the East*, by Hermann Hesse.[80] Hesse's story is about a spiritual journey to the East. On the journey, a servant named Leo carries the bags and does the travelers' chores. There is something special about Leo. He keeps the group together with his presence and songs. When Leo mysteriously disappears, the group loses their way. Later in the book the main character, HH, discovers that the servant Leo was actually the leader. The simple but radical shift in emphasis is from followers serving leaders to leaders serving followers. It is a very old normative view of leadership that can be found in ancient Eastern and Western thought.

Servant leadership has not gotten as much attention as transformational leadership in the literature, but students and business people often find this a compelling characterization of leadership.[81] According to Greenleaf, the servant leader leads because he or she wants to serve others. People follow servant leaders freely because they trust them. Like the transforming leader, the servant leader elevates people. Greenleaf says servant leadership must pass this test: "Do those served grow as persons? Do they *while being served* become healthier, wiser, freer, more autonomous, more likely themselves to become servants?" He goes on and adds a Rawlsian proviso, "*And*, what is the effect on the least privileged in society?"[82] As normative theories of leadership, both servant leadership and transforming leadership are areas of leadership ethics that are open to ethical analysis and provide a rich foundation of ideas for developing future normative theories of leadership.

CONCLUSION: ETHICS AT THE HEART OF LEADERSHIP

In this chapter I have mapped the territory of ethics in leadership studies. I have argued that the definition question in leadership studies is not really about the question, "What is leadership?" It is about the question, "What is *good* leadership?" By good, I mean morally good and effective. This is why I think it's fair to say that ethics lies at the heart of leadership studies. Researchers in the field need to get clear on the ethical elements of leadership in order to be clear on what the term *leadership* connotes.

Existing theories and empirical literature have strong normative implications that have not been fully developed by their authors. A second place for ethics in leadership studies is expanding the ethical implications of these theories and research findings. Normative theories of leadership, such as transforming leadership and servant leadership, are not well developed in terms of their moral implications. They require more analysis as ethical theories and more empirical testing. One reason why the body of research on transformational leadership looks promising is that it contains empirical research on a theory that was constructed to address some of the basic moral challenges of leadership. It offers a richer understanding of leadership than theories that are just about ethics or just about leader behavior.

Leadership ethics can also serve as a critical theory that opens up new kinds of dialogues among researchers and practitioners. Lastly, work in leadership ethics should generate different ways of thinking about leadership and new ways of asking research questions. To some extent, the ideas of servant leadership and transforming leadership have already done this.

The territory of ethics lies at the heart of leadership studies and has veins that run though all leadership research. Ethics also extends to lands waiting to be explored. As an area of applied ethics, leadership ethics needs to take into account research on leadership, and it should be responsive to the pressing ethical concerns of society. Today the most important and most confusing public debate is over what ethical issues are relevant in judging whether a person *should* lead and whether a person is capable of leadership. Research into leadership ethics would not only help us with questions like, "What sort of person should lead?" and "What are the moral responsibilities of leaders and followers?" It should give us a better understanding of what leadership is and what it ought to be.

NOTES

1. These Kohlberg-type studies can be interesting for leadership ethics if you put all these studies together. However, taken one by one, they give a very small snapshot of a group. Kohlberg's work on moral development also has the problems that Carol Gilligan has articulated. A number of philosophers also have problems with Kohlberg's description of the highest stage of development. Nonetheless, some of the most fascinating research that uses this approach is

cross-cultural. For example, see: Sara Harkness, Carolyn Pope Edwards, and Charles M. Super, "Social Roles and Moral Reasoning: A Case Study in a Rural African Community," in *Developmental Psychology*, vol. 17, no. 5 (1981): 595–603. Also see: Anne Marie Tietjen and Lawrence J. Walker, "Moral Reasoning and Leadership Among Men in a Papu New Guinea Society," *Developmental Psychology*, vol. 21, no. 6 (1985): 982–992.

2. Many areas of leadership literature from psychology focus on different types of relationships. For example contingency theories focus on the relationship of the leader and the group in a given situation. See Fred Fiedler, *A Theory of Leadership Effectiveness* (New York: McGraw-Hill, 1967), and Victor H. Vroom and Paul W. Yetton, *Leadership and Decision-Making* (Pittsburgh: University of Pittsburgh Press, 1973). The vertical dyad linkage model focuses on dyads such as the relationship between leaders and managers. See: Fred Dansereau, Jr., George Graen, and William J. Haga, "Vertical Dyad Linkage Approach to Leadership within Formal Organizations: A Longitudinal Investigation of the Role Making Process," *Organizational Behavior and Human Performance*, 13 (1975): 46–78.

3. Some of the most frequently cited ethics texts in leadership articles and books are from business ethics. The reasons for this might be that researchers are often in business schools, business ethics texts are written for a broad audience, and the content of business ethics research into managerial ethics and organizational ethics is relevant to leadership.

4. Joseph Rost, *Leadership for the Twenty-First Century* (New York: Praeger, 1991), 172.

5. James Rachels, *The Elements of Moral Philosophy* (New York: Random House, 1986). Mark Pastin, *The Hard Problems of Management: Gaining the Ethics Edge* (San Francisco: Jossey-Bass, 1986). I am not arguing about the quality of these books, but rather the quantity of research done by Rost.

6. The chapter also contains pronouncements, and generalizations are not well supported. For example, he says: "The first thing that I want to emphasize is that the ethics of what is intended by leaders and followers in proposing changes may not be the same as the ethics of those changes once they have been implemented. This troubling distinction is not often developed in books on professional ethics, but it does turn up time and time again in real life" (Rost, 168). A number of Kantians who write about professional ethics would take issue with this claim.

7. Rost, 177.

8. Ibid., 177. The works cited in his argument are Robert Bellah et al., *Habits of the Heart* (New York: Harper & Row, 1985); William M. Sullivan, *Reconstructing Public Philosophy* (Berkeley: University of California Press, 1986); and Alasdair MacIntyre, *After Virtue* (South Bend, IN: University of Notre Dame Press, 1984). Rost seems to miss the point that all three of these books are reapplications of older traditions of ethics. Bellah et al. and Sullivan make this point clear in their books. Rost does not discuss virtue ethics in this chapter, so it is not clear whether he means to discard this too when he rejects "ethical theory."

9. Ibid., 177.

10. Bernard M. Bass, *Bass & Stogdill's Handbook of Leadership*, 3rd edition (New York: The Free Press, 1990). The quotes are taken from the back jacket of the book.

11. From James MacGregor Burns' book, *Leadership* (New York: Harper Torchbooks, 1978).

12. J. Weber, "Managers and Moral Meaning: An Exploratory Look at Managers' Responses to Moral Dilemmas," *Proceedings of the Academy of Management* (Washington, DC: Academy of Management, 1989), 333–37.

13. K. W. Kuhnert and P. Lewis, "Transactional and Transformational Leadership: A Constructive/Developmental Analysis," *Academy of Management Review*, vol. 12 (1987): 648–57.

14. M. F. Peterson, R. L. Phillips, and C. A. Duran, "A Comparison of Chinese Performance Maintenance Measures with US. Leadership Scales," *Psychologia— An International Journal of Psychology in the Orient*, vol. 32 (1989): 58–70.

15. P. Steidlmeier, *The Paradox of Poverty: A Reappraisal of Economic Development Policy* (Cambridge, MA: Ballinger, 1987).

16. Bass and Stogdill, 906.

17. This is not to say that articles that are cited in Bass and Stogdill are not good, but rather, they are focused studies that taken together would not give the reader much of a perspective on ethics as it pertains to leadership.

18. For example, John Gardner is well known in the leadership area. His leadership paper, "The Moral Aspect of Leadership," was published in 1987. Burns' book was published in 1978 and contained a wealth of references that might have been useful.

19. Bass is working on a 4th edition of *Bass & Stogdill's Handbook of Leadership*, and he promises to offer a more extensive discussion of ethics and leadership.

20. Rost, 27.

21. Ibid., 3.

22. Marta Calas and Linda Smircich, "Reading Leadership as a Form of Cultural Analysis," in James G. Hunt, B. Rajaram Baliga, H. Peter Dachler, and Chester A. Schriesheim, eds., *Emerging Leadership Vistas* (Lexington, MA.: Lexington Books, 1988), 222–26.

23. For example see, Thomas Sergiovanni, *Moral Leadership* (San Francisco: Jossey-Bass, 1992), xiii. Sergiovanni argues that "rich leadership practice cannot be developed if one set of values or one basis of authority is simply substituted for another. What we need is an expanded theoretical and operational foundation for leadership practice that will give balance to a full range of values and bases of authority." He refers to this expanded foundation as the *moral dimension in leadership*.

24. John Gardner, *On Leadership* (New York: Free Press, 1990), 77.

25. Since most of my work has been in business ethics, I use that field as an example. Few philosophers would attempt to write about a topic in business ethics without doing research into that area of business, yet a number of business scholars over the years have felt no discomfort over writing about business ethics without doing research into ethics. If you look at what is considered the best work in business ethics, you will not find research that is only business or only philosophical ethics. A good example of the ideal mix is Ed Freeman and Dan Gilbert's *Corporate Strategy and the Search for Ethics* (Englewood Cliffs, NJ: Prentice Hall, 1988).

26. Extensive work has been done on leadership in political science, but this research is not well integrated into the business/psychology literature. One might argue that because the discussion of leadership is so much a part of political science, it is not noticeable as a separate field, except perhaps for presidential studies. It is, however, interesting to note that Barbara Kellerman's anthology on political leadership is interdisciplinary. See, Barbara Kellerman, ed., *Political Leadership: A Source Book* (Pittsburgh: University of Pittsburgh Press, 1986). It draws from political science, philosophy, economics, history, and sociology. Yet if one looks at the references in Bass and Stogdill, the lion's share of them are from management and psychology and very few from political science or other fields. Extensive work has also been done on leadership in military

academies. For example see, Howard Prince and associates, eds., *Leadership in Organizations*, 3rd edition (West Point, NY: United States Military Academy, 1988).

27. Thomas Kuhn, *The Structure of Scientific Revolutions* (Chicago: University of Chicago Press, 1970), 20.

28. A recent example of a leadership textbook is Richard Hughes, Robert Ginnett, and Gordon J. Curphy, *Leadership: Enhancing the Lessons of Experience* (New York: Irwin, 1993).

29. James G. Hunt has published eight collections of symposia papers on leadership. Note the language in the titles of these books, "Current Developments," "Leadership Frontiers," "The Cutting Edge," "Beyond Establishment Views," and "Emerging Vistas." One senses that Hunt is trying to capture something that keeps falling through scholars' fingers like sand. These are the 8 collections: E. A. Fleishman and J. G. Hunt, eds., *Current Developments in the Study of Leadership* (Carbondale, IL: Southern Illinois Press, 1973); J. G. Hunt and L. L. Larson, eds., *Contingency Approaches to Leadership* (Carbondale, IL: Southern Illinois Press, 1974); J . G. Hunt and L. L. Larson, eds., *Leadership Frontiers* (Carbondale, IL: Southern Illinois Press, 1975); J. G. Hunt and L. L. Larson, eds., *Leadership: The Cutting Edge* (Carbondale, IL: Southern Illinois Press, 1977); J. G. Hunt and L. L. Larson, eds., *Crosscurrents in Leadership* (Lexington, MA: Lexington Books, 1979); J. G. Hunt, U. Sekaran, and C. A. Schriesheim, eds., *Leadership: Beyond Establishment Views* (Lexington, MA: Lexington Books, 1982). J. G. Hunt, D. M. Hosking, C. A. Schriesheim, and R. Stewart, eds., *Leaders and Managers: International Perspectives on Managerial Behavior and Leadership* (New York: Pergamon Press, 1984); James G. Hunt, B. Rajaram Baliga, H. Peter Dachler, and Chester A. Schriesheim, eds., *Emerging Leadership Vistas* (Lexington MA: Lexington Books, 1988).

30. Kuhn, 20.

31. Rost, 6–7.

32. In J. G. Hunt's symposia (opus cited) and in other articles on leadership, scholars constantly lament that they have done so much studying and know so little about leadership. Yet the same scholars who lament this fact do little to change the way that they do research.

33. Rost, 6.

34. Ibid.

35. Ibid., 99.

36. The theory of meaning that I have in mind is from Ludwig Wittgenstein, *Philosophical Investigations*, tr. G. E. M. Anscomb, 3rd edition (New York: Macmillan 1968), 18–20, 241.

37. Rost, 47 from: B. V. Moore, "The May Conference on Leadership," *Personnel Journal*, vol. 6 (1927): 124.

38. Ibid., 47 from: E. S. Bogardus, Leaders and Leadership (New York: Appelton-Century, 1934), 5.

39. Ibid., 48 from: E. B. Reuter, *Handbook of Sociology* (New York: Dryden Press, 1941), 133.

40. Page 50. The bracket part is Rost's summary of the definition from: C. A. Gibb, "Leadership," in G. Lindzey, ed., *Handbook of Social Psychology*, 2 (Cambridge, MA: Addison Wesley, 1954): 877–920.

41. Page 53. From: M. Seeman, Social Status and Leadership (Columbus: Ohio State University Bureau of Educational Research, 1960), p. 127.

42. Page 59, R. N. Osborn and J. G. Hunt, "An Adaptive Reactive Theory of Leadership," in J. G. Hunt and L. L. Larson, eds., *Leadership Frontiers* (Kent, OH: Kent State University Press, 1975), 28.

43. Page 72. From S. C. Sarkesian, "A Personal Perspective," in J. H. Buck and L. J. Korb, eds., *Military Leadership* (Beverly Hills, CA: Sage, 1981), 243.

44. Page 102.

45. Burns criticizes leadership studies for bifurcating literature on leadership and followership. He says that the leadership literature is elitist, projecting heroic leaders against the drab mass of powerless followers. The followership literature, according to Burns, tends to be populist in its approach, linking the masses with small overlapping circles of politicians, military officers and business people. See Burns (1979), 3.

46. One's choice of a definition can be aesthetic and/or moral and/or political (if you control the definitions, you control the research agenda).

47. Rost, 161.

48. Leaders carry their own normative baggage in their definitions. For example:

"A leader is a man who has the ability to get other people to do what they don't want to do, and like it" (Harry Truman).

"Clean examples have a curious method of multiplying themselves" (Gandhi).

"Whatever goal man has reached is due to his originality plus his brutality" (Adolf Hitler).

"If we do not win, we will blame neither heaven nor earth, only ourselves" (Mao). These examples are from G. D. Paige's book, *The Scientific Study of Political Leadership*, 66. They are taken from Barbara Kellerman's *Leadership: Multidisciplinary Perspectives* (Englewood Cliffs, NJ: Prentice-Hall, 1984), 71–72.

49. This is from Ron Heifetz's book *Leadership Without Easy Answers* (Cambridge, MA: Belknap/Harvard University Press, 1998), 17–18.

50. See, Warren Bennis and Burt Nanus, *Leaders: The Strategies for Taking Charge* (New York: Harper Collins, 1985), 45.

51. The leader/manager distinction is a troublesome one in the leadership literature. One problem is that *leadership* is a hot word these days, and the current trend is to put leadership in the title of books on traditional management subjects. If we look at the formal positions of leaders and managers in organizations, the leader's job requires a broader perspective on the operation and on the moral significance of policies and actions of the organization (this is part of the "vision thing"). The manager's perspective is narrower than a leader's. A manager's job is to ensure that people complete a project or set of tasks. In ethical terms, this element of leadership boils down to thinking about actions in terms of how they impact on the organization as a whole and in the long run. In the ethics seminars that I have run for corporate managers, I have noticed that the managers who tend to take a big picture view of particular ethical problems are most often the ones who have been identified as having the greatest leadership potential. So Bennis and Nanus do seem to be right. However, it is not that managers are unethical, but rather that they have a narrower moral perspective that is in part dictated by the way in which they respond to the constraints and pressures of their position. Managers are also subject to Kant's old adage that "ought implies can."

52. Here Aristotle's discussion of excellence (*areté*) would be useful. Aristotle says that excellent actions must be good in themselves and good and noble. See the argument in Aristotle, *Nichomachean Ethics*, Book I, sections 6–8 (1096a12–1098b8). Later in Book II, sections 13–16 (31104b), Aristotle argues that a virtuous person has appropriate emotions along with dispositions to act the right way. Virtue then is being made happy by the right sort of thing.

53. See E. A. Fleishman, "The Description of Supervisory Behavior," *Personnel Psychology*, vol. 37 (1953): 1–6.

54. Results from the earlier and later Michigan studies are discussed in R. Likert's books, *New Patterns of Management* (New York: McGraw-Hill, 1961) and *The Human Organization: Its Management and Value* (New York: McGraw-Hill, 1967).

55. See P. Hersey and K. H. Blanchard, *The Management of Organizational Behavior*, 5th edition (Englewood Cliffs, NJ: Prentice Hall, 1993).

56. It would be worthwhile to look at some of the studies and ask how the subjects with high/high orientations solve ethical problems. Do they tend to find themselves trapped in between deontic and consequentialist approaches to the problem? Are people who score high on the task scale consequentialists when it comes to approaching ethical problems? etc.

57. See Gary Yukl, *Leadership in Organizations*, 2nd edition (Englewood Cliffs, NJ: Prentice Hall, 1989), 96.

58. Old metaethical problems such as David Hume's problem of "drawing an ought from an is," G. E. Moore's naturalistic fallacy and more recent discussions of ethical realism take on a certain urgency in applied ethics. I find that the more work that I do in applied ethics the more I lean toward the position that moral discourse is cognitive in that it expresses propositions that have truth value. However, I am still uncomfortable with drawing moral prescriptions from "scientific" studies of leadership. I have not really worked out a coherent position on these points of moral epistemology. For a good discussion of these issues see, Geoffrey Sayre-McCord, ed., *Essays on Moral Realism* (Cornell: Cornell University Press, 1988). I find David Wiggins' and Geoffrey Sayre-McCord's articles on ethical realism to be particularly compelling.

59. This is the argument that the sciences provide explanation and the humanities understanding. See Chapter 1 of G. H. von Wright, *Explanation and Understanding* (Ithaca: Cornell University Press, 1971).

60. In most journal articles, authors, including this one, offer stipulative definitions. These definitions make clear how concepts are being used in the chapter. They are not meant to be universal definitions.

61. We need a better picture of what a leader ought to be in order to educate and develop leaders in schools and organizations.

62. Burns uses the terms *transforming* and *transformational* in his book. However, he prefers to refer to his theory as *transforming* leadership.

63. I think that Burns is sometimes overly sanguine about the universal truth of these theories of human development.

64. James MacGregor Burns (1978), 42–43.

65. Rost (1991), xii.

66. I am very grateful to Professor Burns for the discussions that we have had on the ethics of leadership. Burns' reflections on his work as a biographer have lead me to this conclusion.

67. For example, see Burns' discussion of Roosevelt's treatment of Joe Kennedy, 32–33.

68. One of the problems with using the values approach to ethics is that it requires a very complicated taxonomy of values. The word *value* is also problematic because it encompasses so many different kinds of things. The values approach requires arguments for some sort of hierarchy of values that would serve to resolve conflicts of values. To make values something that people do rather than just have, Milton Rokeach offers a very awkward discussion of the ought character of values. "A person phenomenologically experiences

"oughtness" to be objectively required by society in somewhat the same way that he perceives an incomplete circle as objectively requiring closure." See Milton Rokeach, *The Nature of Human Values* (New York: The Free Press, 1973), 9.

69. Burns (1978), 426.

70. Ibid., 3.

71. Ibid., 426.

72. The third test has an Aristotelian twist to it. The relationship of leaders and followers and the ends of that relationship must rest on *eudaimonia* or happiness that is understood as human flourishing or as Aristotle says "living well and faring well with being happy." Aristotle, *Nicomachean Ethics*, Book I (1095a19) from Jonathan Barnes, ed., *The Complete Works of Aristotle*, vol. II (Princeton: Princeton University Press, 1984), 1730.

73. Burns (1979), 424.

74. Bernard Bass, *Leadership and Performance Beyond Expectations* (New York: Free Press, 1985). Bernard Bass and Paul Steidlmeier, "Ethics, Character, and Authentic Transformational Leader Behavior," *The Leadership Quarterly* 10, 2 (1999): 181–217.

75. Judith Rosner, "Ways Women Lead," in *Harvard Business Review*, (Nov./Dec. 1990), 99–125.

76. Jay Conger, *The Charismatic Leader: Behind the Mystique of Exceptional Leadership* (San Francisco: Jossey-Bass, 1989), xiv.

77. Bass (1985), 31.

78. For example, see Robert J. House, William D. Spangler, and James Woycke's study "Personality and Charisma in the U.S. Presidency," *Administrative Science Quarterly*, vol. 36, no. 3 (Sept. 1991), 364–396. Their study looks at charisma in terms of the bond between leaders and followers and in terms of actual behavior of the presidents (p. 366). The question that lurks in the background of this research is: Is their relationship, in Burns' terms, morally uplifting? Is the behavior ethical? and, Is the process that takes place in the relationship between these charismatic presidents and their followers humanly enriching?

79. For a very provocative account of charismatic leadership from an anthropological point of view, see Charles Lindholm, *Charisma* (Cambridge, MA: Basil Blackwell, 1990). Lindholm presents several case studies, including ones on Charles Manson and Jim Jones.

80. Greenleaf takes his theory from Hesse. See Robert K. Greenleaf, *Servant Leadership* (New York: Paulist Press, 1977). Hermann Hesse, *The Journey to the East* (New York: Farrar, Straus and Giroux, 1956).

81. The Robert K. Greenleaf Center in Indianapolis works with companies to implement this idea of leadership in organizations. The Robert K. Greenleaf Center, 1100 W. 42nd St., Suite 321, Indianapolis, IN 46208.

82. Greenleaf (1977), 13–14.

2

Moral Leadership and Business Ethics

Al Gini

> Those who really deserve praise are the people who, while human
> enough to enjoy power nevertheless pay more attention to justice
> than they are compelled to do by their situation.—Thucydides

Conventional wisdom has it that two of the most glaring examples of
academic oxymorons are the terms *business ethics* and *moral leadership*.
Neither term carries credibility in popular culture and when conjoined
constitutes a null-set rather than just a simple contradiction in terms.
The reason for this is definitional, but only in part. More significant is
that we have so few models of businesses and leaders operating on
ethical principles. Simply put, the cliché persists because of the dearth
of evidence to the contrary. At best, both these terms remain in the
lexicon as wished-for ideals rather than actual states of being.

A *New York Times*/CBS News poll conducted in 1985 revealed that 55
percent of the American public believes that the vast majority of corporate executives are dishonest, and 59 percent thinks that executive
white-collar crime occurs on a regular basis. A 1987 *Wall Street Journal*
article noted that one fourth of the 671 executives surveyed by a leading
research firm believed that ethics can impede a successful career, and
that more than half of all the executives they knew bent the rules to get
ahead.[1] Most recently, a 1990 national survey published by Prentice Hall

concluded that the standards of ethical practice and moral leadership of business leaders merit, at best, a C grade. Sixty-eight percent of those surveyed believed that the unethical behavior of executives is the primary cause of the decline in business standards, productivity, and success. The survey further suggested that because of the perceived low ethical standards of the executive class, workers feel justified in responding in kind—through absenteeism, petty theft, indifference, and a generally poor performance on the job. Many workers openly admitted that they spend more than 20 percent (8 hours a week) of their time at work totally goofing off. Almost half of those surveyed admitted to chronic malingering on a regular basis. One in six workers surveyed said that he or she drank or used drugs on the job. Three of four workers reported that their primary reason for working was "to keep the wolf from the door"; only one in four claimed to give his or her "best effort" to the job. The survey concluded that the standards equation of the American workplace is a simple one: American workers are as ethical/dutiful in doing their jobs as their bosses and companies are perceived to be ethical/dutiful in leading and directing them.[2]

Sadly, ample evidence suggests that this mutually reinforcing thesis often starts long before one enters the confines of the workplace. Recently one of the teacher/coaches in the Chicago public school system not only encouraged his high school students to cheat in the citywide Academic Decathlon contest, he fed them the answers. According to the eighteen-year-old student captain of the team: "The coach gave us the answer key. . . . He told us everybody cheats, that's the way the world works and we were fools to just play by the rules."[3] Unfortunately, just as workers often mirror the standards set by their bosses, these students followed the guidance of their teacher.

As a student of business ethics, I am convinced that without the continuous commitment, enforcement, and modeling of leadership, standards of business ethics cannot and will not be achieved in any organization. The ethics of leadership—whether they be good or bad, positive or negative—affect the ethos of the workplace and thereby help to form the ethical choices and decisions of the workers in the workplace. Leaders help to set the tone, develop the vision, and shape the behavior of all those involved in organizational life. The critical point to understand here is that, like it or not, business and politics serve as the metronome for our society. And the meter and behavior established by leaders set the patterns and establish the models for our behavior as individuals and as a group. Although the terms *business ethics* and *moral leadership* are technically distinguishable, in fact, they are inseparable components in the life of every organization.

The fundamental principle that underlies my thesis regarding leadership and ethical conduct is age-old. In his *Nichomachean Ethics*, Aristotle suggested that morality cannot be learned simply by reading a treatise on virtue. The spirit of morality, said Aristotle, is awakened in the individual only through the witness and conduct of a moral person. The principle of the "witness of another," or what we now refer to as "patterning," "role modeling," or "mentoring," is predicated on a four-step process, three of which follow:

1. As communal creatures, we learn to conduct ourselves primarily through the actions of significant others;
2. When the behavior of others is repeated often enough and proves to be peer-group positive, we emulate these actions;
3. If and when our actions are in turn reinforced by others, they become acquired characteristics or behavioral habits.

According to B. F. Skinner, the process is now complete. In affecting the actions of individuals through modeling and reinforcement, the mentor in question (in Skinnerean terms, "the controller of the environmental stimuli") has succeeded in reproducing the type of behavior sought after or desired. For Skinner the primary goal of the process need not take into consideration either the value or worth of the action or the interests or intent of the reinforced or operant-conditioned actor. From Skinner's psychological perspective, the bottom line is simply the response evoked.[4] From a philosophical perspective, however, even role modeling that produces a positive or beneficial action does not fulfill the basic requirements of the ethical enterprise at either the descriptive or normative level. Modeling, emulation, habit, results—whether positive or negative—are neither the sufficient nor the final goal. The fourth and final step in the process much include reflection, evaluation, choice, and conscious intent on the part of the actor, because ethics is always "an inside-out proposition" involving free will.[5]

John Dewey argued that at the precritical, pre-rational, preautonomous level, morality starts as a set of culturally defined goals and rules that are external to the individual and are imposed or inculcated as habits. But real ethical thinking, said Dewey, begins at the evaluative period of our lives, when, as independent agents, we freely decide to accept, embrace, modify, or deny these rules. Dewey maintained that every serious ethical system rejects the notion that one's standard of conduct should simply and uncritically be an acceptance of the rules of the culture we happen to live in. Even when custom, habit, convention, public opinion, and law are correct in their mandates, to embrace them without critical reflection does not constitute a complete and formal ethical act and might be better labeled "ethical happenstance" or "ethics by virtue of circumstantial accident." According to Dewey, ethics is essentially "reflective conduct," and he believed that the distinction between custom and reflective morality is clearly marked. The former places the standard and rules of conduct solely on habit; the latter appeals to reason and choice. The distinction is as important as it is definite, for it shifts the center of gravity in morality. For Dewey, ethics is a two-part process; it is never enough simply to do the right thing.[6]

In claiming that workers/followers derive their models for ethical conduct from the witness of leaders, I am in no way denying that workers/followers share responsibility for the overall conduct and culture of an organization. The burden of this chapter is not to exonerate the culpability of workers, but rather to explain the process involved: The witness of leaders both communicates the ethics of our institutions and establishes the desired standards and expectations leaders want and often demand from their fellow workers and followers. Although it would be naive to assert that employees simply and unreflectively absorb the manners and mores of the workplace, it would be equally naive to suggest that they are unaffected by the modeling and standards of their respective places of employment. Work is how we spend our lives, and the lessons we learn there, good or bad, play a part in the development of our moral perspective and the manner in which we formulate and adjudicate ethical choices. As a business ethicist, I believe that without the active intervention of effective moral leadership, we are doomed to forever wage a rear-guard action. Students of organizational development are never really surprised when poorly managed, badly led businesses wind up doing unethical things.

ETHICS AND BUSINESS

Jean-Paul Sartre argued that, like it or not, we are *by definition* moral creatures because our collective existence "condemns" us continuously to make choices about "what we ought to do" in regard to others.[7] Ethics is primarily a communal, collective enterprise, not a solitary one. It is the study of our web of relationships with others. When Robinson Crusoe found himself marooned and alone on a tiny Pacific atoll, all things were possible. But when Friday appeared and they discovered pirates burying treasure on the beach, Crusoe was then involved in the universe of others, an ethical universe. As a communal exercise, ethics is the attempt to work out the rights and obligations we have and share with others. What is mine? What do I owe you?

According to John Rawls, given the presence of others and our need of these others both to survive and to thrive, ethics is elementally the pursuit of justice, fair play, and equity. For Rawls, building on the cliché that "ethics is how we decide to behave when we decide we belong together," the study of ethics has to do with developing standards for judging the conduct of one party whose behavior affects another. Minimally, "good behavior" intends no harm and respects the rights of all affected, and "bad behavior" is willfully or negligently trampling on the rights and interests of others.[8] Ethics, then, tries to find a way to protect one person's individual rights and needs against and alongside the rights and needs of others. Of course, the paradox and central tension of ethics lie in the fact that while we are by nature communal and in need of others, at the same time we are by disposition more or less egocentric and self-serving.[9]

If ethics is a part of life, so too are work, labor, and business. Work is not something detached from the rest of human life, but, rather, "man is born to labor, as a bird to fly."[10] What are work and business about? Earning a living? Yes. Producing a product or service? Sure. Making money or profit? Absolutely. In fact, most ethicists argue that business has a moral obligation to make a profit. But business is also about people—the people you work for and work with. Business is an interdependent, intertwined, symbiotic relationship. Life, labor, and business are all of a piece. They should not be seen as separate "games" played by different "rules." The enterprise of business is not distinct from the enterprise of life and living because they share the same bottom line—people. Therefore, as in the rest of life, business is required to ask the question, What ought to be done in regard to others?

While no one that I am aware of would argue seriously against the notion of ethics in our private lives, many would have it that ethics and business don't or can't mix. That is, many people believe that "business is business," and that the stakes and standards involved in business are simply different from, more important than, and, perhaps, even antithetical to the principles and practices of ethics. Ethics is something we preach and practice at home in our private lives, but not at work. After all, it could cost us prestige, position, profits, and success.

Theologian Matthew Fox maintains that we lead schizophrenic lives because we either choose or are forced to abandon our personal beliefs and convictions "at the door" when we enter the workplace. The "destructive dualism" of the workplace, says Fox, separates our lives from our livelihood, our personal values from our work values, our personal needs from the needs of the community. Money becomes the sole reason for work, and success becomes the excuse we use to justify the immoral consequences of our behavior.[11] This "dualism" produces and perpetuates the kind of "occupational schizophrenia" recently articulated by nationally known jurist Alan Dershowitz: "I would never do many of the things in my personal life that I have to do as a lawyer."[12]

According to ethicist Norman E. Bowie, the disconnection between business and ethics and the dualism of the workplace stem from the competing paradigms of human nature of economists and ethicists. Economics is the study of the betterment of self. Most economists, says Bowie, have an egoistic theory of human nature. Their analyses focus

on how an individual rationally pursues desired tastes, wants, or preferences. Within the economic model, individuals behave rationally
when they seek to strengthen their own perceived best interests. Individuals need only take the interests of others into account when and if
such considerations work to their advantage. Economics, Bowie claims,
is singular and radically subjective in its orientation. It takes all tastes,
wants, and desires as simply given, and does not evaluate whether the
economic actor's preferences are good or bad. The focus remains on
how the individual can achieve his/her wants and desires.

Ethics, on the other hand, is nonegoistic or pluralistic in nature. Its
primary paradigm of evaluation is always self in relation to others. The
ethical point of view, says Bowie, requires that an actor take into
account the impact of his/her action on others. If and when the interests
of the actor and those affected by the action conflict, the actor should
at least consider suspending or modifying his or her action, and by so
doing recognize the interests of the other. In other words, ethics requires
that on occasion we "ought to act" contrary to our own self-interest and
that on occasion a person "ought to" act actively on behalf of the
interests of another. Economists ask, What can I do to advance my best
interests against others? Ethicists ask, In pursuing my best interests
what must I do, what "ought" I do in regard to others? Whereas
economics breeds competition, ethics encourages cooperation.[13]

For R. Edward Freeman, these competing paradigms are firmly en-
trenched in our collective psyches, and give rise to what he calls "The
Problem of the Two Realms." One realm is the realm of business. It is
the realm of hard, measurable facts: market studies, focus groups,
longitudinal studies, production costs, managed inventory, stock value,
research and development, profit and loss statements, and quantitative
analysis. The other realm is the realm of philosophy/ethics. This is the
soft realm, says Freeman, the realm of the seemingly ineffable: myth,
meaning, metaphor, purpose, quality, significance, rights, and values.
While the realm of business can be easily dissected, diagnosed, compared, and judged, the realm of philosophy is not open to precise
interpretation, comparison, and evaluation. For Freeman, in a society
that has absorbed and embraced the Marcusian adage "the goods of life
are equal to the good life," these two realms are accorded separate but
unequal status. Only in moments of desperation, disaster, or desire does
the realm of business solicit the commentary and insights of the realm
of ethics. Otherwise, the realm of business operates under the dictum
of legal moralism: Everything is allowed that is not strictly forbidden.

For Freeman the assertion that "business is business" and that ethics
is what we try to do in our private lives simply does not hold up to close
scrutiny. Business is a human institution, a basic part of the communal
fabric of life. Just as governments come to be out of the human need for

order, security, and fulfillment, so too does business. The goal of all business, labor, and work is to make life more secure, more stable, and more equitable. Business exists to serve more than just itself. No business can view itself as an isolated entity, unaffected by the demands of individuals and society. As such, business is required to ask the question, What ought to be done in regard to the others we work with and serve? For Freeman, business ethics, rather than being an oxymoron, a contradiction in terms, is really a pleonasm, a redundancy in terms.[14] As Henry Ford, Sr., once said: "For a long time people believed that the only purpose of industry is to make a profit. They are wrong. Its purpose is to serve the general welfare."[15]

What business ethics advocates is that people apply in the workplace those commonsensical rules and standards learned at home, from the lectern, and from the pulpit. The moral issues facing a person are age-old, and these are essentially the same issues facing a business—only writ in large script.[16] According to Freeman, ethics is "how we treat each other, every day, person to person. If you want to know about a company's ethics, look at how it treats people—customers, suppliers, and employees. Business is about people. And business ethics is about how customers and employees are treated."[17]

What is being asked of the business community is neither extraordinary nor excessive: a decent product at a fair price; honesty in advertisements; fair treatment of employees, customers, suppliers, and competitors; a strong sense of responsibility to the communities it inhabits and serves; and a reasonable profit for the financial risk-taking of its stockholders and owners. In the words of General Robert Wood Johnson, founder of Johnson and Johnson:

> The day has passed when business was a private matter—if it even really was. In a business society, every act of business has social consequences and may arouse public interest. Every time business hires, builds, sells or buys, it is acting for the . . . people as well as for itself, and it must be prepared to accept full responsibility.[18]

LEADERSHIP

According to Georges Enderle, business leadership would be relatively simple if corporations only had to produce a product or service, without being concerned about employees; management only had to deal with concepts, structures and strategies, without worrying about human relations; businesses just had to resolve their own problems, without being obligated to take the interests of individuals or society into consideration.[19] But such is not the case. Leadership is always about self and others. Like ethics, labor and business leadership is a symbiotic, communal relationship. It's about leaders, followers-constituencies, and all stakeholders involved. And, like ethics, labor and business leadership seems to be an intrinsic part of the human experience. Charles DeGaulle once observed that men can no longer survive without direction than they can without eating, drinking, or sleeping. Putting aside the obvious fact that DeGaulle was a proponent of "the great-person theory" of leadership, his point is a basic one. Leadership is a necessary requirement of communal existence. Minimally, it tries to offer perspective, focus, appropriate behavior, guidance, and a plan by which to handle the seemingly random and arbitrary events of life. Depending on the type of leadership-followership involved, it can be achieved by consensus, fiat, or cooperative orchestration. But whatever techniques are employed, leadership is always, at bottom, about stewardship—"a person(s) who manages or directs the affairs of others—as the agent or representative of others." To paraphrase the words of St. Augustine, regardless of the outcome, the first and final job of leadership is the attempt to serve the needs and the well-being of the people led.

What is leadership? Although the phenomenon of leadership can and must be distinguishable and definable separately from our understanding of what and who leaders are, I am convinced that leadership can only be known and evaluated in the particular instantiation of a leader doing a job. In other words, while the terms *leadership* and *leader* are not strictly synonymous, the reality of leadership cannot be separated from the person of the leader and the job of leadership. Given this caveat, and leaning heavy on the research and insights of Joseph C. Rost,[20] we can define leadership as follows: Leadership is a power- and value-laden relationship between leaders and followers/constituents who intend real changes that reflect their mutual purposes and goals. For our purposes, the critical elements of this definition that need to be examined are, in order of importance, followership, values, mutual purposes, and goals.

FOLLOWERSHIP

As Joseph Rost has pointed out, perhaps the single most important thesis developed in leadership studies in the last twenty years has been the evolution and now *almost* universal consensus regarding the role of followers in the leadership equation. Pulitzer prize–winning historian Garry Wills argues that we have long had a list of the leader's requisites—determination, focus, a clear goal, a sense of priorities, and so on. But until recently we overlooked or forgot the first and all-encompassing need. "The leader most needs followers. When those are lacking, the

best ideas, the strongest will, the most wonderful smile have no effect."[21] Followers set the terms of acceptance for leadership. Leadership
is a "mutually determinative" activity on the part of the leader and the
followers. Sometimes it's cooperative, sometimes it's a struggle, and
often it's a feud, but it's always collective. Although "the leader is one
who mobilizes others toward a goal shared by leaders and followers,"
leaders are powerless to act without followers. In effect, Wills argues,
successful leaders need to understand their followers far more than
followers need to understand leaders.[22]

Leadership, like labor and ethics, is always plural; it always occurs
in the context of others. E. P. Hollander has argued that while the
leader is the central and often the most vital part of the leadership
phenomenon, followers are important and necessary factors in the
equation.[23] All leadership is interactive, and all leadership should be
collaborative. In fact, except for the negative connotation sometimes
associated with the term, perhaps the word *collaborator* is a more
precise term than either *follower* or *constituent* to explain the leadership
process.[24] But whichever term is used, as James MacGregor Burns
wrote, one thing is clear, "leaders and followers are engaged in a
common enterprise; they are dependent on each other, their fortunes
rise and fall together."[25]

From an ethical perspective, the argument for the stewardship responsibilities of leadership is dependent upon the recognition of the
roles and rights of followers. Followership argues against the claim of
Louis XIV, *"L'état c'est moi!"* The principle of followership denies the
Machiavellian assertions that "politics and ethics don't mix" and that
the sole aim of any leader is "the acquisition of personal power."
Followership requires that leaders recognize their true role within the
commonwealth. The choices and actions of leaders must take into
consideration the rights and needs of followers. Leaders are not independent agents simply pursuing personal aggrandizement and career
options. Like the "Guardians" of Plato's *Republic*, leaders must see their
office as a social responsibility, a trust, a duty, and not as a symbol of
their personal identity, prestige, and lofty status.[26] In more contemporary terms, James O'Toole and Lynn Sharp-Paine have separately argued that the central ethical issue in business is the rights of
stakeholders and the obligation of business leaders to manage with due
consideration for the rights of all stakeholders involved.[27]

In his cult classic *The Fifth Discipline*, management guru Peter Senge
has stated that of all the jobs of leadership, being a steward is the most
basic. Being a steward means recognizing that the ultimate purpose of
one's work is others and not self; that leaders "do what they do" for
something larger than themselves; that their "life's work" may be the
"ability to lead"; but that the final goal of this talent or craft is "other

directed."[28] If the real "business of business" is not just to produce a product/service and a profit but to help "produce" people, then the same claim/demand can be made of leadership. Given the reality of the "presence of others," leadership, like ethics, must by definition confront the question, What ought to be done with regard to others?

VALUES

Ethics is about the assessment and evaluation of values, because all of life is value-laden. As Samuel Blumenfeld emphatically pointed out, "You have to be dead to be value-neutral."[29] Values are the ideas and beliefs that influence and direct our choices and actions. Whether they are right or wrong, good or bad, values, both consciously and unconsciously, mobilize and guide how we make decisions and the kinds of decisions we make. Reportedly, Eleanor Roosevelt once said, "If you want to know what people value, check their checkbooks!"

I believe that Tom Peters and Bob Waterman were correct when they asserted, "The real role of leadership is to manage the values of an organization."[30] All leadership is value laden. And all leadership, whether good or bad, is moral leadership at the descriptive if not the normative level. To put it more accurately, all leadership is ideologically driven or motivated by a certain philosophical perspective, which upon analysis and judgment may or may not prove to be morally acceptable in the colloquial sense. All leaders have an agenda—a series of beliefs, proposals, values, ideas, and issues that they wish to "put on the table." In fact, as Burns has suggested, leadership only asserts itself, and followers only become evident, when there is something at stake—ideas to be clarified, issues to be determined, values to be adjudicated.[31] In the words of Eleanor's husband, Franklin D. Roosevelt:

> The Presidency is preeminently a place of moral leadership. All our great Presidents were leaders of thought at times when certain historic ideas in the life of the nation had to be clarified. . . .[32]

Although we would prefer to study the moral leadership of Lincoln, Churchill, Gandhi, and Mother Teresa, like it or not we must also evaluate Hitler, Stalin, Saddam Hussein, and David Koresh within a moral context.

All ethical judgments are in some sense a "values-vs.-values" or "rights-vs.-rights" confrontation. Unfortunately, the question of "what we ought to do" in relation to the values and rights of others cannot be reduced to the analog of a simple litmus-paper test. In fact, I believe that all of ethics is based on what William James called the "will to believe." That is, we choose to believe, despite the ideas, arguments, and reasoning to the contrary, that individuals possess certain basic rights that cannot and should not be willfully disregarded or overridden by others. In "choosing to believe," said James, we establish this belief as a factual baseline of our thought process for all considerations in regard to others. Without this "reasoned choice," says James, the ethical enterprise loses its "vitality" in human interactions.[33]

If ethical behavior intends no harm and respects the rights of all affected, and unethical behavior willfully or negligently tramples on the rights and interests of others, then leaders cannot deny or disregard the rights of others. The leader's world view cannot be totally solipsistic. The leader's agenda should not be purely self-serving. Leaders should not see followers as potential adversaries to be bested, but rather as fellow travelers with similar aspirations and rights to be reckoned with.

How do we judge the ethics of a leader? Clearly, we cannot expect every decision and action of a leader to be perfect. As John Gardner has pointed out, particular consequences are never a reliable assessment of leadership.[34] The quality and worth of leadership can be measured only in terms of what a leader intends, values, believes in, or stands for—in other words, character. In *Character: America's Search for Leadership*, Gail Sheehy argues, as did Aristotle before her, that character is the most crucial and most elusive element of leadership. The root of the word "character" comes from the Greek word for engraving. As applied to human beings, it refers to the enduring marks or etched-in factors in our personality, which include our inborn talents as well as the learned and acquired traits imposed upon us by life and experience. These engravings define us, set us apart, and motivate behavior.

In regard to leadership, says Sheehy, character is fundamental and prophetic. The "issues [of leadership] are today and will change in time. Character is what was yesterday and will be tomorrow."[35] Character establishes both our day-to-day demeanor and our destiny. Therefore, it is not only useful but essential to examine the character of those who desire to lead us. As a journalist and longtime observer of the political scene, Sheehy contends that the Watergate affair of the early 1970s serves as a perfect example of the links between character and leadership. As Richard Nixon demonstrated so well, says Sheehy, "The Presidency is not the place to work out one's personal pathology . . ."[36] Leaders rule us, run things, and wield power. Therefore, says Sheehy, we must be careful about whom we choose to lead, because whom we choose is what we shall be. If, as Heraclitus wrote, "character is fate," the fate our leaders reap will also be our own.

Putting aside the particular players and the politics of the episode, Watergate has come to symbolize the failings and failures of people in high places. Watergate now serves as a watershed, a turning point, in our nation's concern for integrity, honesty, and fair play from all kinds of leaders. It is not a mere coincidence that the birth of business ethics as an independent, academic discipline can be dated from the Watergate affair and the trials that came out of it. No matter what our failings as individuals, Watergate sensitized us to the importance of ethical standards and conduct from those who direct the course of our political and public lives. What society is now demanding, and what business ethics is advocating, is that our business leaders and public servants should be held accountable to an even higher standard of behavior than we might demand and expect of ourselves.

MUTUAL PURPOSES AND GOALS

The character, goals, and aspirations of a leader are not developed in a vacuum. Leadership, even in the hands of a strong, confident, charismatic leader, remains, at bottom, relational. Leaders, good or bad, great or small, arise out of the needs and opportunities of a specific time and place. Leaders require causes, issues, and, most important, a hungry and willing constituency. Leaders may devise plans, establish an agenda, bring new and often radical ideas to the table, but all of them are a response to the milieu and membership of which they are a part. If leadership is an active and ongoing relationship between leaders and followers, then a central requirement of the leadership process is for leaders to evoke and elicit consensus in their constituencies, and conversely for followers to inform and influence their leaders. This is done through the uses of power and education.

The term *power* comes from the Latin *posse*: to do, to be able, to change, to influence or effect. To have power is to possess the capacity to control or direct change. All forms of leadership must make use of power. The central issue of power in leadership is not will it be used, but rather will it be used wisely and well. According to James MacGregor Burns, leadership is not just about directed results; it is also about offering followers a choice among real alternatives. Hence, leadership assumes competition, conflict, and debate, whereas brute power denies it.[37] "Leadership mobilizes," said Burns, "naked power coerces."[38] But power need not be dictatorial or punitive to be effective. Power can also be used in a noncoercive manner to orchestrate, direct, and guide members of an organization in the pursuit of a goal or series of objectives. Leaders must engage followers, not merely direct them. Leaders must serve as models and mentors, not martinets. Or to paraphrase novelist James Baldwin, power without morality is no longer power.

For Peter Senge, teaching is one of the primary jobs of leadership.[39] The "task of leader as teacher" is to empower people with information and offer insights, new knowledge, and alternative perspectives on reality. The "leader as teacher" is not just about "teaching" people how "to achieve their vision." Rather, it is about fostering learning, offering choices, and building consensus.[40] Effective leadership recognizes that to build and achieve community, followers must become reciprocally co-responsible in the pursuit of a common enterprise. Through their conduct and teaching, leaders must try to make their fellow constituents aware that they are all stakeholders in a conjoint activity that cannot succeed without their involvement and commitment. Successful leadership believes in and communicates some version of the now famous Hewlett Packard motto: "The achievements of an organization are the results of the combined efforts of each individual." In the end, says Abraham Zaleznik, "leadership is based on a compact that binds those who lead with those who follow into the same moral, intellectual and emotional commitment."[41] However, as both Burns and Rost warn us, the nature of this "compact" is inherently unequal because the influence patterns existing between leaders and followers are not equal. Responsive and responsible leadership requires, at a minimum, that democratic mechanisms be put in place that recognize the right of followers to have adequate knowledge of alternative options, goals, and programs, as well as the capacity to choose among them. "In leadership writ large, mutually agreed upon purposes help people achieve consensus, assume responsibility, work for the common good, and build community."[42]

STRUCTURAL RESTRAINTS

There is, unfortunately, a dark side to the theory of the "witness of others." Howard S. Schwartz, in his radical but underappreciated managerial text *Narcissistic Process and Corporate Decay*,[43] argues that corporations are not bastions of benign, other-directed ethical reasoning; nor can corporations, because of the demands and requirements of business, be models and exemplars of moral behavior. The rule of business, says Schwartz, remains the "law of the jungle," "the survival of the fittest," and the goal of survival engenders a combative "us-against-them mentality" that condones the moral imperative of getting ahead by any means necessary. Schwartz calls this phenomenon "organizational totalitarianism": Organizations and the people who manage them create for themselves a self-contained, self-serving world view that rationalizes anything done on their behalf and that does not require justification on any grounds outside of themselves.[44] The psychodynamics of this narcissistic perspective, says Schwartz, impose draconian requirements on all participants in organizational life: do your work; achieve organizational goals; obey and exhibit loyalty to your superiors; disregard personal values and beliefs; obey the law when necessary, obfuscate it whenever possible; and, deny internal or external discrepant information at odds with the stated organizational world view. Within such a "totalitarian logic," neither leaders nor followers, rank nor file, operate as independent agents. To "maintain their place," to "get ahead," all must conform. The agenda of "organizational totalitarianism" is always the preservation of the status quo. Within such a logic, like begets like, and change is rarely possible. Except for extreme situations in which "systemic ineffectiveness" begins to breed "organization decay," transformation is never an option.

In *Moral Mazes* Robert Jackall parallels much of Schwartz's analysis of organizational behavior, but from a sociologic rather than a psychological perspective. According to critic and commentator Thomas W. Norton, both Jackall and Schwartz seek to understand why and how organizational ethics and behavior are so often reduced to either dumb loyalty or the simple adulation and mimicry of one's superiors. While Schwartz argues that individuals are captives of the impersonal structural logic of "organizational totalitarianism," Jackall contends that "organizational actors become personally loyal to their superiors, always seeking their approval and are committed to them as persons rather than as representatives of the abstractions of organizational authority." But in either case, both authors maintain that organizational operatives are prisoners of the systems they serve.[45]

For Jackall, all American business organizations are examples of "patrimonial bureaucracies" wherein "fealty relations of personal loyalty" are the rule and the glue of organizational life. Jackall argues that all corporations are like fiefdoms of the Middle Ages, wherein the lord of the manor (CEO, president) offers protection, prestige, and status to his vassals (managers) and serfs (workers) in return for homage (commitment) and service (work). In such a system, advancement and promotion are predicated on loyalty, trust, politics, and personality as much as, if not more than, on experience, education, ability, and actual accomplishments. The central concern of the worker/minion is to be known as a "can-do guy," a "team player," being at the right place at the right time, and master of all the social rules. That's why in the corporate world, asserts Jackall, 1000 "atta-boys" are wiped away with one "oh, shit!"

Jackall maintains that, as in the model of a feudal system, employees of a corporation are expected to become functionaries of the system and supporters of the status quo. Their loyalty is to the powers that be; their duty is to perpetuate performance and profit; and their values can be none other than those sanctioned by the organization. Jackall contends that the logic of every organization (place of business) and the collective personality of the workplace conspire to override the wants, desires, and aspirations of the individual worker. No matter what a person believes off the job, said Jackall, on the job all of us to a greater or lesser extent are required to suspend, bracket, or only selectively manifest our personal convictions.

> What is right in the corporation is not what is right in a man's home or his church. What is right in the corporation is what the guy above you wants from you.[46]

For Jackall the primary imperative of every organization is to succeed. This logic of performance, what he refers to as "institutional logic," leads to the creation of a private moral universe—a moral universe that, by definition, is totalitarian (self-sustained), solipsistic (self-defined), and narcissistic (self-centered). Within such a milieu, truth is socially defined and moral behavior is determined solely by organizational needs. The key virtues, for all alike, become the virtues of the organization: goal preoccupation, problem solving, survival/success, and, most important, playing by the house rules. In time, says Jackall, those initiated and invested in the system come to believe that they live in a self-contained world that is above and independent of outside critique and evaluation.

For both Schwartz and Jackall, the logic of organizational life is rigid and unchanging. Corporations perpetuate themselves, both in their strengths and weakness, because corporate cultures clone their own. Even given the scenario of a benign organizational structure that produces positive behavior and beneficial results, the etiology of the problem and the opportunity for abuse that it offers represent the negative possibilities and inherent dangers of the "witness of others" as applied to leadership theory. Within the scope of Schwartz's and Jackall's allied analyses, "normative" moral leadership may not be possible. The model offered is both absolute and inflexible, and only "regular company guys" make it to the top. The maverick, the radical, the reformer are not long tolerated. The "institutional logic" of the system does not permit disruption, deviance, or default.

MORAL LEADERSHIP

The term *moral leadership* often conjures up images of sternly robed priests, waspishly severe nuns, carelessly bearded philosophers, forbiddingly strict parents, and something ambiguously labeled the "moral majority." These people are seen as confining and dictatorial. They make us do what we should do, not what we want to do. They encourage following the *superego* and not the *id*. A moral leader is someone who supposedly tells people the difference between right and wrong from on high. But there is much more to moral leadership than merely telling others what to do.

The vision and values of leadership must have their origins and resolutions in the community of followers, of whom they are a part, and whom they wish to serve. Leaders can drive, lead, orchestrate, and cajole; but they cannot force, dictate, or demand. Leaders can be the catalyst for morally sound behavior, but they are not, by themselves, a sufficient condition. By means of their demeanor and message, leaders must be able to convince, not just tell others, that collaboration serves the conjoint interest and well-being of all involved. Leaders may offer a vision, but followers must buy into it. Leaders may organize a plan, but followers must decide to take it on. Leaders may demonstrate conviction and willpower, but followers, in the new paradigm of leadership, should not allow the leader's will to replace their own.[47]

Joseph C. Rost has argued, both publicly and privately, that the ethical aspects of leadership remain thorny. How, exactly, do leaders and collaborators in an influence relationship make a collective decision about the ethics of a change that they want to implement in an organization or society? Some will say, "option A is ethical," while others will say, "option B is ethical." How are leaders and followers to decide? As I have suggested, ethics is what "ought to be done" as the preferred mode of action in a "right-vs.-right," "values-vs.-values" confrontation. Ethics is an evaluative enterprise. Judgments must be made in regard to competing points of view. Even in the absence of a belief in the existence of a single universal, absolute set of ethical rules, basic questions can still be asked: How does it affect the self and others? What are the consequences involved? Is it harmful? Is it fair? Is it equitable? Perhaps the best, but by no means most definitive, method suited to the general needs of the ethical enterprise is a modified version of the scientific method: (a) *observation*, the recognition of a problem or conflict; (b) *inquiry*, a critical consideration of facts and issues involved; (c) *hypothesis*, the formulation of a decision or plan of action consistent with the known facts; (d) *experimentation and evaluation*, the implementation of the decision or plan in order to see if it leads to the resolution of the problem. There are, of course, no perfect answers in ethics or life. The quality of our ethical choices cannot be measured solely in terms of achievements. Ultimately and ethically, intention, commitment, and concerted effort are as important as outcome: What/why did leader-followers try to do? How did they try to do it?

Leadership is hard to define, and moral leadership is even harder. Perhaps, like pornography, we only recognize moral leadership when we see it. The problem is, we so rarely see it. Nevertheless, I am convinced that without the "witness" of moral leadership, standards of ethics in business and organizational life will neither emerge nor be sustained. Leadership, even when defined as a collaborative experience, is still about the influence of individual character and the impact of personal mentoring. Behavior does not always beget like behavior in a one-to-one ratio, but it does establish tone, set the stage, and offer options. Although to achieve ethical behavior an entire organization, from top to bottom, must make a commitment to it, the model for that commitment has to originate from the top. Former Labor Secretary Robert Reich recently stated, "The most eloquent moral appeal will be no match for the dispassionate edict of the market." Perhaps the "witness" of moral leadership can prove to be more effective.

NOTES

1. Maynard M. Dolecheck and Carolyn C. Dolecheck, "Ethics: Take It From the Top," *Business* (Jan.-March 1989): 13.
2. James Patterson and Peter Kim, *The Day America Told the Truth* (Englewood Cliffs, NJ: Prentice Hall, 1991), 1, 20, 21, 22.
3. "Quotable Quotes," *Chicago Tribune Magazine*, January 1, 1996, 17.
4. B. F. Skinner, *Beyond Freedom and Dignity* (New York: Alfred A. Knopf, 1971), 107, 108, 150, 214, 215.
5. Stephen R. Covey, *The Seven Habits of Highly Effective People* (New York: A Fireside Book, 1990), 42, 43.
6. John Dewey, *Theory of The Moral Life* (New York: Holt Rinehart and Winston, 1960), 3-28.
7. Jean-Paul Sartre, *Existentialism and Human Emotions* (New York: The Wisdom Library, ND), 23, 24, 32, 33, 39, 40, 43, 44.
8. John Rawls, "Justice as Fairness: Political not Metaphysical," *Philosophy and Public Affairs* 14 (1985): 223–51.
9. The academic issue of which system of ethics best answers the question "what we ought to do" is a moot point and may in fact be an artificial one. However, the reality is, whichever way one decides to answer the question, "what we ought to do" is an endemic requirement of the human condition.
10. Pope Pius XI, "Quadragesimo Anno (On Reconstructing the Social Order)" in David M. Byers, ed. *Justice in the Marketplace: A Collection of the Vatican and U.S. Catholic Bishops on Economic Policy, 1891-1984* (Washington, D.C.: United States Catholic Conference, 1985), 61.
11. Matthew Fox, *The Reinvention of Work* (San Francisco: Harper San Francisco, 1994), 298, 299.
12. "Tempo" section, *Chicago Tribune*, Feb. 1, 1995, 2.
13. Norman E. Bowie, "Challenging The Egoistic Paradigm," *Business Ethics Quarterly*, vol. 1, no. 1 (1991): 1–21.
14. R. Edward Freeman, "The Problem of the Two Realms," speech, Loyola University Chicago, The Center for Ethics, Spring, 1992.
15. Henry Ford, Sr., quoted by Thomas Donaldson, *Corporations and Morality* (Englewood Cliffs, NJ: Prentice-Hall, 1982), 57.
16. Ibid., 14.
17. Freeman, "The Problem of the Two Realms."

18. General Robert Wood Johnson, quoted by Frederick G. Harmon and Gary Jacobs, "Company Personality: The Heart of The Matter," *Management Review* (Oct. 1985e): 10, 38, 74.

19. Georges Enderle, "Some Perspectives of Managerial Ethical Leadership," *Journal of Business Ethics*, 6 (1987): 657.

20. Joseph C. Rost, *Leadership for the Twenty-First Century* (Westport, CT: Praeger, 1993).

21. Garry Wills, *Certain Trumpets* (New York: Simon and Schuster, 1994), 13.

22. Ibid., 17.

23. E. P. Hollander, *Leadership Dynamics* (New York: The Free Press, 1978), 4, 5, 6, 12.

24. In a later article Joseph Rost made a change in his use of the word *followers*: "I now use the word *followers* when I write about leadership in the industrial paradigm. I use the word *collaborators* when I write about leadership in the postindustrial paradigm. This is a change from *Leadership in the Twenty-First Century*, in which I use the word *followers* all the time. The reason for the change is the unanimous feedback I received from numerous professionals throughout the nation. . . . After trying several alternative words, I settled on the word *collaborators* because it seemed to have the right denotative and connotative meanings. In other words, *collaborators* as a concept fits the language and values of the postindustrial paradigm, and so its usage should not be a problem to those who want to articulate a new paradigm of leadership." See Rost, "Leadership Development in the New Millennium," *The Journal of Leadership Studies*, vol. 1., no. 1 (1993): 109, 110.

25. James MacGregor Burns, *Leadership* (New York: Harper Torchbooks, 1979), 426.

26. Al Gini, "Moral Leadership: An Overview," *Journal of Business Ethics* (1997): volume 16, issue 3, pp. 323–30.

27. James O'Toole, *Leading Change* (San Francisco: Jossey-Bass, 1994); Lynn Sharp-Paine, "Managing For Organizational Integrity," *Harvard Business Review* (March-April 1994): 106-117.

28. Peter M. Senge, *The Fifth Discipline* (New York: Double/Currency Books, 1990), 345–52.

29. Christina Hoff Sommers, "Teaching the Virtues, " *Chicago Tribune Magazine*, September 12, 1993, 16.

30. Thomas J. Peters and Robert H. Waterman, Jr., *In Search of Excellence* (New York: Harper and Row, 1982), 245.

31. Burns, Chapters 2, 5.

32. Ibid., xi.

33. William James, *The Will to Believe* (New York: Dover Publications, Inc., 1956), 1–31, 184–215.

34. John W. Gardner, *On Leadership* (New York: The Free Press, 1990), 8.

35. Gail Sheehy, *Character: America's Search for Leadership* (New York: Bantam Books, 1990), 311.

36. Ibid., 66.

37. Burns, 36.

38. Ibid., 439.

39. For Senge the three primary tasks of leadership include: leader as designer, leader as steward, and leader as teacher.

40. Senge, 353.

41. Abraham Zaleznik, "The Leadership Gap," *Academy of Management Executives*, vol. 4., no. 1 (1990): 12.

42. Rost, 124.

43. Howard S. Schwartz, *Narcissistic Process and Corporate Decay* (New York: New York University Press, 1990).

44. Howard S. Schwartz, "Narcissistic Process and Corporate Decay: The Case of General Motors," *Business Ethics Quarterly*. vol. 1, no. 3: 250.

45. Thomas W. Norton, "The Narcissism and Moral Mazes of Corporate Life: A Commentary on the Writings of H. Schwartz and R. Jackall, " *Business Ethics Quarterly*, vol. 2, no. 1: 76.

46. Robert Jackall, *Moral Mazes* (New York: Oxford University Press, 1988), 6.

47. Wills, 13.

Part II

The Moral Relationship Between Leaders and Followers

3

Ethical Challenges in the Leader-Follower Relationship

Edwin P. Hollander

Various streams of thought have converged on the concept of leadership as a process rather than a person or state. This process is essentially a shared experience, a voyage through time, with benefits to be gained and hazards to be surmounted by the parties involved. A leader is not a sole voyager, but a key figure whose actions or inactions can determine others' well-being and the broader good. It is not too much to say that communal social health, as well as achieving a desired destination, is largely influenced by a leader's decisions and the information and values upon which they are based.

The leadership process is therefore especially fraught with ethical challenges. Hodgkinson (1983) considers leadership to be "intrinsically valuational," as "philosophy-in-action." He says, "Logic may set limits for and parameters within the field of value action but value phenomena determine what occurs within the field. They are indeed the essential constituents of the field of executive action . . . If this were not true then leadership behaviour could be routinized and, ultimately, computerized" (p. 202). Gardner (1990), too, sees values as part of "the moral framework that permits us to judge some purposes as good and others as bad" in leadership (pp. 66–67). Rost (1991) stresses the place of ethics in leadership regarding both process and ends.

THE CENTRALITY OF THE LEADER-FOLLOWER RELATIONSHIP

Evidence continues to accumulate about the importance of relational qualities in the unity of leadership-followership (e.g., Hollander, 1992a,b). A major component of the leader-follower relationship is the leader's perception of himself or herself relative to followers, and how they in turn perceive the leader. This self-other perception implicates important ethical issues concerning how followers are involved, used, or abused, especially in a relationship favoring a leader's power over them. Within this dominance motif, followers are essentially seen to be compliant and manipulable in the extreme. An instance of this is a corporate CEO who said that "leadership is confirmed when the ability to inflict pain is demonstrated" (Menzies, 1980). Clearly such abuse of power runs counter to the idea of mutual dependency in a shared enterprise and the value of maintaining personal dignity. Hurting people is usually not the way to get the best from them. Further, abuse deprives a leader of honest information and judgments from cowed subordinates. This can fuel the self-absorption and self-deception that are pitfalls of arbitrary power.

Nevertheless, the leader role is still seen as preeminent, often as *power over* others, rather than as a stewardship, or even as a *service to* others (see, e.g., DePree, 1989). Not least there is the very real problem of what Drucker calls "misleaders" who are dysfunctional. From a ten-year perspective, DeVries (1992) estimates that the base rate for executive incompetence is at least 50 percent. Hogan, Raskin, and Fazzini (1990) found that organizational climate studies from the mid-1950s onward show 60 to 75 percent of organizational respondents reporting their immediate supervisor as the worst or most stressful aspect of their job.

Management performance decrements also can have calamitous consequences to the organization and to others, but not necessarily to the rewards given to these managers. Responsibility for performance is somehow detached from them. A corporation head like Roger Smith, chairman of General Motors from 1981 to 1990, is a good example. He presided over a phenomenal drop of almost 20 percent of his company's share of the U.S. market. For many there and elsewhere, Smith was considered to be rigid and unresponsive to the challenges of consumer needs and foreign competition. Asked by *Fortune* magazine to explain what went wrong, he replied, "I don't know. It's a mysterious thing." Commenting on this statement, Samuelson (1993) says, "As a society, we have spent the past decade paying for mistakes like Smith's" (p. 55). Yet the organization continued its reward pattern: on his retirement the GM board increased his already generous pension to over a million dollars a year.

This dysfunctional system contrasts with one that shows the discipline and unity of purpose represented in "teamwork" aimed at clear performance goals (see, e.g., Hackman, 1989; Katzenbach & Smith, 1993). Achieving teamwork demands a concern for maintaining responsibility, accountability, authenticity, and integrity in the leader-follower relationship. Indeed, the often mentioned "crisis of leadership" usually reveals an absence of these elements (Hollander, 1978b). This normative position has distinctly functional value as a universal perspective applicable to the political *and* organizational spheres. Although this position comes out of a democratic ethos, its generality is evident in the organizational psychology literature on leadership (see, e.g., Gardner, 1990; Hollander, 1978a; Manz & Sims, 1989).

HISTORICAL CONTEXT

Followership is periodically rediscovered as important to leadership, despite a long tradition of usage. The term is variously employed by those who come upon it and declare anew that leadership cannot exist without followership. But the essence of the matter is to recognize that a leader-centric focus is inadequate to understanding the interdependence of leadership and active followership (see, e.g., Hollander & Offermann, 1990; Kelley, 1988; Vanderslice, 1988).

In sixth century B.C.E. China, Lao Tzu wrote about the "wise leader" in his *Tao Te Ching* (see Schmidt, 1975). His philosophy makes a major contribution to the theme of sharing leadership with followers: "The wise leader settles for good work and then lets others have the floor. The leader does not take all the credit for what happens and has no need for fame" (Heider, 1985, p. 162). Similarly, Hegel taught in the eighteenth century that the good leader must incorporate the experience and qualities of the follower, and demonstrate followership in leading.

The late nineteenth century European social philosophers recognized that leading involves a relational process with followers. Interest in crowd behavior, imitation, and the group mind were central to an ethos expressed most notably in the writings of Tarde (1890/1903) and LeBon (1896) in France. Both were influenced by the neurologist Jean Martin Charcot, who drew to Paris such later eminences as Freud and Prince to study with him. Indeed, Prince called his *Journal of Abnormal and Social Psychology* by that name because he saw the two fields as inextricably linked, through his belief in Charcot's idea of the parallel between hypnotic states and the susceptibility of a mob to social influence. It was LeBon, however, who also reported the story of a man chasing after a crowd of protesters saying he had to catch them because he was their leader.

From otherwise different perspectives, Freud (1921) and Floyd Allport (1924) criticized LeBon's view of crowd behavior and, indirectly, Charcot's conception behind it. In *Group Psychology and the Analysis of the Ego* (1921), Freud developed his conception of the followers' identification with the leader as a shared ego-ideal. A significant disciple, Fromm (1941), extended this conception in personality terms, in his contention that, "the psychology of the leader and that of his followers, are, of course, closely linked with each other" (p. 65). Erikson (1975) made an associated point about this linkage in asserting that followers "join a leader and are joined together by him" (p. 153).

CHARISMA AND ITS EFFECTS

Contemporary with Freud's conception of the ego-ideal was the idea of the "charismatic leader," to whom followers are drawn by a special quality. Max Weber (1921), the German sociologist of bureaucracy fame, advanced the concept to account for the loyalty and devotion of followers who are emotionally tied to a leader, especially in a time of crisis (cf. House & Shamir, 1993).

Charisma is not an unmixed good. Hodgkinson (1983) says, "Beware charisma" (p. 187), and Howell and Avolio (1992) have observed the need to distinguish between ethical and unethical charismatic leaders. In the organizational sphere, they cite the dubious ethical standards associated with Robert Campeau, John DeLorean, and Michael Milken, all of whom were acknowledged to have charisma for many of their followers. Unethical leaders are more likely to use their charisma to enhance *power over* followers, directed toward self-serving ends, usually in a calculated manipulable way. Ethical leaders are considered to use their charisma in a socially constructive way to serve others.

When Burns (1978) advanced his concept of the "transforming leader," who changes the attitudes and behavior of followers, he regarded this as having a moral basis yielding beneficial ends. Yet, charisma is *the* quality often imputed to such leaders, although Burns says it "is so overburdened as to collapse under close analysis" (p. 243). Still, charisma has by now become a favored term of almost general approval. In the corporate world, as well as in politics, charismatic leaders are often sought as saviors. But they also may present difficulties, such as tendencies toward narcissism (e.g., Post, 1986) as well as unethical behavior.

Weber (1946) conceived charisma to be one part of acceptance by followers of a leader's various bases for claiming legitimacy, and said, "if his leadership fails to benefit followers, it is likely that his charisma will disappear" (p. 360). Barnard (1938) dealt with this issue in his "acceptance theory of authority," stating conditions that permitted a follower to judge an order as authoritative, thus raising the issue of legitimacy of power (see Hollander, 1993).

THE CONTRAST BETWEEN POWER AND IDENTIFICATION

In his classic conception of power holding, Kipnis (1976) identified four corrupting influences of power affecting the power holder and those in a relationship with that individual. Briefly these "metamorphic effects" are: (a) power becomes desired as an end in itself, to be sought at virtually any cost; (b) holding power tempts the individual to use organizational resources for self-benefit, even illegally; (c) power creates the basis for false feedback and an exalted sense of self-worth; and (d) a corresponding devaluation of others' worth, with a desire to avoid close contact with them. Mulder (1981) has extended the last point, especially in his concept of "power distance." Such distance heightens the gap between leader and followers that exists because of disparities in available information or resources. This gap will be smaller where processes of identification and sharing occur.

Because well-being is at stake, other important features of this relationship are equity, equality, and need, with the potential for perception of injustice (see Deutsch, 1975). These issues are especially salient in a condition where one person depends on another with a great power difference between them. On this point, Emerson (1962) said that the explicit recognition of *dependence* by a lower power person on one of higher power can promote resentment by the former. This effect can undermine mutual efforts, although it has not received as much attention as more tangible rewards, such as markedly different economic benefits (see Bok, 1993). Clearly, the element of trust may be undercut by a leader's self-serving activity, especially the lack of accountability when he or she is manifestly failing.

SELF-SERVING BIASES

Given their traditional superordinate role, leaders may be prone to self-serving biases beyond those that exist in other social relationships. In his analysis of some key psychological processes involved, Greenwald (1985) has presented an interpretation of how the leader's ego or self incorporates several distinctive cognitive biases. These include the self as focus of knowledge; "beneffectance" as the perception of responsibility for desired, but not undesired, outcomes; and resistance to change.

These tendencies are further enhanced by power over others and a sense of being different, with accompanying social distance, and potential manipulation of them as objects. A necessary corrective is for the leader to be attuned to the needs of followers, their perceptions and expectancies. However, the narcissism associated with leaders who draw on the affection of followers, as in "charismatic leadership," often deprives them of this corrective (see Post, 1986). As a counterpart, followers may be vulnerable to perceptual distortions as a feature of the self-serving bias and identification with the leader that can bolster the self (see Hollander, 1992b).

MUTUAL IDENTIFICATION

An alternative view, more in keeping with responsive participation, considers the leader-follower relationship within a mutual identification motif. This includes the prospect of two-way influence, and the perception and counterperception of leader and followers. Cantril (1958) has said that the leader must be able to perceive the reality worlds of followers and have sensitivity to guide intuitions, if a common consensus and mutual trust rather than "mere power, force, or cunning" are to develop and prevail (p. 129).

Identification with the leader is exemplified in Freud's (1921) concept of the leader as a shared "ego-ideal" with whom members of a group mutually identify. They have a common bond on which life itself may depend, as in the military. For instance, according to military historians Gabriel and Savage (1978), inadequate and inattentive leadership were responsible for the failure to maintain "unit cohesion" in the U.S. Army serving in Vietnam. They say,

> . . . the officer corps grew in inverse proportion to its quality. . . [and] could be described as both bloated in number and poorer in quality. . . One result was My Lai. Even the staunchest defenders of the Army agree that in normal times a man of Lieutenant Calley's low intelligence and predispositions would never have been allowed to hold a commission . . . The lowering of standards was a wound that the officer corps inflicted on itself. (p. 10)

They also detail the way that the senior officer corps successfully managed to put themselves farther to the rear of action than before.

By contrast, this identification process is enhanced in those production firms where managers have closer contact with their workforce on the shop floor, and in the cafeteria, often wearing the same company uniform. This pattern illustrates the opposite of distancing employees.

JOINING OR DISTANCING FOLLOWERS

In April 1992, the first page of the *New York Times* Business Section (Hicks, 1992) featured a story about the CEO of U.S. Steel, Thomas Usher. He took the unusual step of unexpectedly going to the offices of the United Steelworkers at the company's largest mill in Gary, Indiana. What he said there was not as interesting as the *fact* of his being there. While acknowledging that, Usher commented that "Our long-term interests are exactly the same. Whether you are a manager or a member of the union, everyone wants to do a good job . . . I think there is a growing realization that we are not going to make it without the union and the union . . . without us" (p. D3).

The Usher view is evidently uncommon among corporate executives, or it would not be so newsworthy. Indeed, the founder of total quality management (TQM), W. Edwards Deming, believed that the enormous financial incentives they receive have destroyed teamwork at many American companies (1992).

Some leaders have become so removed from followers' perceptions and needs that they may cease to be aware of how their actions affect the "team" they wish to foster. A pertinent example of this is seen in the issue of high compensation packages given to American CEOs (see Byrne et al., 1991; Crystal, 1991). *Business Week*, *Forbes*, and *Fortune* are among the major business publications that recently featured articles on this issue.

Criticisms have centered on how these sums greatly exceed the pay of the average worker, as compared to foreign competitors, despite manifestly poor outcomes for some American firms.

> In Japan, the compensation of major CEOs is 17 times that of average workers; in France and Germany, 23 to 25 times; in Britain, 35 times; in America, between 85 and 100-plus times. In 1990, CEO pay rose 7 percent while corporate profits fell 7 percent . . . United Airlines' CEO . . . received $18.3 million (1200 times what a new flight attendant makes) [though] United's profits fell 71 percent. (Will, 1991)

Such disparities may produce even more alienation of followers from their leaders. Although leaders are recognized as needed, they also may be resented for having a position of authority that accords them special benefits, as seen now for instance in the contempt many hold for members of Congress. Least of all, leaders whose performance is substandard, but who remain well rewarded, are unable to encourage good followership by gaining and retaining loyalty and trust. Indeed, it is quite to the contrary, in part due to the inability to show concern for equity to followers.

On the same day that the *New York Times* (March 31, 1993) reported major layoffs of even long-time employees at IBM, it also indicated the pay package for IBM's new CEO. It included $5 million as a bonus for signing, a basic annual salary of $2 million, plus other incentives that would be worth millions more. The article revealed the personal devastation of the employees leaving the company, and the likely psychological toll on those who survived this round of cuts.

Signs of off-the-scale executive compensation exist not only in the private sector, but also in the political realm. Congressional salaries have grown from $30,000 in 1967 to $130,000 in 1991, when they were most recently raised. In that same interval, the average private sector salary has increased from $5,296 to $18,425 (*USA Today*, June 12, 1992, p. 1). Based on the salary differential between the Congress and the public, the distance gap (expressed in absolute dollars) increased disproportionately from $24,704 to $111,575 in less than twenty-five years.

This pattern is observed to extend widely (see, e.g., Bok, 1993). It is even seen in some charitable and nonprofit organizations, and among some university presidents. In the first category is the well-publicized case of the President of United Way of America whose annual salary and benefits, apart from other perquisites, approximated half a million dollars (Hevesi, 1992). Not long after these revelations, he reluctantly agreed to resign, at his Board's urging. Other disclosures were made about his self-dealing activities, including the appointment he created for his son as president of a spinoff firm to market United Way products. Then came word that the most recent president of the largest affiliate of United Way, the Tri-State (New York, New Jersey, Connecticut) division, had resigned in 1989 with a $3.3 million pension payment from that affiliate's funds. Its constituent groups voiced considerable displeasure when that fact surfaced, but much after the payment was made.

In 1991, the president of the University of Pittsburgh retired with a pension plan that included a multimillion dollar package plus a guaranteed annual salary of $309,000 for life. When members of the Pennsylvania legislature, the primary funding source for the University, learned about this through the press, they expressed outrage at the scale of these payments and at having been bypassed by the trustees who approved this package (Reeves, 1991). More pointedly, the campus community was understandably upset over the considerable sum of money given up from institutional funds, which engendered a great loss of confidence in the trustees and their judgment.

LEADER PERFORMANCE

As Drucker (1988) has long noted, leadership *is* performance. The central question is: What earns a favorable judgment on a leader's

performance? Obviously one important answer has to do with success in achieving group goals. But such goals may be set by the leader who thereby defines—and may redefine—the criteria for judgment within the system. In the political sphere, notably the macro-leadership of the presidency, this is "setting the agenda," and frequently involves a process of "getting on the right side on an issue." This usually requires *value expression*, particularly in what the leader says about what is desirable and to be sought. The element of trust also contributes to allowing the leader latitude for action (see Hollander, 1992b).

Other things being equal, positive or negative outcomes are more likely to be attributed to the leader, so that when things go wrong, he or she is more readily faulted and even removed. In Pfeffer's (1977) causal attribution terms, leaders are symbols who can be fired to convey a sense of rooting out the basis for the problem. For Sartre, "To be a leader is to be responsible," but the reality too often is that responsibility and accountability are lacking.

One effect of the attributional view is to make even more explicit the significance of how followers and others perceive the leader, not least regarding expectations about leader competence and motivation. A pointed example of this effect is shown in the work on "derailment" by McCall, Lombardo, and Morrison (1988) with 400 promising managers, seen to be on a fast track. Those who failed to reach their expected potential were more often found to lack skills in relating to others, but not a deficit in their technical skills. Other research by Kouzes and Posner (1987), with a sample of 3400 organizational respondents, dealt with qualities they admired in their leaders, and also found the relational realm significant. Renewed interest in charisma, and now in transformational leadership (Bass, 1985), makes the followers' view even more appropriate for understanding these phenomena.

Hollander and Kelly (1990,1992) used critical incidents, open-ended questions, and rating scales to study responses to good and bad leadership. This research was done with 280 mainly organizationally based respondents, half male and half female. It affirmed the major point that relational qualities were emphasized in reports and evaluations distinguishing good from bad leadership. Most notably, these included providing personal and professional support, communicating clearly as well as listening, taking needed action, and delegating.

Although this research is organizationally based, it has larger implications at the societal level, and resonates with ideas about the effects of power and distance. One point clearly is that leader characteristics have an effect on followers by shaping their perceptions and responses. Indeed, this link between perceptions and behavior tests the ethics of a leader's actions and other attributes as perceived by followers, and their response to those attributes (see e.g., Lord and Mahar, 1990).

How the leader's self-presentation is perceived by followers has broader ethical and performance consequences. These include obvious instances of unfairness, self-seeking at others' expense, weakness, vacillation, and outright misconduct, all of which detract from the leader's standing with followers, as has been previously described. Emler and Hogan (1991) say,

> There is no inbuilt tendency to use power responsibly. You cannot randomly allocate leadership responsibility and expect the interests of justice or society to be well served. Those in charge have a responsibility to make moral decisions greater than those they command . . . [and] those differences become more consequential the further up the hierarchy one goes. (p. 86)

CONCLUSIONS

Clearly there are ethical challenges in the use of authority and power. Among these are the destructive effects on the social contract between the leader and followers. Being a leader allows more influence and power over others' outcomes and events more broadly. The leader also has many benefits and privileges, including higher financial rewards and the freedom to keep at a distance, if desired. But these benefits come at the price of responsibility and accountability to followers (see Hollander, 1978b). Where the leader is seen to be power-oriented, exploitative, and self-serving, especially in the face of failures, the goal of mutual identification is hardly attainable. Instead, followers may feel alienated and ultimately take their allegiance elsewhere. That prospect poses an essential challenge today.

ACKNOWLEDGMENTS

This chapter is based upon a presentation made on July 8, 1993, in the Ethics Symposium at the Sixteenth Annual Scientific Meeting of the International Society of Political Psychology, Cambridge, Massachusetts. The assistance of Elisa H. Schwager and Ketty Russeva in the preparation of this chapter is gratefully acknowledged.

REFERENCES

Allport, F. 1924. *Social psychology*. Boston: Houghton Mifflin.
Barnard, C. I. 1938. *The functions of the executive*. Cambridge, MA: Harvard University Press.
Bass, B. M. 1985. *Leadership and performance beyond expectations*. New York: Free Press.
Bok, D. 1993. *The cost of talent*. New York: Free Press.

Burns, J. M. 1978. *Leadership*. New York: Harper & Row.

Byrne, J. A., W. C. Symonds, and J. F. Siler. 1991. CEO disease. *Business Week*, 1 April, 52–60.

Cantril, H. 1958. Effective democratic leadership: A psychological interpretation. *Journal of Individual Psychology* 14: 128–38.

Crystal, G. 1991. *In search of excess: The overcompensation of American executives*. New York: W. W. Norton.

Deming, W. E. 1992. Quoted in *The Economist*, 1 February, 19.

DePree, M. 1989. *Leadership is an art*. New York: Doubleday Dell.

DeVries, D. L. 1992. Executive selection: Advances but no progress. *Issues & Observations* 12:1–5.

Deutsch, M. 1975. Equity, equality, and need: What determines which value will be used as the basis of distributive justice? *Journal of Social Issues* 31:137–49.

Drucker, P. F. 1988. Leadership: More doing than dash. *Wall Street Journal* 6 January, 14.

Emerson, R. M. 1962. Power-dependence relations. *American Sociological Review* 27: 31–41.

Emler, N., and R. Hogan. 1991. Moral psychology and public policy. In *Handbook of moral behavior and development*, Vol. 3. *Applications*, edited by W. M. Kurtines and J. L. Gewirtz. Hillsdale, NJ: Lawrence Erlbaum.

Erikson, E. H. 1975. *Life history and the historical moment*. New York: W. W. Norton.

Freud, S. 1921/1960. *Group psychology and the analysis of the ego*. New York: Bantam. First published in German in 1921.

Fromm, E. 1941. *Escape from freedom*. New York: Rinehart.

Gabriel, R., and P. Savage. 1978. *Crisis in command*. New York: Hill and Wang.

Gardner, J. W. 1990. *On leadership*. New York: Free Press/Macmillan.

Greenwald, A. 1985. Totalitarian egos in the personalities of democratic leaders. Symposium Paper, International Society of Political Psychology Annual Meeting, Washington, D.C., June 20.

Hackman, J. R. 1989. *Groups that work (and those that don't)*. San Francisco: Jossey-Bass.

Heider, J. 1985. *The Tao of leadership*. Atlanta, GA: Humanics New Age.

Hevesi, D. 1992. United ways challenge method used to divide their donations. *The New York Times*, 20 March, B4.

Hicks, J. P. 1992. The steel man with kid gloves. *The New York Times*, 3 April, D-1.

Hodgkinson, C. 1983. *The philosophy of leadership*. Oxford, England: Basil Blackwell.

Hogan, R., R. Raskin, and D. Fazzini. 1990. The dark side of charisma. In *Measures of leadership*, edited by K. E. Clark and M. B. Clark. West Orange, NJ: Leadership Library of America.

Hollander, E. P. 1978a. *Leadership dynamics: A practical guide to effective relationships*. New York: Free Press/Macmillan.

Hollander, E. P. 1978b. What is the crisis of leadership? *Humanitas* 14:285–96.

Hollander, E. P. 1992a. The essential interdependence of leadership and followership. *Current Directions in Psychological Science* 1: 71–5.

Hollander, E. P. 1992b. Leadership, followership, self, and others. *Leadership Quarterly* 3: 43–4.

Hollander, E. P. 1993. Legitimacy, power, and influence: A perspective on relational features of leadership. In *Leadership theory and research: Perspectives and directions*, edited by M. Chemers and R. Ayman. 29–47. San Diego: Academic Press.

Hollander, E. P., and D. R. Kelly. 1990. Rewards from leaders as perceived by followers. Paper presented at the meeting of the Eastern Psychological Association, Philadelphia, March 30.

Hollander, E. P., and D. R. Kelly. 1992. Appraising relational qualities of leadership and followership. Paper presented at the 25th International Congress of Psychology, Brussels, July 24.

Hollander, E. P., and L. R. Offermann. 1990. Power and leadership in organizations: Relationships in transition. *American Psychologist* 45:179–89.

House, R., and B. Shamir. 1993. Toward the integration of transformational, charismatic and visionary theories. In *Leadership theory and research: Perspectives and directions*, edited by M. M. Chemers and R. Ayman. 81–107. San Diego: Academic Press.

Howell, J. M., and B. J. Avolio. 1992. The ethics of charismatic leadership: Submission or liberation? *Academy of Management Executive* 6:43–54.

Katzenbach, J. R., and O. K. Smith. (1993). *The wisdom of teams: Creating the high-performance organization.* Cambridge, MA: Harvard Business School Press.

Kelley, R. E. 1988. In praise of followers. *Harvard Business Review* 88:142–48.

Kipnis, D. 1976. *The powerholders.* Chicago: University of Chicago Press.

Kouzes, J. M., and B. Z. Posner. 1987. *The leadership challenge: How to get extraordinary things done in organizations.* San Francisco: Jossey-Bass.

LeBon, G. 1897. *The crowd: A study of the popular mind.* 2d ed. London: T. F. Unwin.

Lord, R. G., and K. J. Maher. 1990. Leadership perceptions and leadership performance: Two distinct but interdependent processes. In J. Carroll (Ed.), *Advances in applied social psychology: Business settings.* Vol. 4. Edited by J. Carroll. Hillsdale, NJ: Erlbaum.

Manz, C. C. and H. P. Sims. 1989. *Super-leadership: Leading others to lead themselves.* Englewood Cliffs, NJ: Prentice Hall.

McCall, M. W., M. M. Lombardo, and A.M. Morrison. 1988. *The lessons of experience.* Lexington, MA: Lexington Books.

Menzies, H. D. 1980. The ten toughest bosses. *Fortune* 101: 62–9.

Mulder, M. 1981. On the quantity and quality of power and the Q. W. L. Paper presented at the International Conference on the Quality of Work Life, Toronto.

Pfeffer, J. 1977. The ambiguity of leadership. In *Leadership: Where Else Can We Go?* edited by M. W. McCall, Jr., and M. M. Lombardo. Durham, NC: Duke University Press.

Post, J. M. 1986. Narcissism and the charismatic leader-follower relationship. *Political Psychology* 7:675–88.

Rost, J. C. 1991. *Leadership for the twenty-first century.* Westport, CT: Praeger.

Reeves, F. 1991. Pitt misled us, lawmaker asserts. *Pittsburgh Post-Gazette*, 25 April.

Samuelson, R. 1993. The death of management. *Newsweek*, May 10, 55.

Schmidt, K. O. 1975. *Tao Te Ching.* Lakemont, GA: CSA Press.

Stacey, Julie. 1992. "Piece of the Pie," *USA Today* June 12, p. 1A.

Steinberg, Jacques. 1993. "Among the first to fall at IBM." *New York Times*, March 31, section B, page 1.

Tarde, G. 1903. *The laws of imitation* (translated from 2d French edition by E. C. Parsons; original, 1890.) New York: Holt.

Vanderslice, V. J. 1988. Separating leadership from leaders: An assessment of the effect of leader and follower roles in organizations. *Human Relations*, 41:677–96.

Weber, M. 1921. The sociology of charismatic authority. Republished in translation (1946) in H. H. Gerth, and C. W. Mills (eds. and trans.), *From Max Weber: Essays in sociology.* New York: Oxford University Press.

Will, G. 1991. Corporate raiders. *Boston Globe*, 2 September, p. 15.

4

Leadership and the Problem of Bogus Empowerment

Joanne B. Ciulla

Empowerment conjures up pictures of inspired and confident people or groups of people who are ready and able to take control of their lives and better their world. The empowered are the neighbors in a community who band together and take action to drive out drug dealers, the long-time welfare mother who gets a job and goes on to start a business, and the child who learns to read and to ride a bike. Power is a relationship between people with mutual intentions or purposes.[1] Empowerment is about giving people the confidence, competence, freedom, and resources to act on their own judgments. Hence, when a person or group of people are empowered, they undergo a change in their relationship to other people who hold power and with whom they share mutual goals. In a community, empowering citizens changes their relationship to each other and to other holders of power such as business and government. In a business, empowering employees changes their relationship to each other, management, and the work process.

You can hardly pick up a business book today without seeing the words *leadership, empowerment, trust,* or *commitment* either on the cover or in the text. Gone are the bosses of the industrial era. Organizations have entered a new age where employees are partners and part of the team. Not only are managers supposed to be leaders, but all employees are leaders in their own way. This is good. It's democratic. It shows respect for persons and it sounds very ethical. So why isn't everyone happy? Why do business leaders worry about trust and loyalty? Why are employees cynical? One reason is that people are less secure in their jobs because of downsizing, technology, and competition from the global labor market. The other reason, and focus of this chapter, is that in many organizations, promises of empowerment are bogus. The word *bogus* is often used by young people to express their anger, disappointment, and disgust over hypocrisy, lies, and misrepresentations. This is how people feel when they are told that they are being empowered, but they know that they are not. When leaders promise empowerment, they raise the moral stakes in their relationship to followers. Failure to deliver can lead to even greater cynicism about leadership, alienation, and abdication of moral responsibility by employees and/or citizens.

When you empower others, you do at least one of the following: You help them recognize the power that they already have, you recover power that they once had and lost, or you give them power that they never had before. In his study of grassroots empowerment, Richard Couto says there are two main kinds of empowerment. The first kind he calls psycho-political empowerment. It increases people's self-esteem and results in a change in the distribution of resources and/or the actions of others. In other words, empowerment entails the confidence, desire, and, most important, the ability of people to bring about real change. This is probably what most people think of when they think of empowerment. Couto calls the second form of empowerment psycho-symbolic empowerment. It raises people's self-esteem or ability to cope with what is basically an unchanged set of circumstances.[2] More often than not, leaders promise or appear to promise the first kind of empowerment but actually deliver the second.

In this chapter I argue that authentic empowerment entails a distinct set of moral understandings and commitments between leaders and followers, all based on honesty. I begin by looking at the cultural values behind the idea of empowerment, particularly as it applies in the workplace. My primary focus will be on business organizations, but much of what I have to say about the moral aspects of empowerment applies to leaders and followers in community, nonprofit, and political contexts as well. I briefly outline how the idea of empowerment has evolved over the past fifty years of management theory and practice. Using critical analysis of this history and the ways in which empowerment is manipulative and unauthentic I talk about the moral aspects of empowerment and their implications for leadership.

THE SOCIAL VALUES BEHIND EMPOWERMENT

The idea of empowerment has its charm. Americans treasure democracy and its accompanying values of liberty and equality. If democracy were the only goal of empowerment, Americans would have the most democratic workplaces in the world, but they don't. As Tom Wren points out, ever since American independence, there has been a conflict between the values of equality and authority.[3] This tension is clearly evident in all organizational life. However, there are other values in our culture that shape the leadership and values of the workplace. Charles Taylor identifies three values of the modern age that he says cause tremendous personal anxiety and social malaise. They are individualism, instrumental reason (which causes disenchantment with the world), and freedom (which people seem to be losing because of individualism and instrumentalism).[4] Ideally, empowerment is what makes humans triumph over the anxiety they have over these values and provides the antidotes to the social malaise.

In the workplace are constant tensions among individualism, freedom, and instrumental value and/or economic efficiency (I count these as two aspects of the same value). In a society where people value individualism and freedom, the challenge of leadership in organizations is the challenge of leading a flock of cats, not sheep.[5] This means leaders have to use more powerful means of control than they would in a culture where people live in accepted hierarchies. For example, Americans were first smitten with Japanese management because it was effective and seemed so democratic. What they failed to realize was that the Japanese could afford to be democratic because the social controls imposed by hierarchy and community were internalized in workers, hence requiring less overt control by managers. American business leaders face the challenge of maintaining control without overtly chipping away at individualism and democratic ideals. This is why the language of empowerment is so attractive.

Economic efficiency and instrumentalism are the most powerful and divisive values in the workplace. They trump all other values, and our current faith in the market makes it difficult to sustain plausibly any other ethical values in an organization. The market is a mean, ruthless boss. Instrumentalism, or the value of getting the job done, is more important than the means and people used to get it done. Business leadership is effective if it gets results. Leaders and their organizations are successful if they make the most amount of money or do the most amount of work in the least amount of time. Not only are the ends more important than the means, but there is little if any room for things that have intrinsic but noninstrumental value in business. The greatest of all impediments to empowerment in business, and increasingly in all areas of life, is economic efficiency. It acts on rules that refuse to take into account special circumstances.

In addition to the values of instrumentalism, individualism, and freedom, I add a fourth social value that I call "niceness." It might sound strange to say that our culture values niceness at a time when there seems to be little civility. Niceness is not civility. Historian Norbert Elias traces the origin of civility to the sixteenth-century Dutch philosopher Erasmus. His book *De Civilitate Morum Puerilium* (*On Civility in Children*) is dedicated to a prince's son. It chronicles the proper behavior of people in society with a special emphasis on outward physical behavior. In short, it is an etiquette book on properly blowing one's nose, eating at the table, and relieving oneself. Published in 130 editions and translated into English, French, Czech, and German, Erasmus' book established the concept of civility as behavior that was considerate of other people in a society.[6] Kant later points out that civility is not morality (because it doesn't require a good will), but the similitude of morality—an outward decency.[7] Civility is the behavior that citizens should have toward their fellow citizens. It includes an obligation of citizens to be polite and respectful of the private rights of others.

Whereas the concept of civility develops as a form of outward consideration for others (e.g., not picking your nose in public), niceness is used as a means of gaining the favor and trust of others by showing a willingness to serve. Niceness fits the description of courtly behavior from which we get the term *courtesy*. This selection from the *Zeldler Universal Lexicon of 1736* captures the basic elements of commercial niceness:

> The courts of great lords are a theater where everyone wants to make his fortune. This can only be done by winning favor with the prince and the most important people of his court. One therefore takes all conceivable pains to make oneself agreeable to them. Nothing does this better than making the other believe that we are ready to serve him to the utmost capacity under all conditions. Nevertheless we are not always in a position to do this, and may not want to, often for good reasons. Courtesy serves as a substitute for all this. By it we give the other so much reassurance, through our outward show, that he has a favorable anticipation of our readiness to serve him. This wins us the other's trust, from which an affection for us develops imperceptibly, as a result of which he becomes eager to do good to us.[8]

There are other distinctive facets of niceness that are embedded in the observations of social critics since the mid-twentieth century. The first element of niceness is the belief that social harmony means lack of conflict. In *An American Dilemma* Gunnar Myrdal explains one facet of niceness. He argues that American social scientists derived their idea of social harmony from liberalism based on the Enlightenment ideal of communum bonum or common good. Radical liberals wanted to reformulate corrupt institutions into places where natural laws could function. The radical liberal, who could be a communist, socialist, or anarchist, wanted to dismantle power structures of privilege, property, and authority. In the utopia of the radical liberal, the concept of empowerment would not be useful. People wouldn't need to be given power or made to feel powerful, because the restraints that institutions had on their lives would in theory be removed. However, the dominant view in the social sciences (and certainly among those who were management theorists) was conservative liberalism. The conservative liberal took society as it was and, under the influence of economics, adopted the idea of social harmony as stable equilibrium.[9] The social scientists studied empirically observable situations and terms such as *balance, harmony, equilibrium, function,* and *social process.* They pretended that these terms gave a "do-nothing" valuation of a situation, but behind these words carry a veiled set of value judgments. Myrdal notes:

> When we speak of a social situation being in harmony, or having equilibrium, or its forces organized, accommodated, or adjusted to each other, there is almost inevitable implication that some sort of ideal has been attained, whether in terms of "individual happiness" or "the common welfare."[10]

Traditionally, management theorists have tacitly accepted the valuations behind these terms. Empowerment, like harmony, is assumed to be a good that brings about individual happiness. Social harmony in an organization meant accommodating and adjusting to people. Conflict or disharmony was a sign of failed leadership. Niceness comes out of this one-dimensional picture of stable equilibrium and harmony. If no one complains and yells at work, then there is social harmony. Furthermore, the "do-nothing" value-free stance of social scientists is in part responsible for some of the manipulative theories and practices in management.

David Riesman captured another root of niceness in his 1950 description of the emerging American character. In *The Lonely Crowd,* Riesman described inner-directed people who can cope with society because they are directed by internal, general goals implanted in them by their elders. Riesman observed that these people are becoming far and few between. Inner-directed people have less need for empowerment because they have what they need built in. The more prevalent character type identified by Riesman is the other-directed person.

These people are shallower, friendlier, and more uncertain of themselves.[11] Other-directed people take more of their clues on values and goals from the outside: They want to be liked and have a strong need to belong.

In his book, Riesman described a society dominated by other-directed people, in which manipulative skill overshadows craft skill and expense accounts overshadow bank accounts. Business is supposed to be fun and managers are supposed to be glad-handers who joke with secretaries and charm their bosses and clients. Most important, Riesman noted the trend that continues today of rewarding highly skilled people with management positions and power over other people. Hence the skilled engineer who gets promoted has to become a skilled glad-hander. The growth of the service industry shaped this character type into the model leader-manager and employee. To be successful in a service one has to be friendly, likable, and nice. Since Riesman's day, bank accounts matter more and expense accounts are smaller. What remains the same is the powerful value of the glad-hand. Our society may be less civil, and perhaps because of it niceness has been commercialized into the courtly norm of friendly bosses, bankers, and waiters all intent on gaining favor with customers and superiors to facilitate a smooth transaction.

As practiced in business, niceness consists of not getting into conflict and behaving in a commercially friendly fashion. Since people don't seem to behave this way naturally, we need the help of the therapist to attain niceness. In *The Triumph of the Therapeutic*, Philip Rieff says that truth has become a highly personal matter he calls "psychic truth."[12] He thinks that *therapeutic effectiveness* has replaced the value of truth in our culture. Truths that make people feel better and help them adjust and fit in are far more desirable than truths that rock the boat. If our culture places more importance on psychic truths than on real truths, and if some "truths" or therapeutic fictions are effective because they make people happier, then leaders have an obligation only to make people feel empowered. They don't have to give them actual power.

It is obvious why niceness, based on therapeutic lies and conflict-free environments and a kind of bland friendliness that we experience when we go the store or a bank, is one of the values that lurks behind the history of empowerment in business for an obvious reason. Leaders often prefer the nice kind of empowerment over the kind that leads to chaos and loss of control. As I have said, there are empowerment and bogus empowerment. I describe bogus empowerment as the use of therapeutic fictions to make people feel better about themselves, eliminate conflict, and satisfy their desire to belong (niceness), so that they will freely choose to work toward the goals of the organization (control of individualism) and be productive (instrumentalism). Leaders who offer bogus empowerment are unauthentic, insincere, and disrespectful of others. They believe that they can change others without changing themselves.

EMPOWERMENT AND THE ORGANIZATION MAN

C. Wright Mills offers one of the clearest articulations of bogus empowerment:

> The moral problem of social control in America today is less the explicit domination of men than their manipulation into self-coordinated and altogether cheerful subordinates.[13]

Mills believed that management's real goal was to "conquer the problem of alienation within the bounds of work alienation."[14] By this he meant that the problems of the workplace had to be defined and solved in terms of the values and goals of the workplace itself. By controlling the meanings and the terms under which alienation was conquered and satisfaction found, employers could maintain control without alienating workers. William H. Whyte echoed Mills' concern about psychological manipulation in *The Organization Man*, only Whyte zeroed in on people's need to belong. The workplace of the late 1950s is both radically different from and strikingly the same as today's workplace. Whyte criticized the social ethic that makes morally legitimate the pressure of society against the individual. The social ethic rationalizes the organization's demand for loyalty and gives employees who offer themselves wholeheartedly a sense of dedication and satisfaction. The social ethic includes a belief that the group is a source of creativity. A sense of belonging is the ultimate need of the individual, and social science can create ways to achieve this sense of belonging.[15]

Whyte feared that psychologists and social engineers would strip people of their creativity and identity. He attacked the use of personality tests to weed out people who don't fit in. He also challenged the notion that organizations should be free from conflict. The critique of the workplace in Whyte's book is similar to the critiques that liberals have of communitarianism. Community-oriented life looks good, but it is ultimately oppressive and authoritarian. In the 1950s social critics worried about the conformity of people to institutions and the values of suburban life. Today we worry about lack of consensus about values and the breakdown of urban and suburban communities. There is an increasing effort in the workplace to build teams and emphasize the value of groups. No one seems worried about loss of creativity and submission of individual identity to group identity. Managers care more about the problem of the individual who isn't a team player, and a majority of management theorists today believe that groups and teams are the foundation of all that is good and productive.

Whyte says, "The most misguided attempt at false collectivization is the attempt to see the group as a creative vehicle."[16] Contrary to popular management thinking today, Whyte does not believe that people think or create in groups. Groups, he says, just give order to the administration of work. Whyte describes an experiment done at the National Training Lab on leaderless groups. Theoretically, when the group "jelled," the leader would fade into the background, to be consulted for his expertise only. These groups resulted in chaos but as Whyte puts it, the trainers hoped that the resulting "feeling draining" of the group would be a valuable catharsis and a prelude to agreement.[17] According to Whyte, the individual has to enter into the process somewhere. If everyone wants to do what the group wants to do, and nothing gets done, then the individual has to play a role in the process. However, Whyte wonders if we should openly bring individuals into the process or "bootleg" it in an expression of group sentiment. Basically, he sees the leaderless group as intellectual hypocrisy. The power and authority of groups simply mask the real power and authority of leaders.

Whyte urges people to cheat on all psychological tests given during job interviews and at the workplace. He takes a strong stance against the organization and what he sees as the social scientist's coercive idea of belongingness. Another famous illustration of the struggle against the organization is in Sloan Wilson's novel *The Man in the Gray Flannel Suit*, published a year before Whyte's book. In the novel a personnel manager asks the main character, Tom Rath, to write an autobiography in which the last line reads, "The most significant thing about me is . . ." Rath, revolted by the exercise, debates whether to say what the company wants to hear (the therapeutic lie) or write about his most significant memory, concerning a woman he met during the war. Caught between truth and fiction, Rath holds on to his dignity by stating the facts—his place of birth, his schooling, and the number of children in his family. He writes that the most significant thing about him is the fact that he is applying for the job. He also says that he does not want to write an autobiography as part of his application.[18]

Rath draws a fine line between himself and the organization. Whyte misses the moral in the first scene of Wilson's book: Telling the truth strikes a much stronger blow for individual dignity than beating the organization at its own game. Wilson's novel resonates with students today because all of them at some time will have to decide how truthful they have to be in a job interview or with an employer and how much of themselves they are willing to give to an organization. It is sometimes hard to tell the truth when you want someone to like you. The thin line is not about the amount of hours or work one does. It is the boundary that people draw between their inner self and the parts of them needed to do their job. It is the line that allows a person to be both an individual and part of a group. In the modern workplace it isn't always easy to draw this line; some workplaces use programs with the language of leadership and empowerment in them to erase the line between the two parts.

THE RACE FOR THE WORKER'S SOUL

In the 1960s, the centralized bureaucratic organization of the 1950s gave way to the sensitive approach to management. The National Training Labs developed sensitivity training and T-Groups to transform bossy managers into participative ones. After much crawling around on the floor together and getting in touch with their inner feelings, few managers were transformed. During the 1970s and 1980s, management fads designed to capture the souls of workers bombarded the workplace. Fueled by global competitive pressures, managers were ready to try anything to get people to work hard and be productive. In 1981, William Ouchi's *Theory Z* and Richard Pascal and Anthony Athos' *The Art of Japanese Management* were best-sellers. The "new" idea from Japan was job enrichment and quality circles—after all, it worked for the Japanese. In 1982, the mystical Eastern touch of these two books gave way to Thomas J. Peters and Robert H. Waterman's blatantly evangelical *In Search of Excellence*. Peters and Waterman realized outright that the role of a manager is to make meaning for employees and create excitement. They argued that excellent organizations do not produce the conformist described by Whyte. They assure us that, "In the very same institutions in which culture is so dominant, the highest levels of true autonomy occur. The culture regulates rigorously the few variables that do count, and it provides meaning." Nonetheless, in these organizations "people are encouraged to stick out, to innovate."[19] If a strong culture provided meaning, it could reach to the very souls of employees, hence allowing for great freedom and creativity within the boundaries of the culture and the meanings provided by the culture. This kind of organization is designed to foster Mills' cheerful subordinates.

Popular books on management and leadership exert more influence on the way organizations are run than do most studies done by scholars in the fields. Another 1982 best-seller was Kenneth Blanchard's *The One-Minute Manager*. Blanchard's adult fairy tale portrayed a kindly and therapeutic manager who inspired fealty and commitment. It makes the manager into a combination Mr. Rogers–Captain Kangaroo.

Some companies required all of their managers to read it; it sold over three million copies. In the 1990s real softies can regress and read what Winnie the Pooh has to say about management.[20] The fairy-tale format continues to be popular. Books such as *Zapp! The Lightning of Empowerment* and *Heroz: Empower Yourself, Your Coworkers, Your Company* by William C. Byham and Jeff Cox take the form of heroic and inspiring fables.[21] The fables include knights and dragons and demonstrate how sharing power with workers can revitalize a company. Stephen Covey is the top evangelical crusader of leadership literature in the 1990s. A recent article described "Coveyism" as "total quality management for the character, re-engineering for the soul."[22] Covey preaches that businesses have to focus on making employees "feel good" about the organizational structures in which they work.

In the 1980s and 1990s the word *leadership* began taking the place of the word *management* in business books. The semantic change is also a conceptual change from the idea of a manager as a boss who commanded and controlled the process of production to the leader who inspires people to work toward mutual goals. Joe Rost says that in the old industrial paradigm, leadership was nothing more than good management.[23] Empowerment is at least implied in most recent articulations of leadership in business books today. What is confusing about this literature is that it continues to be written for people who usually hold the position of manager. In ordinary discourse, people talk about managers who lead and managers who manage. The carefully crafted distinctions made in the scholarly leadership literature are not always present in popular discourse. What we do see in ordinary discourse is that leadership has positive connotations and is sometimes used as an honorific, whereas management is either neutral or slightly negative.

The management fads of the 1980s and 1990s have appealed to business leaders (and those who aspire to be business leaders) because they make them feel powerful, inspiring, adventuresome, and lovable, all at the same time. The lovable leader is an attractive image, especially given the lack of respect and trust for authority figures in our society. Lovable leaders are nice because they are democratic and they do not openly exert power over others. Practicing lovable leadership requires some therapeutic fictions. CEOs of large corporations have spent fortunes on consultants and training programs. The goal of most of the programs has been to make work more enjoyable and participatory and to push power relationships between employees and management into the background. All of this is done in hope of creating a more competitive business. Sometimes these programs have backfired.

In 1987, the California Public Utilities Commission asked Pacific Bell to stop its leadership-development program. The program intended to move away from the old AT&T culture, empower low-level managers and give them more responsibilities, cut middle managers, and become more customer-focused. At Pacific Bell 23,000 of 67,000 employees took the two-day training.[24] Charles Krone created the Leadership Development program that came to be called "Kroning." This New Age program is aimed at getting all employees to use the same language and think at all times about the six essentials of organizational health: expansion, freedom, identity, concentration, order, and interaction. The program was based vaguely on the Armenian mystic Gurdjieff's Law of Three, which teaches that there are no constraints that can't be reconciled.[25]

After a two-month investigation of this $40 million training program, the commission reported that employees complained of brainwashing. An employee survey turned up repeated descriptions of the program as Big Brother, thought control, and mind restructuring. Employees also claimed that the Krone program used obtuse language and unnecessary concepts that made some people feel stupid. The irony was that the investigation discovered that a large majority of employees expressed a love of and commitment to Pacific Bell and mistrust of its management.[26] A Meridian survey of 2000 Pacific Bell employees concluded that top managers at Bell "blame the employees for the lack of productivity and are trying to make them think better. However, the Pacific Bell workforce already knows how to think."[27]

Thirty years after *The Organization Man*, corporations spent 30 billion dollars on training. Most of the training was in skills, but in 1986 about $4 billion went to programs such as Krone's and Werner Erhard's rehashed EST franchise called Transformation Technologies Inc. In 1987, *California Business* surveyed 500 corporate owners and presidents and found that half their companies used some form of consciousness-raising.[28] These programs focused on the same themes espoused today: empowerment, leadership, and positive thinking. They are distinctive because they used such unorthodox training techniques as meditation, biofeedback, and hypnosis. For example, a company called Energy Unlimited escorted executives across hot coals as a means of empowering people. While many of these programs now look silly to the outsider, they gained serious followers among corporate managers. Their impact on other employees is unclear. We rarely hear about cases in which employees complain about a company motivational program. That's why the Krone's scandal is so interesting. Most employees are a captive audience: Their success in the organization is contingent on buying into these programs. Motivational human potential courses often create a short-lived sense of euphoria among employees and/or a Hawthorn effect. They raise the expectation that employees will be enriched and empowered; however, after the dust settles, everything seems the same until the next initiative.

Did these attempts to redistribute power and responsibility in the organization succeed? On the one hand, employees were being promised more power and control over their work; on the other hand, some felt that they were being manipulated by the training programs. The standard answer given today is programs to empower employees often failed because supervisors and line managers did not want to give up power.

EMPOWERMENT AND PARTICIPATION

Discussions of worker participation, including such issues as empowerment and the team approach, derived from two sources: industrial relations research and management research (largely based on organizational behavior). On the industrial relations side, discussion in the 1970s focused on workplace democracy. Admirable models of workplace democracy included democratic worker councils employed at the time in Yugoslavian industries. These councils allowed workers to play an active part in all facets of the business. Employees even elected their own managers. Other researchers in the 1960s and 1970s studied worker cooperatives in hopes of finding clues to constructing new forms of truly democratic organizations.[29] The workplace-democracy advocates wanted employees to have control of the organization as a whole and to discover new possibilities for organizing work.[30] Behind their thinking was the idea that participation was central to democracy, where citizens had a say in all significant institutions, including family, school, and work.[31] Worker participation fit Couto's model of psycho-political empowerment. However, back in the Cold War era, real democracy in the workplace was considered un-American.

Researchers on the management side focused on quality of worklife and job enrichment and motivation. They were interested in giving employees more discretion over the actual task that they performed, not over the organization itself. A major emphasis was on making the employee feel good about work. This approach, which is the one usually emphasized in business schools, aimed toward therapeutic effectiveness and tended to fall into Couto's category of psycho-symbolic empowerment. One of the biggest problems with empowerment schemes is that the language used often raises unrealistic expectations about how much power and control employees actually gain over their work. They also fail to see any change in their relationship to other power holders. When employees discover the limits of their participation, they are disappointed. (One also wonders if people have addictive and/or insatiable desire for power.) For example, people in a quality circle could suggest changes on the production line, but not changes in their work hours. Many managers were ambivalent about giving away their own supervisory power. The Japanese never had these problems because supervisors usually headed up quality circles.[32]

It is useful to compare the impetus for and terms of participatory schemes in other countries with those in the United States. In his study of the macropolitics of organizational change, Robert E. Cole tells us that in the 1960s, Japan, Sweden, and the United States gave small groups more discretion to make work more interesting, attract employees looking for satisfying work, and motivate employees. The Japanese called innovations such as quality circles *decentralization of responsibility*. These small-group structures did not challenge the hierarchical structure of the organization. Sweden, in contrast to Japan, challenged the hierarchy of managerial authority and cast the early debate over these innovations in the political terms of *joint influence* and *democratization*. In the United States, while there were some union supporters of industrial democracy, discussion of empowerment was categorized in terms of *participation, quality of worklife, leadership*, and *employee involvement*.

Cole's study compares the amount of control given the workers and the success of the programs in different countries. The study concludes, "the Swedish tried more and accomplished less, while the Japanese tried less and accomplished more. By contrast, the Americans tried still less and accomplished very little."[33] The Japanese and the Swedes were clear about the boundaries of employee involvement. In Japan the aims were aesthetic: to give workers autonomy to make their work more challenging and enjoyable. The Swedes wanted to bring real democracy into the workplace. The Americans had goals similar to those of the Japanese. However, the language used by Americans, their adversarial labor climate, and cultural values of individualism and freedom made the scope of these programs appear to reach beyond the aesthetic aspects of work and hint at a greater say in the organization. Most participatory schemes were really benevolent ways of motivating people by making work more satisfying. What wasn't clear was whether a boring job in a democratic workplace was better than an interesting job in an undemocratic one. Americans tended to assume that the latter was the case.

The 1935 Labor Relations Act recognized the need to protect workers from bogus empowerment of participatory programs. Under it, quality circles and other similar participatory schemes are illegal unless employees have the right to choose their representatives and have a genuine voice in decisions. The Act prohibited "sham unions" or in-house unions formed by employers attempting to keep out real unions. Since it is obvious to most people today that employers have to forge a cooperative partnership with employees to be competitive, the 1935 Act looks like an atavism that ought to be eliminated. However, the law recognized that companies prefer cooperation and participation of their employees on their own terms. Most important, companies fear the loss of control that would come with unionization. In most businesses, empowering employees does not change the balance of power within the organization. Unions are still the only institution in history that ever addressed the asymmetry of power between employers and employees. Unions can be a strong form of empowerment because they give employees an independent voice that terrifies most employers. Businesses have always had such an intense fear of unions that one has to question what they mean when they talk about empowerment.

TEAMS AND QUALITY

Management language in the 1990s is a continuation of terms that started in the 1960s. The term *empowerment* replaces terms such as *worker involvement*. The emphasis on power gets at what managers failed to deliver despite their claims over the past thirty years. What has become abundantly clear in research done on productivity is that workers do a better job when they have a say in the way they do their work, the redesign of their jobs, and the introduction of technology into the workplace. Yet, over the past twenty years, managers have been constantly amazed by this phenomenon, which tells us something about the respect they have had for their employees.

The twentieth century began with scientific management with its physical control over production. It will end with total quality management (TQM) and its social control over production. They are two sides of the same coin. Scientific management separated the mind from the body of the worker to mass produce goods. TQM puts workers together in teams to produce quality goods and services. Both systems assert a high level of control at all phases of production (albeit using different means of control), and both systems have been extremely successful at improving production of goods and services.

Teams are a powerful form of social control. Peer pressure from the group keeps everyone in line and pulling his or her weight. Teams affect the individual more directly than does the larger culture of the organization. If the group puts out a measurable product it can "keep score," which makes it accountable and allows for direct feedback and reinforcement. Hence, it is not surprising that along with excitement over teams some businesses engender a religious fervor for TQM. Originating from statistical quality control, TQM pieced together quality circles, team approaches, and leadership into a new philosophy that required leaders "to accept TQM as a way of life."[34]

In his book on leadership and TQM, Richard Pierce advises frontline supervisors to act like leaders and become "more participatory and less authoritarian." According to Pierce, participatory means listening to employees' ideas, and when appropriate, implementing their ideas. The author goes on to say that employees, too, have to change. They need to know "that improved quality performance on their part, while vital, may bring no added compensation ('what's in it for me?'), but in the long run, productivity and quality improvement are necessary for survival."[35] Behind TQM is the idea of reinstating a craft ethic in workers, which includes pride in workmanship and the intrinsic value of a job well done. While this is a positive and rewarding model of work, it cannot be isolated from the context in which a job is done and the kind of work that is done. In this setting, the manager does not want employees to behave as if they are engaged in an economic transaction. Yet the employer bases most of his or her decisions regarding the employee on economic considerations. This is a good example of a therapeutic fiction: Everyone pretends that work is not guided by the values of instrumentalism and economic efficiency.

A great attraction of TQM for business leaders is that it gives the impression that they are ceding control and being democratic (and nice), but they end up with more control. Furthermore, TQM has been very effective in improving the quality of goods and services. However, TQM theorists are not satisfied at stopping with improved quality. They assert that quality is a matter of ethics and that it requires ethical leaders at the top giving customers what they want. One writer concludes that "companies have a moral obligation to live up to the promises they have made in advertisements, product brochures, and annual reports."[36] Ethical commitment in TQM focuses largely on a company's obligations to customers. True believers assume that TQM is intrinsically ethical because employees are empowered to participate in decisions and management listens to their employees. This is a fairly thin description of an ethical arrangement. The key issue here is, What is the relationship of employees to management? Listening to employees and allowing them to participate in decisions does not mean that their relationship to management or each other has changed, especially if the listening and participation take place between parties of unequal power. Furthermore, TQM says that managers should treat employees like customers. This is a therapeutic fiction. Can a business really treat employees like customers? It's a nice idea, but it breaks down in practice.

In a recent book documenting the wonders of teamwork in various organizations, Kimball Fisher emphasizes the importance of authenticity. He says that the key values of a team leader are belief in the importance of work, a belief that work is life, a belief in the "aggressive" development of team members, and a conviction to "eliminate barriers to team performance." Team leaders have to be themselves, or authentic, Fisher quotes a manager as saying. "The distinction between the work person and the family person is unhealthy and artificial."[37] In today's volatile economic environment, rhetoric like this rings false because, as Robert Frost said, "Home is the place where, when you have to go there, /They have to take you in."[38] We don't have many workplaces that do that. Team leaders also know that no matter how hard they or their team work, it may still not be enough. Kimball is right that authenticity is a fundamental part of leadership, but he is unauthentic in his denial of the distinction between work and the family. People may choose to lead lives with no distinction between work and home, but this choice is up to the individual and often rests on the nature of his or her work.

SINCERITY AND AUTHENTICITY

At this point, some readers may be irritated by the unkind portrayal of management practices that most people consider a vast improvement over scientific management and traditional bureaucratic forms of work. Clearly there are sincere and committed business leaders all over America who really care and do their best to make work more rewarding for employees. I am not claiming that all the management theories and programs of the past fifty years have been designed to fool the American worker, nor am I saying that all of the social scientists behind these theories and the consultants who develop these programs are evil manipulators. Yet I do ask the irritated reader to consider the irony of the effort put into empowerment programs in an era of downsizing, when the ultimate fate of workers is not decided by business leaders but by the invisible hand. I have painted this dark picture to underscore the bankruptcy of empowerment without the honesty necessary for authentic empowerment. Clearly not all empowerment programs are intended to manipulate people and some leaders really do want to empower their followers. However, to do so they must be sincere and authentic.

In his book *Sincerity and Authenticity* Lionel Trilling tells us that the public value of sincerity, like the concept of civility, emerged during the sixteenth century, a period of increasing social mobility in England and France. The art of acting with guile and expressing certain false emotions publicly became a tool for taking advantage of new social opportunities. Trilling says that sincerity was devalued when mobility and acting became accepted behaviors in a mobile society. People considered the sincere person stupid and unsophisticated. Audiences were no longer interested in seeing plays about "hypocrite-villains and conscious dissemblers."[39] It was more interesting to read or watch plays about people who deceived themselves. Authenticity replaced the notion of sincerity as a subject of dramatic interest.

The question of authenticity takes us back to Mills, Whyte, and Wilson's *Man in the Gray Flannel Suit*. Mills believed that people had to sell their personalities to work in bureaucratic organizations; Whyte was concerned with the toll of conformity on the individual; and in the opening scene of Wilson's novel, Tom Rath is both sincere, in that he tells the truth, and authentic in that he tries to come to grips with who he is. Nevertheless, the remainder of the novel is really about his struggle to be truthful to himself. It's ironic that the phrase "man in the gray flannel suit" has come to characterize a boring, conformist organization man. Tom Rath is anything but that. He is a man wrestling with the organization and struggling to be honest with himself and others.

According to Trilling, we have deprecated the value of sincerity by treating it as such a common commodity in society and the marketplace. If this is true, then the really valuable emotional commodities are authenticity and "true" emotions. Thus, either people who serve customers will require even better acting skills, or training will have to dig even deeper into the employee to evoke the appropriate real emotions. If training programs could get at people's real feelings—find the "hot buttons"—employees would either no longer have to act, or they could engage in "deep acting." This may be the real reason for the use of intrusive motivational programs like the Krone program. It also lurks in the background of the ideology of strong cultures. Make the workplace your family and carry to it all the sense of caring and responsibility that you feel naturally for family members. Although this sounds sinister, it is true that most organizations want their employees to have a certain "genuine" feeling about their work, the people that they work with, and the organization. At Pacific Bell, employees really cared and were concerned about the company. Perhaps one thing that we learn from the Krone case is that attempts at engineering appropriate attitudes and emotions can actually undercut genuine feelings for a company. If a workplace is run honestly, people do care and are friendly; however, their emotions have to be free to be real. Nonetheless, the broader issues at stake remain the line between motivation and manipulation of emotions, and the claims that an organization can make on the inner self and emotions of an employee.

The principle of authenticity applies to organizations as well as individuals. Often motivational programs and leadership programs are just polite lies within a company. Quality of work life and employee involvement programs and redesigned jobs benefit employees by making their work more interesting. They intend to make employees feel empowered and feel that the organization cares about their development. Nonetheless, there is a difference between feeling empowered and really being empowered. One wonders if employees willingly buy into the fiction of empowerment because of their own need to believe that they have power and control. If so, symbolic empowerment works because employees are unauthentic.

REALITY AND TRUTH

The obvious difference between authentic and bogus empowerment rests on the honesty of the relationship between leaders and followers. Honesty entails a set of specific practical and moral obligations and is a necessary condition for empowerment. In the beginning of the chapter, I outlined three social values behind empowerment: individualism, freedom, and instrumentalism and economic efficiency. The fourth value, which encompasses the first three, I have called niceness. I characterized the value of niceness as a kind of self-interested social harmony, commercial friendliness, and therapeutic truth. All the values color the way that people view the context of their work. To empower people, leaders must take into account the social and economic conditions under which they operate.

The issue for most businesses is not democracy in the workplace or the workers' need for self-esteem or self-fulfillment. Plainly and simply, it is competitiveness. According to today's conventional wisdom, businesses of the twenty-first century have to be lean, mean, and flexible. This condition requires a flatter organization structure and employees willing to learn and change with the changing demands of their job, the market, and technology. Companies must innovate constantly, which means workers need the flexibility and work ethic of the old craft guilds.[40] This is what TQM tries to do and why there is so much discussion about commitment.

In this new business environment, in a sense employees already have more power than they had in the past and employers have less. Information is a source of power. On the one hand, the use of and access to information technologies in the workplace give employees far more power than they had in the past. On the other hand, computerized control systems can impose even stricter discipline on workers and replace layers of management. Competition is the reality of company life and the market rules the lives of business leaders. Business leaders, especially those who are responsible to stockholders, have significantly less power and control over their firms than in the past. The decisions of even those with the best of intentions are dominated by the demands of the market.[41] Internal power shifts occur not necessarily because one group intentionally gave up power, but because the demands of technology and economic efficiency required a new distribution of power. Power also decreases in organizations because of flattened organizational structure. Why does this matter? It matters because empowerment requires good faith. It is a kind of giving. You don't tell people that you are giving them power that they have already gotten through structural and technological changes.

Perhaps the greatest obstacle to empowerment today is downsizing, despite low unemployment figures. Although most workers remain unaffected by it, downsizing strikes fear into the hearts of all workers because it reminds them of the fundamental way in which they are totally powerless over their lives when business leaders act as if they are powerless to do anything but downsize. It would seem virtually impossible to empower people in organizations that do not make a strong commitment to keeping their workers employed through good times and bad. In their enthusiasm for downsizing, some companies may discover that they have demoralized workers who lack the security necessary to produce the creative and innovative products needed to be competitive in the world market.

The second requirement for empowerment in the workplace is a commitment by employers to go to great lengths to protect employees' jobs. For example, consider the case of Malden Mills. On December 11, 1995, the factory burned down. Owner Aaron Feuerstein distributed Christmas bonuses. Furthermore, for the next three months he continued to pay his employees their full salaries while the factory was being repaired. If job security is related to empowerment, there is a sense in which Feuerstein's workers felt more empowered than those who took part in the AT&T and Xerox leadership programs that same year. One can write this off as old-fashioned paternalism, but I doubt that any company initiative could produce in employees the trust, commitment, and self-esteem of the employees at Malden Mills. While many companies try smoke and mirrors, moral action is stronger and longer lasting than therapeutic intervention. The great moral leaders of business choose moral commitment to people and society over economic efficiency. When they come out ahead, they demonstrate to other business leaders that when employees really are the most important resource, ethics really pays.

EMPOWERMENT AS A RECIPROCAL
MORAL AGREEMENT

When leaders really empower people, they give them the responsibility that comes with that power. But this does not mean that with less power, leaders have less responsibility. This point is often misunderstood. Perhaps one of the most ethically distinctive features of being a leader is responsibility for the actions of one's followers. For example, transformational leaders don't have less responsibility for their followers when they transform them; the followers have chosen to take on more. Couto offers a good example of a bogus empowerment relationship. He listened in amazement as a hospital administrator "told federal health-policy makers about her hospital's patient advocacy program that empowered low-income patients to find means to pay their hospital bills."[42] Is the administrator really giving people power, or is she simply unloading the hospital's moral responsibility on them? In the workplace, employees can take full responsibility only if they have the power and access to resources to influence outcomes. Empowerment programs that give employees responsibility without control are cruel and stressful. Authentic empowerment gives employees control over outcomes so that they can be responsible for their work.

When empowering employees, leaders must keep their promises. The best way to do this is to make promises that they can keep. When leaders empower employees, they need to be clear about the extent of that power and avoid the temptation of engaging in hyperbole about the democratic nature of the organization. An organization can always give employees more responsibility, but employees feel betrayed when they discover that they have been given less than the leadership's rhetoric implied. A leader who keeps his or her promises establishes dependability necessary for trust.

Modern leadership consists of two ideals, trust and power, that often conflict with each other.[43] Trust has taken over from authority as the modern foundation of leadership. The moral concepts behind empowerment—responsibility, trust, respect, and loyalty—are reciprocal moral concepts; that is, they exist only if they are part of the relationship between followers and leaders. Like all the other moral principles that I have been examining in relationship to leadership and empowerment, they are related to truth and honesty. Honesty is one way to resolve the tension between power and trust. It is morally wrong to lie because lying shows lack of respect for the dignity of a person. This is why bogus empowerment is so devastating. Employees are made to feel foolish about falling for inflated claims and undelivered promises. Leaders lose credibility and respect because they have blatantly failed to respect their employees. Business leaders often overlook the reciprocal nature of these moral concepts, particularly the notion of loyalty or commitment. If leaders don't demonstrate in substantive ways that they are loyal and committed to their employees through good times and bad, they simply cannot expect employees to be loyal to them, and therapeutic interventions will be short-lived at best.

Last, if leaders are to establish a moral relationship with employees that allows for authentic empowerment, they need to think about constructively reapplying the traditional values behind empowerment. They must consider how to protect individualism even in team settings. Individualism has taken a beating by the communitarians in recent years, but there are some ethically important aspects to individualism, such as recognition and tolerance of difference and diversity.[44] Teamwork without tolerance of differences in opinion, gender, racial, or cultural background is unacceptable. Morally imaginative business leaders will challenge the dogma of instrumentalism and economic efficiency that sometimes mindlessly dominates all business decisions. It is difficult to say whether employees are more or less free on the job today then they were in the past. While many are liberated from harsh physical toil and a dictatorial boss, others are caged in by competition, insecurity, and peer pressure. Empowerment means more than discretion on the job. It also requires freedom to choose and freedom from emotional manipulation.

To empower people authentically, business leaders have to be ready to overthrow some of the aspects of niceness. The truth is not always pleasant. It can disrupt the harmony of an organization and introduce conflict. When you really empower people, you don't just empower them to agree with you. Employees don't always feel good when they hear the truth and leaders don't like to deliver bad news. As a result of the therapeutic fictions that are part of niceness, managers aren't forthright in their assessment of employees' work and teachers aren't forthright about the quality of their students' work. Assessment inflation makes people feel good in the short run, but it does not build the self-esteem necessary for empowerment in the long run.

I close with the notion of authenticity. Leaders cannot empower people unless they have the moral courage to be honest and sincere in their intention to change the power relationship that they have with their followers. If leaders want to be authentic about empowering people, they must first be honest with themselves. Too many leaders are not authentic. They talk about empowerment and participation and even believe that they are participatory, but in practice they lead in autocratic ways. Employees are "empowered" to organize their work but when they do, management steps in and tells them how to do it their way.

James MacGregor Burns points to Franklin Roosevelt's decision to support the Wagner Act as an example of authentic empowerment. According to Burns, Roosevelt knew that the Act gave a substantial amount of power to the people. He didn't necessarily like this fact; nevertheless, he supported the Act.[45] Authentic empowerment requires leaders to know what they are giving away and how they are changing the relationship between themselves and their followers. This is the only way that they can commit to keeping their part of the empowerment relationship. It is difficult for leaders to give away their own power and even more difficult for them to take away power from others.

Leadership is a distinct kind of moral relationship between people. Power is a defining aspect of this relationship. Whenever there is a change in the distribution of power between leaders and followers, there is a change in the specific rights, responsibilities, and duties in the relationship. Both sides have to be honest when they make these changes and have to understand fully what they mean. Bogus empowerment attempts to give employees or followers power without changing the moral relationship between leaders and followers. Empowerment changes the rights, responsibilities, and duties of leaders as well as followers. It is not something one does to be nice in order to gain favor with people. Over the past fifty years, business leaders have tried to harness the insights of psychology to make people feel empowered. These attempts have often failed and led to cynicism among employees because business leaders have ignored the moral commitments of empowerment. Without honesty, sincerity, and authenticity, empowerment is bogus and makes a mockery of one of America's most cherished values, the freedom to choose.

NOTES

1. James MacGregor Burns, *Leadership* (New York: Harper & Row, 1978), 13.
2. Richard Couto, Grassroots Policies of Empowerment. Paper given at the annual meeting of the American Political Science Association, Sept. 1992, 13.
3. J. Thomas Wren, Historical background of values in leadership, Kellogg Working Papers, 1996.
4. Charles Taylor, *The Ethics of Authenticity* (Cambridge, MA: Harvard University Press, 1991), 2–9.
5. James O'Toole, *Leading Change* (San Francisco: Jossey-Bass, 1994).
6. Norbert Elias, *The History of Manners* (New York: Pantheon Books, 1978), 53–55.
7. Immanuel Kant, "Idea for a Universal History with a Cosmopolitan Intent," *Perpetual Peace and Other Essays*, tr. Ted Humphrey (Indianapolis: Hackett Publishing, 1983), 31–32.
8. Elias, 9.
9. Gunnar Myrdal, *An American Dilemma*, vol. 2 (New York: Harper & Row, 1962), 1046–47.
10. Ibid., 1055.
11. David Riesman, *The Lonely Crowd* (New Haven: Yale University Press, 1950), 14–21.
12. Philip Rieff, *The Triumph of the Therapeutic* (New York: Harper & Row, 1966), 137. A similar point is made in Robert Bellah et al. *Habits of the Heart* (Berkeley, CA: University of California Press, 1985), Chapt. 2.

13. C. Wright Mills, "Crawling to the Top," *New York Times Book Review*, Dec. 9, 1956.

14. C. Wright Mills, *White Collar* (New York: Oxford University Press, 1951), 232-237.

15. William H. Whyte, Jr., *The Organization Man* (New York: Simon & Schuster, 1956), 6–7.

16. Ibid., 51.

17. Ibid., 54.

18. Sloan Wilson, *The Man in the Gray Flannel Suit* (New York: Arbor House, 1955), 14.

19. Thomas J. Peters and Robert H. Waterman, Jr., *In Search of Excellence* (New York: Warner Books, 1982), 105.

20. Roger E. Allen, *Pooh on Management* (New York: Dutton, 1994).

21. William C. Byham and Jeff Cox, *Zapp! The Lightning of Empowerment* (New York: Harmony Books, 1990); *Heroz: Empower Yourself. Your Coworkers. Your Company* (New York: Harmony Books, 1994).

22. "Confessor to the Board Room," *The Economist*, Feb. 24, 1996.

23. Joseph C. Rost, *Leadership for the Twenty-First Century* (Westport, CT: Praeger, 1991).

24. *Telephony*, June 22, 1987, 15.

25. Annetta Miller and Pamela Abramson, "Corporate Mind Control," *Newsweek*, May 4, 1987.

26. Ibid., 6.

27. Sanford Bingham, *Management*, July 1987, 14.

28. *Venture*, March 1987, 54.

29. Two good studies of cooperatives are Joyce Rothschild and Allen Whitt, *The Cooperative Workplace* (New York: Cambridge University Press, 1986) and Edward S. Greenberg, *Workplace Democracy* (Ithaca: Cornell University Press, 1986).

30. For example, see Martin Carnoy and Derek Shearer, *Economic Democracy: The Challenge of the 1980s* (Armonk, NY: Sharpe, Inc., 1980); and Gerry Hunnius, G. David Garson, and John Case, eds., *Workers' Control* (New York: Vintage Books, 1973).

31. See Carol Pateman, *Participation and Democratic Theory* (London: Cambridge University Press, 1970).

32. Robert E. Cole, "The Macropolitics of Organizational Change: A Comparative Analysis of the Spread of Small-Group Activities," in Carmen Sirianni, ed., *Worker Participation and the Politics of Reform* (Philadelphia: Temple University Press, 1987), 39–40.

33. Ibid., 40.

34. See Richard S. Johnson, *TOM: Leadership for the Quality Transformation* (Milwaukee: ASQC Quality Press, 1993).

35. Richard J. Pierce, *Leadership. Perspective and Restructuring for Total Quality* (Milwaukee: ASQC Quality Press, 1991), 11.

36. Ibid., 13.

37. Kimball Fisher, *Leading Self-Directed Work Teams* (New York: McGraw-Hill, 1993), 105–109.

38. "The Death of the Hired Man," in *The Poetry of Robert Frost*, ed. Edward C. Lathem (New York: Holt, Rinehart and Winston, 1979), 38.

39. Lionel Trilling, *Sincerity and Authenticity* (Cambridge, MA: Harvard University Press, 1972), 13.

40. This description comes from Michael J. Piore and Charles F. Sable, *The Second Industrial Divide* (New York: Basic Books, 1984), 282–307.

41. Anthony Sampson, *Company Man* (New York: Times/Random House, 1995), 260.

42. Couto, 2.

43. See Francis Sejersted, "Managers as Consultants and Manipulators: Reflections on the Suspension of Ethics," *Business Ethics Quarterly*, vol. 6, no. 1 (Jan. 1996): 77.

44. Taylor, 37.

45. My thanks to James MacGregor Burns for this example and for his other helpful comments on this chapter.

5

Ethical Leadership, Emotions, and Trust: Beyond "Charisma"

Robert C. Solomon

I am a novice on the subject of leadership, but after fifteen years of research and consulting in business ethics, I have become convinced that morally sensitive leaders are the essential feature of any good organization. I have never been a leader—although one hopes that teachers and especially philosophy teachers might share a few of the attributes of leaders in terms of inspiration and impact—and I confess that, while I pride myself on my trustworthiness and loyalty, I have never been much of a follower either. Too many leaders, as Voltaire complained of heroes, "are so noisy." Perhaps that is why I have never before delved into the subject as I should, for so much of what I have noticed about leadership is the noise.

Much of the noise has to do with the well-known but little understood phenomenon of Weberian charisma, the excited appeal supposedly generated and accordingly cultivated by leaders. *Charisma*, in other words, has much to do with emotion, but not just the emotion generated by leaders. It is also, first and foremost, the passion *of* the leader. It is strange, then, that the nature of emotion, the very heart of charisma, should have been so long neglected by leadership scholars. What has also been neglected, along with emotion, is the intimate relationship between emotion and ethics. This relationship speaks to several of the more controversial debates about leadership: the role and desirability of charisma, the nature of leadership itself, the dangers of evil leaders (the "Hitler problem"[1]), the nature of ethical leadership, and the nature of the relationship between leaders and the led. (I prefer the word "led" mainly by virtue of its length. I do not deny that following may be as active and autonomous a choice as leading, and in a sense, perhaps more so.[2]) In this chapter, therefore, I approach the topic of leadership by way of an often exciting but rarely analyzed set of connections: the connection between emotions and leadership; the connection between emotions and ethics; and, consequently, the connections among emotions, leadership, and ethics. To summarize, ethical leadership is essentially based on an emotional relationship, with the emphasis on charisma replaced by the much more mundane (but no less evasive) notion of trust. Whereas charisma is celebrated as a mysterious attribute of a leader, trust, obviously, is a relationship between a leader and his or her followers. The practical applications will, I hope, be obvious. The focus on leadership will bear fruit only if, unlike some lovelorn cowboys, we don't go looking for leaders in all the wrong places.[3]

THE ROLE OF EMOTIONS IN LEADERSHIP

Emotions are rarely the focus of discussions on leadership. When they are discussed, it is usually in terms of their arousal.[4] Emotions tend to be dismissed or ignored in almost every realm of "hard-headed" business, political, philosophical, and scientific discussion. Emotions, after all, are "subjective." They are, according to the popular prejudice, "squishy," "ineffable," "hard to get hold of." They are—because they are "inner" and "private"—unmeasurable. Answers to survey questions, by contrast, are readily quantifiable, easily subject to statistical analysis, and need deal with emotions only in an indirect way. ("Do you have confidence in the leaders of your organization?" "Do you approve of the direction in which the country is going?") By contrast, I would like to explore the role of emotions in a direct manner, in part through what one might call "phenomenology," an appeal to our shared experience. This does not mean that I am describing only my own emotions, nor does it mean that I think it worth placing too much faith on the much-touted "method" of "empathy" or *Verstehen* that has played such an enormous role in the history of anthropology and sociology. But what has emerged from my research on emotions over the years are the conclusions that many, if not most, emotions are cognitively and evaluatively rich and insightful, not the brute forces or mere "arousal" discussed by many theorists. In short, emotions are essential to ethics, and emotional sensitivity, rather than only rationality and obeying the rules, is what ethics is all about. Furthermore, emotions are largely socially constituted, not in their biological origins, perhaps, but in their aims, expressions, and nuances.[5] In terms of the present discussion, this means that emotions should be understood in terms of emotional relationships.

There are ordinary and extraordinary leaders who often but not always correspond or fail to respond to ordinary and extraordinary situations. It is not surprising that much of the literature on leadership focuses on extraordinary leaders in extraordinary times, for example, Lincoln, Churchill, and Truman, to limit ourselves to three relatively recent Anglo-American examples. At such times (in the course of a civil war, a world war, the use of the first thermonuclear bomb), the emotions of all the world are extraordinary as well. Extraordinary emotions motivate and provoke extraordinary behaviors, which in turn produce and provoke even more extraordinary emotions. In extraordinary situations, predictions are extraordinarily difficult to make, if only because the extraordinary is by its very nature also relatively rare. How people behave in war, under fire, in circumstances in which their everyday bearings and sources of security and routine have been destroyed or rendered irrelevant, continues to be a matter for extensive study; but the behavior of supposedly ordinary people is no less fascinating than the behavior of the most distinguished and extraordinary leaders.

What do I know of the emotions of a Martin Luther King, facing down the dogs and bullhorns of a well-armed and hostile Alabama police force? For that matter, what do I know of the emotions of those who stood with him, trusted him, confident in the face of their own fear that what they were doing was both important and effective? What can I imagine of the emotions of a Roosevelt or Churchill, a Stalin or a Mao, or, for that matter, a Reverend Moon or a David Koresh or their benighted followers? Accordingly, I want to approach the subject of emotion in leadership in rather ordinary situations. But by understanding such ordinary feelings and emotions, we need not pretend that we are easily capable of imagining or projecting ourselves into dramatic, tragic, or heroic situations that in fact lie quite beyond most of our experiences. That, I think, is part of the difficulty of understanding the greatest as well as the most evil leaders. What we tend to understand is just those aspects of their personalities that are most common, most like ourselves, most "human-all-too-human," as Nietzsche called it. The extraordinariness escapes our study. By examining ordinary situations, however, we can bypass such captivating but perhaps impossible questions such as, Why can we not now find or produce an extraordinary leader of the ilk of a Lincoln, Churchill, or a Truman? One probable answer, of course, is that we do not want and will not allow for one.

But our society is filled with leaders—heads of departments, agencies, associations, and corporations. It would be a mistake to dismiss them all as something less than real leaders, as mere "managers," because they do not have that sparkle and celebrity usually identified as "charisma." My focus is on corporate executives and institutional administrators, university presidents and deans, cabinet ministers, and trade union leaders rather than on heroes. What sorts of emotions enter into their success and failure? The too familiar reply is couched in terms of "cool": the lack of emotion, an imperviousness or immunity to emotions. In other words, the less prone to "emotional" behavior, the more effective the leader. (In Taoism, one is taught that lessened emotional involvement results in a more intuitive response, but then the Taoists did not believe in leaders.) First, I would like to undermine and utterly reject that viewpoint. Second, I would like to insist that a rich and energetic emotional life is very different from the rather unflattering notion of behaving "emotionally," that is, "out of control." Leadership intimately involves the former, not the latter.[6]

A dominant theme in the current literature is the search for an all-encompassing definition (paradigm, model) of leadership.[7] I am not interested in joining the search here, nor am I impressed with the use of singular definitions to analyze complex and ambiguous social phenomena.[8] But I would like to make a point or two about the underlying emotional themes that are to be found in virtually all of such attempts to define *leadership*. I have highlighted certain terms recurring. I have also retained the distinctively male references in brackets to remind us of how embarrassingly sexist the field has been. This is not incidental to my point, of course. The assumption that leaders are men (with distinctively "masculine" virtues) as opposed to women (whose "feminine" features almost inevitably include some form of sentimentality or supposedly excessive emotionality) explains, in part, why the emotions have been ignored in favor of such dispassionate notions as "influence" and bureaucratic "management skills." This also goes some distance in explaining, I would suggest, why the distinction between "leader" and "manager" has been so problematic in the recent literature. So long as leadership is defined instrumentally or simply in terms of change vs. status, without explicit reference to and analysis of the emotions involved both in leading and in being led, the distinction is a negligible one, and leadership might just as well be reduced to the role of a mere "organizer."[9]

Consider the following definitions of leadership:[10]

1. "the ability to *impress* the will of the leader on those led and *induce* obedience, *respect, loyalty*, and cooperation" (B.V. Moore, 1927);
2. "an ability to *persuade* or direct [men]" (Reuter, 1941);

3. "authority *spontaneously* accorded [him] by [his] [fellow] group members" (C.A. Gibb, 1954);
4. "acts by a person which *influence* other persons in a shared direction" (M. Seeman, 1960);
5. "discretionary *influence*" (R.N. Osborn, J.G. Hunt, 1975);
6. "a [man] who has the ability to get other people to do what they don't want to do, and *like* it" (Harry Truman).

I have highlighted the terms *impress, induce, respect, loyalty, persuade, spontaneously, influence,* and *like* because they all strongly suggest (although obviously do not entail) emotional evocation. To be sure, there are skills and techniques of leadership (whether learned or "natural"), but leadership is not just instrumentality—"getting things done." It is also *moving* people, in both senses of that term. It involves stimulating their emotions, and it involves motivating them. Burns is perhaps most explicit about this, and his terms *exploiting tensions, raising consciousness,* and *strong values,* all suggest strong emotion. What are *strong values,* for example? They are values deeply held, values that are deemed important, but also, therefore, values with enormous emotional significance. *Transactional* leadership is, for him, a highly emotionally charged and infectious process. So, too, even when Joseph Rost employs the much more modest terminology of *an influence relationship* we immediately want to know *what kind of influence,* and some reference to emotions and affections is unavoidable.[11]

According to much of the recent literature, a leader is one who inspires and motivates, not just resolves or "manages." (The disdain heaped on the concept of *management* as a result of the search for *leadership* is a phenomenon that requires a detailed investigation of its own.) I think we might well distinguish between moral leadership and *moral leadership,* where the latter is truly inspirational and deeply emotional and the former is routine moral sensitivity. The latter may be what fascinates us, but the former, I would argue, is much more important for maintaining ethical organizations, institutions, and communities. To limit the honorific phrase *ethical leadership* to moral heroes is, again, to deny or demean what is perhaps most substantial to ethics and leadership, and no less based on emotion. More to the point here, however, one might notice that, in terms of the above definitions, most of the emotions of leadership tend to fall on the side of the led, the "followers," rather than the leader. This suggests an unfortunate paradigm, one unhappily much in evidence in the behavior of any number of demagogues. They certainly provoke emotions, often violent and extremely effective and well-directed emotions, but they often evidence very little of those same passions themselves. Thus we should avoid the temptation to suggest that leadership does not so much involve emotions (i.e., the emotions of the leader) as it does the emotional impact or effect of the leader on the led. This would reduce leadership to manipulation, perhaps even to creating appearances that affect followers, perhaps to mere "acting," and raise the question of *authenticity*. The emotions of leadership must, in part, be the emotions of the leader. He or she is not a puppeteer, a strategic manipulator of other people's feelings. He or she is, first of all, the subject of passions.

Leadership is the very opposite of "control," and to say that leadership is a matter of emotions is not to say that it is a matter of emotional control or, for that matter, manipulation either. Control is a quasi-mechanical term, and, in human relationships, implies at the very least some sort of coercion, which virtually every leadership theorist has rightly distinguished from leadership. For example, leadership through naked terror—imperatives backed up by threats—is hardly leadership. Thus we do not think of those military commanders who threaten to shoot their own troops if they retreat as "leaders." So, too, "manipulating" emotions, as if they were circuits simply to be stimulated, is not leadership either. If Hitler had wholly relied on the Gestapo and threats of violence against his own people, or if he had only pressed the red buttons of prejudice against gypsies and Jews, his "leadership" would not be so problematic. He would not be considered a leader at all. But instead, he evidently did inspire real devotion and action, although the values he represented and the horrible results of his leadership haunt our use of this term.[12] Because emotions are often (mis)conceived as involuntary, appealing to people's emotions is too easily (mis)conceived as trying to control or manipulate them; thus our highly negative reactions to mawkish leadership pleas and overt appeals to our baser passions. But emotions occupy an intermediate and problematic position between straightforward voluntary rational decision making and the merely mechanical. For example, zombies and robots may be commanded to behave without reference to their "will," but we do not think of someone as a "loyal follower" if he or she is merely a zombie or a robot.

Thus we talk in politics as well as romance about "winning hearts." When Harry Truman defines leadership as getting people to do something they did not want to do initially and "liking" it, he is not conferring retrospective approval or necessarily any kind of enjoyment. Rather, he captures in the simplest language the idea that emotional behavior is voluntary behavior, and what leaders do with their followers to "move" their emotions in the direction already passionately chosen by the leader. This choice, however, need not be thought out or fully understood (although one might argue, not always convincingly, that the more thought and understanding, the better the leader). This brings to the surface a rather difficult point about *knowledge* in leadership. It is often said that leadership is a skill or set of skills (which it certainly is) and that skills by their very nature require knowledge. This is so, but such "know-how" is not always articulated or propositional knowledge. Just as people need not know the direction in which they are being led, it does not follow that the leaders themselves know the direction in which they are leading. Hegel captured that lack of clarity in his stunning phrase "the cunning of reason." Tolstoi illustrated the thesis in detail in his unflattering treatment of the principals in the 1812 Napoleonic invasion of Russia and the battle of Borodino in particular. But "not knowing the direction" does not mean "in complete ignorance." The leader may well be "feeling his way along" or "following his intuitions," and his followers may know only that they trust him and are faithfully following. To be a bit polemical, we might say that too much is made of the role of knowledge in leadership and not enough of such emotional features as trust and loyalty. More plainly, knowledge (for example, managerial knowledge) is effective in leadership only insofar as that knowledge is in the service of the appropriate emotions.

The demand, that "knowledge be in the service of the appropriate emotions," is the beginning of an all-important answer to the most devastating challenge to the role of emotions in leadership. It is often noted that Hitler inspired at least as great devotion as Roosevelt and considerably more than Lincoln, and so the question is raised how one set of emotions can be judged superior to another. In ethics in general, this is often referred to as the problem of "relativism," that is, whether a set of values held sacred by a community is thereby *right and proper for them*, and beyond criticism from anyone else. This assumes that there are no common "nonrelative" values, or, in the case of emotions, that there are no standards for emotion apart from those already contained within the emotion. But there are such common values, and there are such standards: social harmony and well-being, to begin with. Thus we might suggest a criterion to distinguish between effective but evil leadership and ethical leadership: the promotion of harmony and the public good. But these characteristics are not self-contained within a society, nor can they apply to one part of a society without including consideration of all other parts as well. "Us vs. them" leadership, I would argue, always contains at least the potential for evil (although when an oppressed group is struggling against an oppressor group, this danger may remain invisible for some time). The "appropriate emotions," therefore, will be those that are conducive to these larger concerns as well as sensitive to the nuances of the current situation. An ethical leader, in short, is one who shares with his or her followers the emotions of fairness, mutual well-being, and harmony. In corporations, all of this might well be stated in terms of real concerns for "stakehold-ers" rather than the tempting but ultimately divisive focus on "the bottom line." In politics, it would be stated in terms of the urgency of winning elections. The "appropriate emotions" in ethical leadership motivate not the grudging decision to sacrifice profits or lose an election but rather the overriding passion to do the right thing.

FALSE LEADS: THE MYTH OF CHARISMA

The term *charisma* is shorthand for the emotional power of certain rare leaders, but it is, unfortunately, without ethical value and without much explanatory value either. It is one of the most frequently recurrent terms in discussions of leadership. Derived in its current usage from the Ger-man sociologist Max Weber, it is, perhaps, the only such term that so explicitly refers to the emotional quality of leadership, albeit at consid-erable cost to clarity, imbued as the term is with mystery and magic. It is also used at great cost to an adequate understanding of emotions, since the very notion of charisma connotes an irrational as opposed to a ratio-nal influence. Although Weber is noted for his analysis of institutions and bureaucracy in terms of "rationality," he himself was an ethical noncognitivist and viewed rationality and rationalization as a costly "disenchantment" with the world. At the end of his famous book *The Protestant Ethic and the Spirit of Capitalism*[13] he argued that rationalism is destructive of value, an "iron cage" in which both freedom and meaning are sacrificed to efficiency. One should not be surprised, therefore, that for him charisma offered a significantly religious promise.[14]

The Weberian term is defined by the *American Heritage Dictionary* as follows: " 1.a. A rare personal quality attributed to leaders who arouse fervent popular devotion and enthusiasm. b. Personal magnetism or charm. 2. Theology. An extraordinary power, such as the ability to perform miracles, granted to a Christian by the Holy Spirit."

The theological dimension of the term is to be noted, especially in Weber's classic use of the concept, as is the idea that charisma is by its very nature "rare." Its nature does not invite analysis; in fact, it discour-ages it. Even careful analytic writers like Robert Nozick are reduced to such impoverished New Age metaphors as an "aura."[15] It will not do to take the nature of charisma as given, trying only to understand its use and effects.[16] The fact that it is rare (and "blessed") encourages gratitude and reverence rather than critical analysis, and its kinship to "magnetism and charm" tends to foreclose any meaningful investiga-tion. Indeed, James MacGregor Burns warns that the "term is so over-used it threatens to collapse under close analysis."[17]

Bernard Bass describes charisma as displayed by leaders "to whom followers form deep emotional attachments and who in turn inspire their followers to transcend their own interests for superordinate goals."[18] This is true, perhaps, but what are these emotional attachments? How do they work? What are their vicissitudes? The mysterious origins of charisma also invite a serious worry: What happens when this "blessing" turns into a curse and serves evil rather than good (the "Hitler Problem" again)? How do we know that the gift is from God rather than from Satan, except by the results?[19] Thus C. Hodgkinson warns, "Beware charisma,"[20] and Michael Keeley, in a powerful essay, attacks "transformational leadership" precisely on the grounds that it gives too much credence to charisma and too little to the madisonian "checks and balances" that control or contain charisma.[21] Charisma, according to such authors, is a dangerous genie to let out of the bottle. But few of them pay much if any attention to what charisma actually is, leaving unanalyzed charisma's enviable status as "an extraordinary power" (if not exactly "the ability to perform miracles"), "a rare personal quality" of leaders "who arouse fervent popular devotion and enthusiasm."

I argue that charisma is not anything in particular. It is not a distinctive quality of personality or character, and it is not an essential implement of leadership. Rather, it is a misleading even if exciting concept that deflects us from the emotional complexity of leadership that might better occupy our attention. Charisma is not a single quality, nor is it a single emotion or set of emotions. It is a generalized way of pointing to and emptily explaining an emotional relationship that is too readily characterized as fascination but should be analyzed more fundamentally in terms of trust. Within the range of what is usually identified as "charisma," I would want to distinguish:[22]

What the leader is saying. Is it the message itself that is fascinating? Steve Forbes smartly suggested a simplified "flat tax" at precisely the time that most American taxpayers were brooding over, struggling with, and hating the brain-twisting annual exercise called "filling out your 1040." It is not surprising that people were fascinated, and other candidates quickly adopted the idea. The attention Forbes received had nothing to do with charisma. Often a good idea—even sound common sense—will evoke sufficient emotion that the praise goes to the speaker when it is the idea that is really being endorsed. (Ross Perot's appearance in 1992 is probably a case in point.)

The rhetorical persuasiveness of how he or she says it. Martin Luther King was a brilliant orator, although that by itself is not what made him a great leader. More recently, Pat Buchanan, while more of a curmudgeonly televangelical than a voice of hope, has obviously found the "hot buttons" of a substantial portion of the American public. Rhetorical skills alone do not count as charisma, or many English professors would be leaders. Nevertheless, rhetorical skills certainly play a considerable role in what is called charisma. Such skills may make a mediocre message—and the speaker—much more memorable than the ideas themselves deserve.

The hopes, wishes, and fears of the audience. Obviously, what gets said is fascinating not just for its own sake; it speaks to powerful emotions on the part of the audience. But this by itself says more about the receptivity of the audience than the character of the speaker—riling people up is not yet leading them. Yet, insofar as leadership is an emotional relationship that concerns the future, responding to hopes, wishes, and fears may well be interpreted as charisma by an appreciative audience. Paranoia, notably, produces some of the most "charismatic" leaders.

His or her degree of enthusiasm, "infectiousness." What is obviously an aspect of the personality of a leader is his or her ability to excite and transmit emotion, even against the initial resistance or opposition of others. A recent analysis of Franklin Roosevelt suggests "his remarkable capacity to transmit his internal strength to others."[23] Enthusiasm is certainly high up on the list of ingredients of charisma, and enthusiasm plus infectiousness takes us a long way to understanding what is meant by the term. Motivational speakers are often called "charismatic," but we should note again that this does not imply leadership.

Such personality traits as charm, intelligence, and sincerity. Much of what passes for charisma is in fact some combination of much more easily understood character traits. "Charm" may be difficult to define (although literature abounds with some excellent witticisms, such as "charm is getting what you want without asking"). Much of John Kennedy's famous charisma was, no doubt, a combination of his straightforward charm and his good looks. Inevitably, a fascinating or comforting leader is characterized as "attractive," "sexy," "fatherly," or "motherly." (A concept that deserves some rigorous analysis is *presence*. While this term shares many of the problems of *charisma*, at least it is rarely confused with magic. It is, for example, highly correlated with such mundane features as height.)

"Celebrity." These days celebrity is often confused with leadership, and it is celebrity, not leadership, that attracts the attribution of charisma. But celebrity clearly requires no particular virtues or characteristics other than merely being much in the news, often on television, the butt of popular jokes and late-night humor, or being readily recognized. (Indeed, the talking heads who do nothing but read the news headlines on television are typically viewed as celebrities.) This is what Jay Conger calls *attribution*. What does this have to do with leadership?

The nature of the situation or "context." Sometimes an individual who stands up or comes through in terrifying, dangerous, promising, or hate-filled circumstances may thereby get accepted as a leader. (Boris Yeltsin facing the tanks is an apt example.) This is not charisma; the circumstances, rather than any particular quality of the character in question, supply the aura of seeming greatness, at least for a while.

Change. Many leadership theorists (e.g., Burns, Rost) note presiding over change as an essential ingredient in leadership. Whether this is so, being visibly "in charge" of change is itself often conflated with the dynamism of charisma. But, as in Tolstoi, there is always the question of where the action really is, in the leader or in the change itself. True, there is much to be said about managing change, and much to be debated about the ability of any leader to bring about change without the forces of society already mustered, but the dynamics of change itself may be readily confused with the dynamic character of the leader.

Resemblance/continuity. In contrast, sometimes charisma may be little more than continuity, a carryover, an echo of previous leadership or, perhaps, the result of an enduring myth or faulty memory. George H. W. Bush had enough seeming charisma to carry him through one presidential election, but it quickly became apparent that this was merely the fading continuation of the Reagan "magic." Harry Truman, by contrast, suffered from comparison with his great predecessor. Regardless of whether he had his own degree of charisma, he had to establish his reputation for leadership from a decidedly disadvantaged position.

What is called charisma may be some blend or mixture of all these different ingredients, and no doubt more besides, but that is not the point of this crude dissection. I suggest that charisma doesn't refer to any character trait or "quality" in particular, but is rather a general way of referring to a person who seems to be a dynamic and effective leader. And as a term of analysis in leadership studies, I think that it is more of a distraction than a point of understanding.

THE EMOTIONAL CORE OF LEADERSHIP: TRUST

Charisma distracts us from looking at the relationship between the leader and the led and, in particular, the relationship of trust. The mistake is not so much that charisma is dangerous in the "wrong" leaders, but rather that it is a distorted perspective on leadership. The word *trust* appears in virtually every current book on leadership, and it is taken as commonplace that without trust, leadership is impossible. This has not always been the case. Machiavelli, for example, suggests that leaders should strive to be feared, not loved. But trust is hard to analyze, and it is hard to say anything very useful about it. Francis

Fukuyama has published a 400-page book simply entitled *Trust*,[24] but one is hard put to find any discussion of the subject in those many pages. Fukuyama utterly ignores the dynamics of trust, the ways in which trust is created and cultivated, particularly between cultures and rival subcultural groups. Nevertheless, many of the examples of what Fukuyama calls "spontaneous sociability" are revealing.

Several standard definitions of trust (e.g., N. Luhmann and B. Barber) characterize it primarily in terms of *expectations*,[25] but this is only half the story. It also involves decisions and the dynamics of a relationship. Trust, in other words, is an emotional relationship, as is leadership. Putting it more succinctly, leadership is an emotional relationship of trust.

Niklas Luhmann distinguishes trust from confidence, noting that we trust (or don't trust) people but have (or do not have) confidence in institutions. This points to an important distinction, but it does not yet reach it. The distinction between persons and organizations is convenient and obvious but often, especially in business and organizational ethics, misleading or counterproductive. Organizations and institutions have many features of persons (not least, that in the eye of the law they are persons, with fiduciary obligations, rights and responsibilities). As such, we trust them (or not) much as we would trust a person who had made us a promise or with whom we had agreed upon a contract. On the other hand, we sometimes have confidence in people we do not or would not trust; for example, bureaucrats who are known for their fairness and efficiency but are personally unknown to us. We may also have confidence in someone precisely because we do not trust him or her; for instance, when we place our confidence in the double-dealing habits of an old enemy, or "have confidence" that our friend M will fail to quit smoking this time as he has failed in every one of the last thirty-one attempts to do so. (This use of "have confidence" is not wholly ironic.)

The distinction that Luhmann is after has been stated by Laurence Thomas, among others, who distinguishes between trust and prediction.[26] We predict that something will happen. We trust that someone will do something. The distinction is between mechanism and agency, nature and persons. Trust, in other words, is not predicting that something will be the case. This, it seems to me, is fairly obvious, yet it has taken up a substantial portion of the literature (perhaps just because it is so seemingly straightforward). Here, I think, is where Luhmann is aiming us as well, although he mislocates the cleavage. Organizations and institutions are not mechanisms, no matter how efficiently (that is, "mechanically") they may be constructed. Organizations and institutions are people, working together. Those people, and consequently the organizations and institutions they create, are agents. Thus they have obligations, rights, and responsibilities. What they will do is not simply a matter of probabilities. It is a matter of trust. This is why the common-sensical notion (advocated by Luhmann and adopted by Barber) that trust is first of all a set of expectations is misleading. It is this, of course, but it is much more than this. Trust, as opposed to prediction or confidence, presupposes a relationship. And relationships by their nature involve much more than a calculation of probabilities and outcomes. They involve values and emotions, responsibilities, and the possibility of not only disappointment but betrayal.

Trust is an umbrella term. It is not an emotion as such, although in certain situations it can manifest itself as a very powerful emotion, notably and most dramatically in the case of betrayal, but also in its positive display. One way of describing this feature of trust is to say that, by its very nature, it is part of the *background* of our social activities.[27] To say that trust is not as such an emotion is not, however, to remove it from the realm of emotion. Quite the contrary. Trust is the framework within which emotions appear, their precondition, the structure of the world in which they operate. Without trust, there can be no betrayal, but, more generally, without trust, there can be no cooperation, no community, no commerce, no conversation.[28] And in a context without trust, of course, all sorts of emotions readily surface, starting with suspicion, quickly escalating to contempt, resentment, hatred, and worse. Thus *trust* characterizes an entire network of emotions and emotional attitudes, both between individuals and within groups and by way of a psychodynamic profile of entire societies. (This is Fukuyama's theme in *Trust*.) In such large contexts, one might even say that trust is something of an "atmosphere," a shared emotional understanding about who is or who is not to be included, contracted, "trusted."

One reason to argue that trust is not as such an emotion is to get rid of the uncritical picture of trust as a "warm fuzzy feeling" of the sort so disdained by hard-headed ethicists and leaders of all sorts. Thus I would disagree with John Dunn when he argues that trust is a human passion or sentiment.[29] It is not, say, like compassion. It is not even an attitude. Not that I object to warm, fuzzy feelings. On the contrary, sentimentality can be a powerful (although easily exploited) quality of leadership and one that is often neglected in the more "macho" emphasis on charisma. But to think of trust as a particular feeling—not to mention a mawkish feeling—is to demean it and to give a misleading characterization of what trust entails. Trusting does not indicate a "softness," a gullibility, or a weakness. It is a strength, a precondition of any alliance or mutual understanding. It is not a vulnerability, except insofar as, by the very nature of the case, someone who is trusted is thereby in a position to betray that trust. And trust is, I would argue, necessarily a reciprocal relation. This is not to say that Franklin can only trust Benito if Benito trusts Franklin as well, but it is to say that trust is a relationship and not merely an attitude. If Franklin "trusts" Benito but Benito has no relation to Franklin, I am tempted to say that this cannot be a matter of trust at all, but rather predictability or confidence.

One might think of trust in negative terms, as, for example, a suspension of fear or a suspension of certain thoughts. However, while this notion captures an important insight (namely, that trust as such doesn't *feel* like anything in particular), it fails to capture the important positive dimensions of trust, because it fails to appreciate the nature and character of emotion. Put one way, perhaps too starkly, emotions are not feelings, except in the most generic and, for the most part, vacuous sense of that term (as any felt mental state or experience). Even anger, which would seem to be as profoundly "felt" as any emotion, is not just a feeling or even primarily a feeling. It is an attitude toward the world, specifically directed at a person, action, situation, or state of affairs. More accurately, anger is a systematic set of judgments, judgments of blame, especially, that cast their target in a particular role, put him or her on trial, or consider him or her for punishment.[30] Trust, by way of this perspective, is a certain *conception* of the world and other people. It is a way of seeing, a way of estimating and valuing. Thus it establishes a framework of expectations and agreements (explicit or not) in which actions conform or fail to conform. A leader, one might surmise, is one who succeeds in establishing or sustaining a framework of trust. Indeed, perhaps the increasingly evasive distinction between attentive leaders and actively participating followers has not to do with the recommendation or initiation of actions but rather with the primary responsibility for such a framework.[31]

Trust can also be a decision. To talk about trust as background brings it dangerously close to something that is taken for granted, something that is either there or not there (Fukuyama's general assumption about "high trust" and "low trust" societies). But as we all know from our own experience, trust can be a very conscientious, extremely difficult, and deliberative decision. We meet someone new, or we find ourselves in a new situation with someone we do not know very well. Something comes up. Something must be done. We have to decide: Do we trust this person? In such cases, we establish a framework that was not in place before. Of course, there will be a more general framework within which this relationship and this situation takes place, and that general framework will influence and may well define the boundaries of the decision. One does not want to be too deterministic about this. Some of the most important trust decisions, in particular, decisions to trust a new leader, are made in defiance of an existing trust or distrust situation. But trust is not always in the background. Sometimes, such as when we have to decide whether to trust someone, it may be very much in the foreground. Indeed, it may be the definitive aspect of the situation. In leadership, the establishment of trust by a new president just taking office, for example, may be the most important factor in his or her success or failure.

But then, trust is also dynamic.[32] As such, it can clearly be talked about in terms of emotion, but it turns out to be something more than an emotion. It is more of a family of emotions, negotiations, deliberations, and decisions. For example, a woman has all of the evidence imaginable that her husband has been and is still being unfaithful. She refuses to accept that evidence—or, rather, she refuses to accept it *as evidence*—and thus refuses to accept the obvious conclusion. One might glibly say that this is self-deception, a blatant attempt to refuse to recognize what she in fact clearly knows.[33] But I would argue that it can also be a conscious decision and not deception at all. It is not that the woman refuses to acknowledge (if only to herself) what she knows. It is rather that she has decided to trust her husband, regardless of his behavior (which can then be conveniently ignored or pushed to the side). So, too, I want to argue, while leaders may be said to earn the trust of their followers, it is the followers who have the capacity to give that trust. Trust thus becomes a part of the dynamics of the relationship between those who would be leaders and their followers, even when the leadership position is independently determined, as it usually is. (CEOs, supervisors, officers, deans, and college presidents—at least in Texas—are placed in their positions by such higher authorities as boards of directors and generals, not by those whom they are to lead.)

One problem in analyzing trust is a certain ambiguity, much of it due to the above background-foreground contrast. Because trust covers so many situations, however, one is tempted to try to sharpen the edges and define trust in terms of its context or content. Thus Benjamin Barber distinguishes three different meanings of *trust* by virtue of the object or content of that trust: first, a general meaning regarding social expectations; second, a "competence" sense of trust, that one has the skills and knowledge to carry out one's responsibilities (e.g., a doctor, an explosives expert, a White House economist); and third, a "partnership" or "fiduciary" sense, in which one is trusted to carry out certain duties or obligations, as a result of a certain relationship, usually by virtue of some commitment, contract, or agreement.[34] I find such distinctions troubling, mainly because I think that it is a problem to distinguish kinds of trust on the basis of trust's object or content, but also because one's obligations and one's expected competencies are usually correlated in a logical way ("ought implies can," says Kant in a phrase of admirable brevity). Furthermore, it is not clear in what sense the two "specialized" senses of trust are not just that—not different meanings or senses of trust but only more specific instances of trust in general.

And, as if to underscore the problem of multiplying senses needlessly, much of Barber's book is spent criticizing alternative accounts of trust on the grounds that they conflate the latter two senses of *trust*, which gets in the way of some of his genuinely interesting observations about trust in practice, in the family, in politics, and (in a less obvious sense) in business.[35] What he does not discuss, unfortunately, is the central role of trust in leadership (as opposed to politics) as such.

What I am suggesting is that different dimensions (not "senses") of trust be distinguished not on the basis of the object or content of trust, but on its social role, its role as an emotion, and its role as background. In many situations, paradigmatically in the primordial situation in which as infants we trust our parents, trust might best be considered part of the background. It is present and taken for granted throughout in every transaction. It is not at issue and not in question. Often, such trust relationships are unrecognized as such, until, that is, the trust is breached. For example, banks have been the target of distrust and abuse by American populists and political activists since the last century. President Andrew Jackson even sought to outlaw them. And yet, the amount of trust taken for granted by anyone who has any business with banking at all is astounding. We trust that the money we deposit will be returned to us as promised. We trust that the bills and most checks we receive are valid and genuine. The fact that we ask for a "bank check" or "cashier's check" for absolute security is further evidence of our trust in banks, however great our distrust may be on some more abstract level.[36] And yet, we all have seen the consequences of even a minor bank scare. Not just that bank but all banks are suddenly under scrutiny, under suspicion.[37] Banking depends on trust—not as an issue, but as background. Trust has already been compromised once it has become an issue, once the question, Is my money really safe in that bank? has come up. So, too, once a leader comes under suspicion, no matter that the charges against him may be malevolent and/or political, trust in him as a leader is already compromised. Thus the political effectiveness of raising the Whitewater issue, which proclaims itself to be a question of Clinton's character but in fact is intended to be and obviously has succeeded in casting doubt on his trustworthiness as a leader.

The emotional dimension of trust is more explicit, more dynamic. Here trust is an active relationship and transaction rather than the background of relationships and transactions. This is most evident when it is most in question, for example, at the negotiating table between two bitter and mutually distrustful enemies (the Bosnians and the Serbs, the Israelis and the Syrians). Trust here involves decisions. One decides to trust the other, however tentatively. It is here that the dynamic of trust gets really interesting, for even the slightest hint of betrayal can be met by the most awesome response. We can also witness the evolution or growth of trust, typically not in a single all-or-nothing decision but rather in incremental increases, although it may be generations before trust is sufficiently established to blend into the background. Sometimes, miraculously, mutual trust can just become a fact. Indeed, what I find most fascinating about trust is the human tendency to trust, despite all of the cynicism and suspicion to the contrary. Most people, in the absence of any clear warning or traumatic past experience, tend to be trusting. Trust in general is not so much an achievement as an assumption. It is the initial state rather than a result. People would rather trust than not (and, obviously, would rather be trusted than not). If this is so, it lends an interesting twist to all of the current questions about a "crisis of trust" in American leadership. In a recent column, Alexander Cockburn sagely suggests that this "crisis" in fact reflects people's resentment and distrust of pollsters and professors rather than of one another.[38] He also adds that the American people have always distrusted their leaders. Based on my own reading, I believe this to be false, and so one is moved to ask what particular and obviously effective obstacles to trust are operative in the current political environment. Watergate and Vietnam have obviously worn out their explanatory power.

We talk a great deal about *earning* trust, but I would suggest that *giving* trust is a more promising avenue of pursuit. Earning trust is, ultimately, encouraging trust to slip into the background. Giving trust is a dynamic decision, the transformation of a relationship of the most basic and sometimes most difficult kind. This, I would suggest, is central to any conception of "transforming" or "transformational leadership," indeed, to any leadership at all. But this places an enormous burden on the led. Their decision to trust or not to trust makes leadership possible, and I believe much of the traditional talk about charisma as "a special quality" might better be viewed as the endowment or the projection of such a quality, by way of the people who then "find" that property worthy of following. When it is not part of the background, trust is something that has to be given. But for most leaders in most situations, certainly today, trust cannot be presumed to be part of the background. Thus they must make considerable effort in the name of earning people's trust, but earning usually entails desert, and the history of politics makes all too clear that life in politics is not fair. Ultimately, perhaps, in politics there is no such thing as deserving the people's trust. One is trustworthy, or one is not. One is trusted, or one is not. But whether or not trust can be earned, it can be wisely or foolishly given. Thus it is those who would follow, not those who would lead, who are the ultimate power in any leadership relationship.

CONCLUSION: WHETHER 'TIS BETTER TO BE LOVED OR FEARED

Whether it is "better to be loved or feared" is, of course, one of the more famous questions raised by Machiavelli in *The Prince*, and his answer was unambiguous. Better to be feared, he said, but what should be obvious, even within that grim framework, is that the emotional choices are woefully incomplete. One need not fear a leader to obey, nor need one love a leader to trust. Indeed, the extremes of emotion all too often tend to provoke the extremes of reaction, which Machiavelli clearly sees, and neither provides a very promising guide to leadership, much less ethical leadership. Charisma is designed to solve the problem by providing an emotional intermediary that salvages the power of fear and love but dispenses with the liabilities of both: the hatred generated by fear, the fickleness invited by love. But charisma serves this purpose only by introducing opacities and misunderstandings of its own. Thus I have suggested, albeit briefly, that trust would be a much better emotional vehicle for the discussion of leadership than charisma.

NOTES

1. Can an evil leader be an effective leader? It is tempting to reject the stipulative definition: that is, define a "leader" or a "good/effective leader" as an "ethical leader," thus stipulating Koresh and Hitler out of consideration. But making ethics a necessary condition for leadership simply begs the question, What distinguishes between good and bad (even evil) leaders? The second temptation to avoid is a pseudo-Weberian religious analysis, such that the quality of charisma, which is deemed essential to true leadership, is by its very nature "blessed." We know (as did Weber) that the voice of God seems to be heard by some very unlikely and unlikable ears. For a good discussion of this, see R. Heifetz, *Leadership Without Easy Answers* (Cambridge: Harvard University Press, 1994).

2. One can often choose to be a follower without being chosen, but one cannot be a leader without being chosen, in some sense, to lead (even those who, in Shakespeare's phrase, have leadership "thrust upon them").

3. I have benefited from several excellent books in the field: Heifetz; Jay A. Conger, *The Charismatic Leader* (San Francisco: Jossey-Bass, 1989); and, of course, James MacGregor Burns, *Leadership* (New York: Harper, 1978).

4. For example, Heifetz, who begins *Leadership Without Easy Answers* with "Leadership arouses passions," 13. Conger remarks, "They [charismatic leaders] touch our emotions," xi.

5. Robert C. Solomon, *The Passions* (New York: Doubleday, 1976; Indianapolis: Hackett, 1993).

6. The role of emotionality in leadership, as opposed to emotions, is complex. An interesting illustration is crying, an explicit display of becoming emotional. Senator Ed Muskie reputedly lost his bid for the Democratic nomination for the presidency when he cried at a press conference during the primaries. Jimmy Carter cried upon losing the 1980 election to Ronald Reagan; his act was treated with considerable disdain. Congresswoman Pat Schroeder cried in pub-

lic about the same time, but reactions were more mixed, ranging from "just like a woman" to "crying shows strength."

7. See Joseph C. Rost, *Leadership for the Twenty-First Century* (New York: Praeger, 1991).

8. In fact, I would argue that the misguided search for definitions in the social sciences more often paralyzes than clarifies research. Precipitous attempts at definition distort and falsify both hypotheses and data and provoke debates which, by the very nature of the case, cannot be resolved before the research is well under way. The hidden model here, I believe, is that of Socrates, developed twenty-five hundred years ago. Socrates also searched by definitions, but he believed that a definition would yield a "numenal" (almost mystical) insight into the true nature of reality. But without the fantastic metaphysics that accompanies this belief, the search for definitions is not much more than the naive sophomoric demand that we "define our terms." The truth is that a proper definition comes at the end, not at the beginning of an intensive research program. Even then, it should be considered no more than a summary account of "work in progress." This applies to wholly technical, stipulative terms, and certainly to loaded historical terms like "leadership."

9. This language is particularly prominent in the work of James MacGregor Burns, who distinguishes between "transactional" and "transformational" leadership on this basis. There is a political sense in which the term *organizer*, however, operates very much like the term *leader* and connotes the passionate "transformation" of a cause rather than coldly bureaucratic efficiency. Labor organizers, for example, would be a case in point, as opposed to the purely managerial 1934 E. S. Bogardus definition quoted by Rost: "Leadership is a process in which the activities of many are organized to move in a specific direction by one" (Rost, 47). See also Joanne Ciulla, "Leadership Ethics: Mapping the Territory," *Business Ethics Quarterly*, vol. 5, no. 1 (Jan. 1995): 11.

10. I have taken the following definitions from Ciulla and Rost.

11. At one point, Burns attacks Rost on the supposed need for consensus and comments that consensus erodes leadership. It is worth speculating why this might be so. Consensus is usually the outcome of negotiation and compromise, typically "cool-headed" rather than enthusiastic. Thus, we encounter a somewhat traditional philosophical question: Can such cool-headed reason motivate action, or does consensus, while it may promote harmony and even efficiency, stifle the passionate urge to do something difficult, even seemingly impossible? In other words, does consensus undermine the emotional appeal of, as well as the need for, leadership?

12. Despite decades of denial, that the German people in general were fully knowledgeable participants in Hitler's vision is now generally believed. See, for example, Daniel Goldhagen, *Hitler's Willing Executioners: Ordinary Germans and the Holocaust* (New York: Knopf, 1996).

13. First published in 1904, it appeared in English in 1930 (New York: Scribner).

14. See Hans Gerth and C. Wright Mills, eds., "The Sociology of Charismatic Authority," in *From Max Weber: Essays in Sociology* (New York: Oxford University Press, 1946), 245 ff.

15. Robert Nozick, *Philosophical Explanations* (New York: Simon & Schuster, 1990).

16. See Conger.

17. Burns, 243.

18. See Ciulla.

19. Jim Jones and David Koresh are examples. If not for the ultimately lethal consequences, would such figures ever have been considered "leaders"?

20. Quoted by Edwin P. Hollander, "Ethical Challenges in the Leader-Follower Relationship," *Business Ethics Quarterly*, vol. 5, no. 1 (Jan. 1995): 57.

21. Michael Keeley, "The Trouble with Transformational Leadership," *Business Ethics Quarterly*, vol. 5, no. 1 (Jan. 1995): 57.

22. I should say here that I am indebted to Jay Conger's work on charismatic leadership, although my analysis is quite different from his and I do not give "charisma" the centrality that he does.

23. Robert Wilson, ed., *Character Above All* (New York: Simon & Schuster, 1996).

24. New York: Free Press, 1995.

25. Niklas Luhmann, *Trust and Power* (New York: John Wiley, 1980), 80; Bernard Barber, *Logic and Limits of Trust* (New Brunswick: Rutgers University Press, 1983), 2, 71.

26. Laurence Thomas, *Living Morally* (Philadelphia: Temple University Press, 1989); Annette Baier, *Moral Prejudice* (Cambridge: Harvard University Press, 1994).

27. The concept of the "background" comes from Heidegger and his analyses of human practices in general, but it is also explained in a more analytic framework by John Searle in his book *Intentionality* (Cambridge: Cambridge University Press, 1983).

28. Of course, there can be banter and all kinds of "speech," but the number of "speech acts" that simply break down is mind-boggling, and not only those that depend on trust that the other person is telling the truth.

29. In Diego Gambetta, *Trust* (Oxford: Blackwell, 1988), 73.

30. I have argued this analysis of anger at much greater length in my book *The Passions* (New York: Doubleday, 1976; Indianapolis: Hackett, 1993) and in numerous articles, e.g., "Getting Angry," in Richard Schweder and Robert LeVine, eds., *Culture Theory* (Cambridge: Cambridge University Press, 1984).

31. Burns, Jan. 22, 1996.

32. Thus, Dunn also insists that trust is a "modality" as well as a human passion. See Gambetta.

33. I have discussed this sort of self-deception as an active and necessary ingredient of social relations in "Self, Deception and Self-Deception," in Roger Ames, ed., *Self and Deception* (New York: SUNY Press, 1997).

34. The last definition follows Talcott Parsons, to whom Barber is obviously indebted. See Parsons on trust as a consequence of commitment in his *Politics and Social Structure* (New York: Free Press, 1969), 4.

35. Barber seems to conflate "trust" with "confidence," a distinction he borrows from Luhmann, who talks about trust in "the market."

36. The difference between practical trust and theoretical distrust is a fascinating topic in its own right, especially in leadership studies. It is often noted, for example, that Americans now claim to distrust their government at the same time that their demands and expectations of government are at an all-time high. Attitudes toward banks and banking—except for those rare eccentrics who prefer to keep their cash under the mattress—is another case in point. "In God We Trust" is printed on American money. The awkward truth, however, is that "In Government We Trust" is the necessary precondition of the value of any currency.

37. The Bank of New Zealand scare of 1990 threatened to undermine that entire economy, not to mention the current difficulties of the big Tokyo banks.

38. Alexander Cockburn, *The Nation* (Feb. 1996).

Part III

The Morality of Leaders: Motives and Deeds

6

Should Leaders Be Selfish or Altruistic?

Letters on Leader Motivation

Bruce J. Avolio and Edwin E. Locke

LETTER 1: WHY LEADERS SHOULD BE SELF-INTERESTED

Dear Bruce:

I would like to convey to you some of my thoughts on the issue of whether leaders should be self-sacrificial (altruistic) or egoistic (selfish). I will defend the view that leaders (and everyone else) should be selfish. However, before I can discuss this issue intelligently, I need to define my terms.

Let me begin with the term *self-sacrifice* or altruism. (Technically, these concepts are not identical. The concept of self-sacrifice itself does not specify whom the beneficiary of the sacrifice should be [e.g., God, animals, trees]. Altruism says the beneficiary should be other people or society. This is what people typically mean when they advocate self-sacrifice.) Many people are confused about the meaning of sacrifice. Some, for example, claim that there is no such thing as self-sacrifice because all people do what they really "want" to do: that is, they choose the path

with the strongest valence or expected value. Clearly, there is an equiv-
ocation here. All actions are certainly motivated by something, but the
issue is: motivated by what principle? It is obvious that although both
Mother Teresa and Thomas Edison were motivated to act, they were
motivated by very different and opposite moral principles. Mother
Teresa turned herself into an ascetic, selfless scarecrow whose sole
function in life was to tender to the poor. Thomas Edison flamed with
a burning passion to invent; his focus was not on the social good that
his lightbulb could achieve (although he was aware of its commercial
possibilities); it was on the lightbulb. He was motivated by the selfish
love of creation.

Another misconception is that self-sacrifice or altruism are synonymous with helping others. Helping others is not necessarily self-sacrificial. It can be done for selfish motives. For example, an individual
may help his or her spouse or children out of love for them; for the
same reason, individuals may not help people they do not personally
value. An employee may help a co-worker because it is in his
self-interest to see that the project gets finished and the company
succeeds. A passerby may help a stranded motorist out of benevolence
or good will.

What, then, does self-sacrifice actually mean? It means the sacrifice
of a higher value to a lower one. "Sacrifice does not mean the rejection
of the worthless but of the precious . . . [It is] the surrender of that which
you value in favor of that which you don't" (Binswanger, 1986, p. 429,
quoting Ayn Rand). Sacrifice to whom? Altruism (literally, otherism)
means the sacrifice of oneself to others. "The basic principle of altruism
is that man has no right to exist for his own sake, that sacrifice to others
is the only justification of his existence, and that self-sacrifice is his
highest moral duty, virtue and value" (Binswanger, 1986, p. 4, quoting
Ayn Rand).

So if a leader wanted to be truly altruistic, he or she should pick
a role (job, career) he does not want or value, make a product he or
she has no personal interest in, expect no rewards for his or her
achievements, and devote himself or herself to serving the wants of
his or her customers and employees without any hope of pleasure or
gain. Would anyone want to be a leader under such circumstances?
I cannot imagine why.

Now let us consider the alternative to altruism. Obviously, it is
selfishness. The concept of selfishness has been even more misunderstood than that of altruism. Consider how the so-called "selfish"
leader is typically portrayed. He or she takes the job, not because he
or she loves the work, but because he or she wants power. He or she
is not at all averse to lying to get his or her way, and may even enjoy
it. He or she keeps promises only if it is convenient at the time. He

or she may hire smart people but is sure to take credit for their accomplishments and blame them when things go wrong. He or she becomes infuriated if a subordinate disagrees with him or her. He or she likes to lead by threat and intimidation. He or she is desperate to see his or her name in the press and boasts of his or her own greatness. He or she insists on a huge salary that is unrelated to the success of the company; if he or she has stock options, he or she makes sure (through repricing the options) that he or she makes money even if the stock goes down. He or she lets people compete for his or her favors and rewards those who bow to him or her and flatter him or her while punishing those who do not. He or she fudges the numbers, if he or she thinks he or she can get away with it, to make profits look good in the short run. He or she uses company money for personal expenses. He or she relishes the perks of the office and loves to be driven to VIP parties in his or her chauffeured limousine. Oh, and one more, thing: This type of leader inevitably fails, when the bottom line gets too bad to hide; typically, he or she is fired in disgrace, his or her career in tatters.

Now, let us take a closer look at selfishness. Selfishness literally means to act in one's own interest. The concept does not specify either how to discover one's interests or how to achieve them. Many people believe that selfishness consists simply of doing whatever one *feels* like doing at the time (e.g., hedonism, pragmatism). Clearly, this is false. Just because one "wants" to do something does not mean it is in one's actual self-interest to do it. Taking dope or driving while drunk is an obvious example. Spending money heedlessly is another. The leader in the preceding example is yet another example. The leader did what he or she "wanted" to do and ruined his or her career as a result.

To understand what self-interest actually consists of and how it is discovered, we must understand people's nature. Unlike the lower animals, people cannot survive by functioning at the sensory percep-tual level, using the pleasure-pain mechanism as their only guide. They do not possess instincts. They have to learn how to survive in the long range. Their main means of survival is reason. Through reason, they need to develop a moral code, a code of values selected by choice to guide their choices and actions. The purpose and need of a moral code are to enable one to live successfully. Life is the ultimate and objective standard of value in ethics. "It is only the concept of 'Life' that makes the concept of 'Value' possible" (Rand, 1964, p. 16). I must stress that only individuals exist and pursue values; society is not an entity but a collection of individuals.

The concept of egoism refers to the fact that individuals must be the beneficiary of their moral code and, therefore, of their own actions. Observe the fundamental contradiction in the doctrine of altruism: In response to the fact that one needs a moral code to live, it declares that one must sacrifice one's life to others. This is like advocating poison as a response to the observation that one needs food. Altruism sets one's moral code against oneself; it is the code of death. This is not an exaggeration. Who is considered the paragon of morality in the Western world?—Jesus, who gave up his life for humankind, including for people who were not even born yet. What countries most consistently demanded that individual citizens sacrifice themselves for the good of the state?—Nazi Germany and Soviet Russia.

I am sure you can see another contradiction in the code of altruism. If it is good to sacrifice to others, is it not selfish (i.e., evil, immoral) of others to accept it? Should they not, in turn, sacrifice to others, thus setting up a chain of endless sacrifices with no one gaining anything in the end? Every altruist knows quite well that it is a code that cannot be practiced consistently, else everyone would die. This means that moral perfection is impossible; the emotional consequence of this is a state of permanent guilt. That, of course, is the real purpose of the code of altruism. Those who feel guilty about value achievements such as earning wealth can readily be induced to give much of it up for the sake of those who have not earned it.

I have shown so far that one should be the beneficiary of one's own moral code. Now I address the issue of how one actually achieves one's own survival. The answer is: through virtue. The highest virtue is rationality—the unconditional adherence to reason as people's only source of knowledge and only guide to action (Peikoff, 1991). To reject reason is, in the end, to reject reality (i.e., to reject facts including one's own nature). Implicit in the virtue of rationality are a number of other virtues:

- Honesty: the refusal to fake reality;
- Integrity: loyalty to one's rational judgment in action;
- Independence: acceptance of the responsibility of using one's own rational judgment to sustain one's own life;
- Productiveness: acceptance of the responsibility of producing or earning the material values that one's life requires;
- Justice: rationality with regard to other people, judging them in accordance with the facts by a rational standard;
- Pride: recognition of the fact that one is a being of self-made soul, a soul that seeks its own moral perfection.

Observe that these life affirming, egoistic virtues are vastly different from conventional notions of virtue, which stress faith (over reason), self-sacrifice (over egoism), conformity (over independence), compassion (over justice), and humility (over pride).

Now let us apply these virtues to the notion of leadership. What would truly egoistic leaders be like and how would they act?

- They would take a job (career) that they selfishly enjoy. They would discover this by trying out different types of activities, discovering what they like, and identifying the reasons for it. They would not choose this work out of duty or obligation.
- If they chose to become a leader, they would look at reality, gather facts, and try to discover how their business could succeed using their best rational judgment.
- They would hire the best people they could, including those who might argue with them, because they would know that they were not omniscient and that brainpower was essential to their own success.
- They would be consistently honest in all their dealings because they would know that when people try to fake reality, reality fakes out the faker in the end.
- They would act true to their word because they would know that subordinates and customers would not trust a leader who said one thing and did another.
- They would listen to, and even welcome, reasoned disagreement and good advice, but in the end would make the key decisions themselves.
- They would not ask the government for special favors and subsidies (as opposed to the freedom to run their business without interference) because they would want to earn the profits that they get.
- They would treat employees and clients justly because they would know that people who are treated unjustly would not want to work for or with them. They would be delighted if they made many others rich and customers happy, even though they would not be working primarily to serve them but for their own pleasure. Their focus would be on the principle of trade.
- They would take pride in the success of their business and would not feel unearned guilt for a single penny of their earned wealth even if it amounted to billions.

I think you can see that this leader is radically different from both the altruistic leader (if such a person could even run a profit-making firm) and the pragmatic, amoral, "big shot" who tries not to earn money but to get away with some money before he or she gets caught. The conventional belief that a leader either has to be a self-sacrificing servant of others or a conniving wheeler-dealer is a classic example of the fallacy of the false alternative. My choice is: neither of the above. A truly rational leader takes the actions that will make his or her business succeed in the long run. Virtue is not the enemy, to be escaped whenever possible, but a tool of success.

This is not to say that virtue alone is a guarantor of success. It is not. You also need business and industry knowledge, management skills, financing, a reasonably free economy, energy and ambition, intelligence, confidence, passion for work, and other characteristics (Locke, 2000). Nevertheless, virtue is critical. Given the presence of these other factors, the true (i.e., rational), egoist is the type of leader I would most like to work for.

A major source of confusion occurs for people when a leader is a mixture of virtue and vice. Some leaders are genuinely able and brilliant and have certain virtues, but they are not consistent. They may love the limelight too much, be honest most but not all of the time, listen to others at times but often become overbearing and arrogant, give some credit where credit is due but often minimize the legitimate contributions of others. This is most likely to occur in leaders who have had early success and come to think of themselves as infallible. They may become egocentric; their own ego rather than reason and reality becomes the central focus of their lives. This happened to Henry Ford in his later years and to others and usually presages business failure or at least a downhill slide. They forget the thinking processes that made them successful and come to assume that everything they feel is automatically true. I am no fan of such people; they have abandoned reason to their own detriment.

Does anyone really practice true egoism? I will mention one example. BB&T, a banking company headquartered in North Carolina, explicitly practices the virtues that I listed above (Locke, 2000). The bank is very successful. If I were a new MBA with an interest in banking, would I want to work there? You bet.

Sincerely,

Edwin A. Locke

LETTER 2: WHY LEADERS SHOULD MAKE SACRIFICES

Dear Ed:

I enjoyed having the opportunity to read your thoughts on whether leaders should be more selfish. The ideas that you presented were quite intellectually stimulating for me, in the sense that we describe this

now, the greater good of my group of followers and myself would be best served.

I believe there are very few leaders who do not question the utility of their sacrifices, even when it is for all the right reasons. There are some, however, who probably do not even consider it a sacrifice, but rather what they are able to contribute to the common good of their group, community, and society. The lens through which they view their actions does not label them self-sacrifices or losses at all, but rather as contributions, which they feel they are supposed to make to their followers.

Let us take Candy Lightner as one potentially complex example, who said, "I'd rather have ten people working with passion than a thousand people working with interest." Candy Lightner's life was fundamentally changed when her teenage daughter was killed in a motor vehicle accident involving a drunk driver. Was it in her selfish interest to start Mothers Against Drunk Driving? Or, was it a life sacrifice that she was now enduring to make a difference for other parents? As a parent, it is difficult for me to see her actions as being motivated by selfish interest alone. Whether it is selfish or self-sacrifice or both, the net result is still more than a 60 percent reduction in teenage drunk-driving fatalities over the last decade. As this example shows, human behavior typically is more complex than a rational model of decision making can always account for or fully explain.

I believe the actions of this mother can be seen as selfish, self-interested, and self-sacrificing, depending on your perspective and maybe depending on where she was in her own healing process. Perhaps, what best distinguishes her actions is the intent that underlies them. At one extreme, a mother losing a child may want "revenge" against all drunk drivers and could energize a national movement to place all offenders in jail for life. Her motives are driven by hatred and revenge, and we could say that they are selfish, in the more traditional sense. In the middle range, we have someone who is going through the healing process and is turning her grief into passion to make a difference for the good of the community. Still selfish perhaps, but at a much higher moral level. Finally, we have someone who is so purely altruistic in the traditional sense, he or she can think only of the good of the community. Any amount of time he or she puts into a movement is seen as contributing to the good of the community—a level of selfishness that is so highly moral, it is hard not to define it as altruism.

Perhaps there is a point where common ground can be achieved in our discussion of self-sacrifice, selfishness, and self-interest. One way to create common ground is to consider "banding" around self-interest. What I mean by banding is that at one extreme, people pursue their selfish interest very narrowly defined. Characterizing this tendency, Drucker (1999) remarked that we tend to suffer from single cause interest groups, who subordinate the common good for their own aggrandizement. The banding idea can be simply stated: Does the leader really care about anyone else but himself or herself? If not, it does not necessarily mean that achieving his or her self-interests is necessarily bad for others; it can actually be good. However, I suspect that the probability of such selfishness resulting in solutions that are good for all is likely to be lower.

Should leaders be selfish, and if so, under what conditions? In U.S. culture, there is more of an orientation toward self-interest being "okay." Yet, as Johns (1999) pointed out, if an individual or group comes to believe that its approach, goal, or mission is superior, then it risks developing a self-serving bias. Failure is not our fault, but rather the fault of all those who keep us from achieving our superior objectives. Salancik and Meindl (1984) used this form of self-serving bias to explain why companies frequently attribute success to themselves and failure to external events in their annual report.

Another potential risk in advocating selfishness is how it will play on the development of interdependence. The need for interdependence and the means by which it is achieved in organizations are, in part, dependent on how they are perceived (Weick & Roberts, 1993). Can we develop interdependence through the exact alignment of selfish interests? Or, should we now explore the collective selfish interests of groups as a basis for motivating interdependence? This to me seems like a very delicate balance to achieve and depends, in large part, on how each party's selfish interests are perceived to coincide with another party's selfish interests.

Where we seem to have total agreement is around the issue of honesty and virtue. I believe that leaders must create high levels of transparency in their organization for their followers to fully understand the intent underlying their actions. If transparent, then the leader must also be willing to be vulnerable and challenged by others. You must be able to defend your "selfish interests" as the best alternative for the group. If you are both transparent and vulnerable, then you better be honest or virtuous. Obviously, people know what is going on, they can question the leader, and therefore the leader better be doing the "right thing." If the first three conditions are met, then the goal of the leader is to get followers to identify with what he or she most wants to achieve. One way to get them to identify with what is most important is to show what the leader is willing to sacrifice or give up to achieve the mission or vision. This is only one approach, but one often chosen by many leaders.

I close my letter as I end a two-week stay in Singapore. Each morning when I went down for coffee, I saw a box on the counter. The box had a sign asking for a donation to Mother Teresa's charity. I personally reflected on Mother Teresa's sacrifices as being a demonstration of the importance she associated with her vision. I have passed many similar donation boxes on counters around the world, but today I was motivated to show my support for her vision, in "exchange" for what she was willing to sacrifice. Maybe our selfish interests were aligned for a moment, and then again maybe not.

LETTER 3: WHY SELF-INTEREST IS MORE ETHICAL THAN ALTRUISM

Dear Bruce:

Thank your for your reply to my letter. You brought up many issues. The main theme of your letter seemed to be the issue of conflicts of interest in society, business, and the military, so these are the issues I will focus on in my reply. Before I address these issues, let me correct one important error in your reply. I did not say the Nazis were selfish; I said just the opposite, that Nazism (and all forms of statism) is based on the principle of self-sacrifice, the sacrifice of the individual to the state. (Hitler himself, of course, was just a criminal.)

Much of your reply involved the issue of alleged conflicts of interest among people in society and between leaders and followers. You also implied that selfishness is a subjective concept so that when conflicts occur, there is no way we can resolve them ("Whose definition of selfishness do we accept?"). You concluded from all this that sometimes some people need to sacrifice for some greater good or "higher" value. Of course, if everything is subjective, then there are as many "higher values" as there are pressure groups, and society reduces to Hobbes' war of all against all, with the biggest gang or pressure group winning out in the end. (Our country is not too far from this state right now.) My view is very different.

Rand (1962) once made the startling claim that there can be no conflicts of interest among rational men. What is the basis for this assertion? She identified four considerations.

Reality
A wish or desire or emotion is not primary but is caused by one's (subconscious) ideas, including values. For a rational person, desires are not the starting point in deciding how to act or what is good. One first has to identify and validate a proper code of morality. I addressed this issue in my first letter. It is not rational to hold a wish based on an

invalid premise (e.g., one that is wrong because it contradicts reality, such as wanting something you have no right to).

Context
A rational person thinks long range, not just for the range of the moment. It may be tempting to steal your neighbor's new car, but such an act leads not to happiness but to jail. Similarly, a rational person does not desire ends divorced from means. In a free society, the proper means of getting what you want is voluntary trade.

Responsibility
A rational person takes responsibility for knowing the conditions required to achieve his goals. For example, an employee knows that to be employable, he or she needs to acquire relevant skills. A manager knows that to make the business succeed, he or she must make the organization an enjoyable place for the employees to work.

Effort
A rational individual knows that all values must be produced by human effort and that one person's efforts to achieve values are not made at the expense of those who do not exert effort.

Now consider Rand's application of these principles to a classic case of alleged conflict, the case of two men who apply for the same job (Rand, 1962, p. 35):

1. "Reality." The mere fact that two men desire the same job does not constitute proof that either of them is entitled to it or deserves it.
2. "Context." Both men should know that if they desire a job, their goal is made possible only by the existence of a business concern able to provide employment that that business concern requires the availability of more than one applicant for any job, and that competition for the job *is* to their interest, even though one of them will lose in that particular encounter.
3. "Responsibility." Neither man has the moral right to declare that he does not want to consider all those things; he just wants the job.
4. "Effort." Whoever gets the job has earned it (assuming that the employer's choice is rational). This benefit is due to his own merit, not to the "sacrifice" of the other man who never had any vested right to that job.

Now consider the wider, political context. Ayn Rand's (and my own) view of the proper rules for a free society is that people should be (politically) free to do whatever they want so long as they do not physically harm others. Thus, criminal behavior, which means the initiation of force (including fraud), is ruled out. This means a society governed politically by the principle of individual rights. In this context, if a given individual who is not a criminal chooses to be irrational, one does not have to deal with him. Rights include the right to use one's own property as one sees fit. Thus, if a property owner wanted to build a house that blocked your view, that would be permitted. A property owner would also have the right to destroy the habitat of the 12-toed salamander on his property, even if it were the last one on Earth. An owner would not have the right, however, to spew poisonous gases or dump dangerous chemicals onto his neighbor's land or into his or her water supply. Having a proper, objective view of the concept of rights would eliminate millions of so-called conflicts that exist today as a result of the total perversion of the concepts of rights, which today means anything any powerful influence group "wants" at the expense of some other group. (The "mixed" economy is one aspect of this perversion.)

If people are rational, think in principles, and do not violate the rights of others, then there are no fundamental conflicts of interests between people. And no one needs to be sacrificed to anyone. Rational people, of course, may disagree (e.g., over the terms of a contract), but then it is the interest of both parties to adjudicate the disagreement objectively in the courts.

Business Leadership

Now let us apply these principles to the issue of business leadership. If both leader and follower respect each other's legitimate rights to trade freely with others, then there are no criminal issues to cause conflict. If one party is irrational, the other party is free not to deal with him or her.

The rational leader will neither want to sacrifice his or her legitimate interests to the employees nor to sacrifice the employees' interests to his or her own. The rational leader will not take the job unless it is personally important to him or her. To get and keep good employees, the leader will want to appeal to the employees' self-interest; that is, if you come to work here, I will give you mentally challenging work and the chance to grow, fair rewards, competitive benefits, etc. He or she will not think just of the range of the moment (that is, I will work them to the bone and make my results look good to my boss this quarter), but also of the long-range consequences of his or her actions (e.g., what will happen if the best people all quit). His or her goal will be to merge the interests of all parties so that everyone gets something out of it and the organization prospers. The ideal relationship is mutual trade to mutual benefit.

You argue that self-sacrifice is a way that leaders can show that they are committed to their values. This is the direct opposite of the truth; showing your commitment to your values by self-sacrifice is a contradiction. To show your commitment to a value or goal, you go after it with all the reason and passion at your disposal. Yes, you give up lesser values, but this is not a sacrifice if they are, in fact, less important. As I noted in my first letter, all actions involve choice. Action is only self-sacrificial if you give up a greater value for a lesser one. The ultimate proof of commitment is not what you give up but what actions you take to achieve the value in reality.

You seem to assume that it is a sacrifice if a leader gives up something in the short term for the sake of the long term. Not necessarily. Let us say a founding CEO agrees to take no salary for two years until his company gets off the ground. This a not a sacrifice if the leader (a) loves his or her job and the company, (b) sees this step as necessary to make the business viable at the start-up stage, and (c) expects to make up the lost salary later in stock options and the like. It is a sacrifice if the CEO has no personal interest in the company or its products and works short and long term only to selflessly serve society, like Mother Teresa. Mother Teresa, who was truly selfless, may be an ideal role model to you, but not to me. She worshipped poverty; I admire those like Bill Gates, who worship production.

You mention the issue of leader and follower maturity. Maturity is important; to me it means the ability to hold a rational, long-range context in the face of the emotions of the moment, but it is only helpful if the people involved hold rational, life affirming values.

I believe that a bigger problem today than immaturity is amorality. No one segment of society has any monopoly on this trait. Many people just seem to have no moral principles at all; they are "pragmatists." For example, I asked the members in my organizational behavior class this spring to raise their hands if they knew anyone who had cheated in college. (To prevent self-incrimination, I did not ask them about themselves.) One hundred percent of the students raised their hands. I asked them if they realized that this meant those people were getting their degrees by fraud. They looked at me like I was from another planet. By comparison, I did not know anyone who cheated when I went to college (which is not to say there were no such people). Pragmatists do whatever "works" for the range of the moment; this is not rational or selfish because pragmatism is not, in fact, practical. Living short range works for the lower animals but not for humans. For a detailed discussion of this issue in relation to the virtue of honesty, see Locke and Woiceshyn (1995).

You say that my concept of rational self-interest (from Ayn Rand) is too idealistic. I certainly agree that it is idealistic. I believe in moral ideals, but not the ones that are conventionally taught (see Locke, 2000), especially not self-sacrifice. The ideal of self-sacrifice is antilife and antihappiness (Rand, 1957). I believe that a person's highest moral purpose is the achievement of his or her own happiness on this Earth and that if people are rational and respect individual rights, they can live together in society and in organizations happily, harmoniously, and nonsacrificially.

The Military

I am glad you brought up the topic of the military. It is one dear to my heart, and one that I have published an op ed on (see AynRand.org). Yes, soldiers, by the nature of their profession, have to be willing to die for their country, but it does not follow that this is a sacrifice. It depends on what they die for. It was disgraceful to send our brave soldiers to die in Vietnam; that was a pointless, self-sacrificial war if there ever was one. But it is not a sacrifice if the soldiers are fighting for the protection of our country against an aggressor. The New Hampshire motto, "Live free or die," names the essence of the proper view; it is better to die fighting for your freedom than to live as a slave. This puts a solemn responsibility on our politicians: They should never send our soldiers to risk their lives unless our national interest is clearly at stake. I am assuming here an all-volunteer army in which the people who join are those who love their country and want to be soldiers. (Am I in favor of using American soldiers to police the world? Definitely not!)

As to military pay, if the pay is so low that soldiers cannot make a decent living, which is certainly true today, then the solution is simple: raise their wages! I suspect that the reason their pay has been held at such disgracefully low levels is that the politicians *expect* them to sacrifice not only their lives but their standard of living as well. You call the problem of military pay a "dilemma" because "society" wants soldiers to work for peanuts and the soldiers want to selfishly live a decent life. You ask, "How do we resolve this dilemma?" But the dilemma disappears if society does not ask for a sacrifice it has no right to demand or expect. Pay the soldiers what they are worth and there will be no shortage of fighting men and women.

Conclusion

Let me end with some comments on two other issues you brought up. First, the Candy Lightner (who founded Mothers Against Drunk Driving) story, which you seem to use in a way that obfuscates the issues. The main problem with this example is that we do not know this woman's psychology or moral philosophy, so there is no way of knowing whether or not she was acting in her self-interest. There can be many motives for such an endeavor, but it seems quite clear that self-interest was involved in the sense that this issue had great personal meaning to her.

My favorite example of "giving" is Michael Milken, the great financier, who contracted prostate cancer after the government sent him to jail on trumped up charges for the sin of making too much money. He has donated many millions to prostate cancer research, and he has a very selfish reason for it—he wants to live!

Second, what of the issue of "banding," which you define as, "Does the leader care about anyone else but himself or herself?" Making yourself your highest value does not preclude liking and loving other people; in fact, a firm sense of pride and identity is a prerequisite to loving another. To quote Howard Roark from *The Fountainhead*, "To say 'I love you' one must know first how to say the 'I'" (Rand, 1952, p. 376). Love, in fact, is the most selfish of all emotions; it means that you consider another person to be an important value to you, that the other person's happiness and welfare are critically important to your life and happiness. To be unable to love another person is to be unable to value. Narcissism is not egoism but a psychological abnormality.

LETTER 4: WHY ALTRUISM IS A NECESSARY PART OF LEADERSHIP

Dear Ed:

Nothing has been said in our exchange thus far that has fundamentally changed my views about altruism, self-sacrifice, and selfishness. They are each fundamental parts of what constitutes human nature in general and in the particular case of human nature we refer to as leadership. Yet, I have wondered whether our different views could be integrated into something more interesting than a simple checklist of differences. For example, Selye (1974) suggested combining altruism and egoism, labeling it "altruistic egoism." It is certainly possible for a vision to be articulated in such a way that it represents what is good for all people and yet still serves the selfish interests of the leader, as you suggest in your first letter: *to act in one's own interest*. Perhaps we can agree that when a leader's own interests are in line with the collective interests of his or her organization, any further discussion of our differences becomes moot. Where these interests are incompatible, or one interest comes before the other, is where our arguments, and I would add that the study of leadership, get quite interesting.

So how do we take our positions and turn them into research ideas? One area of research to explore could involve how certain leaders are able to inspire followers to extraordinary efforts, even when it is apparent that the leader's self-interest has nothing to do with his or her followers' needs or interests. How do such leaders motivate followers to substitute their own interests for the sake of the leader's interests, especially when the substitution takes them down vs. up Maslow's need hierarchy? Under what extreme conditions is such behavior more or less likely to occur? What type of impression management techniques do such leaders use to motivate followers to support the leader's self-interest? Some leaders fake sacrifice and it seems to motivate others to believe in their message. If they can fake it to gain such effects, how does real sacrifice affect different followers' motivation to perform beyond expectations? Are some more or less prone to the allure of self-sacrifice?

My experience in working with organizations around the world suggests to me that the case of complete alignment across all individual interests is less common than the clash of individual interests. This condition was the basis for my earlier comment about your arguments for egoistic leadership being too idealistic. Alignment is the less typical case, as evidenced by the rising need for negotiators, conflict management consultants, and compensation analysts. Moreover, even in the situation where there is some basis to argue that each party's self-interests can be "objectively" satisfied, the reality is that some people will still not see their situation as being equitable. Although my self-interests may be absolutely and objectively the same as yours, I may not view them as being equivalent. Research on equity theory and sensitivity to equity differences inform us that these differences in perception are quite common.

Clearly, *self interests*, *selfishness*, and *altruism* are in the eye of the beholder, which makes our task of explaining the motivational impact of leaders on followers much more complex than simply saying that leaders need to be more selfish. Even if we accept that argument, the degree of selfishness that will motivate different followers will be affected by differences in their respective motivational states. Indeed, my reference to Nazi Germany was meant to suggest that many people in Germany took Hitler's message and translated it into satisfying their selfish interests in many ways, including stealing from others. I do not believe this behavior represented self-sacrifice for the German nation.

A long line of research on transformational leadership has shown that it can *augment* transactional leadership in predicting performance (Avolio, 1999; Bass, 1998). We draw from this work the conclusion that transformational leadership activates the higher-order needs of followers, which then induces them to transcend their self-interests for the sake of the overall organization's needs, interests, and goals. By transcending self-interests, we meant "to rise above," as self-interests are frequently by definition, not necessarily the best alternative for everyone in the group either "objectively" or "subjectively."

Let me share a recent example that highlights my concerns regarding how we judge *self-interested* vs. *altruistic* leadership. At the end of the third presidential debate between Vice President Gore and Governor Bush, one of the commentators, who is an historian named Doris Kearns Goodwin, remarked that each candidate kept saying what he did, and what he would provide for each of us. But neither candidate asked what we should all be willing to sacrifice to achieve our collective goals as a nation. She compared these two candidates to several great presidents of the past, and conveyed her disappointment of how they each paled in comparison to those earlier presidents. She was disappointed in their selfishness, traditionally defined.

Maybe self-sacrifice is on the wane, or at the very least it is something our political leaders should not ask of us, out of fear of losing popular support. Nevertheless, her comments were framed in terms of disappointment about the stature of these two candidates. Asking us to be willing to delay our self-interests, or to even sacrifice for the good of our own children, was in her opinion a normative expectation for presidential aspirants. It is a frame set and way of thinking that shapes how people interpret the actions of leaders. This presidential historian is not unique in invoking this frame set to judge the leadership of each candidate. And this has been one of my central arguments throughout our discussion. Selfish or altruistic leadership is not only in the eye of the beholder, it is also determined in part by organizational and cultural norms. Smirich and Morgan (1982) made this point by describing leadership as follows: "Leadership as a phenomenon is identifiable within its wider context as a form of action that seeks to shape its context." Weick (1979) referred to this as the "punctuation of contexts," where a leader frames the context in such a way that followers are able to use that framing as a point of reference for interpreting their own actions (Smirich & Morgan, 1982). Your inability to interpret Candy Lightner's behavior as being selfish or self-sacrificing supports the position that we cannot always judge leaders on a purely rational basis.

Leadership not only shapes the context in terms of how it is interpreted, it also is shaped by the context in terms of how it is perceived. For example, in African humanistic philosophy, a person is not considered a person unless discussed in relationship to some other person. They refer to this core linkage as the basis of an individual's *vital force*. How might this cultural lens and context affect how we operationally define and measure *selfishness*, *self-serving*, and/or *altruistic* behavior, as compared to the normative lens in our culture? Exploring what constitutes selfish or altruistic behavior in Muslim, African, and Asian cultures, as opposed to our Western culture, might shed some further light on the importance of the context to how followers interpret exemplary (or abysmal) leadership. House and Aditya (1997) indicated that nearly 98 percent of leadership research has been done in Western contexts, so neither you nor I know how culture will affect perceptions of selfishness. This remains an important area for experimental and field research to explore, especially in light of the globalization of economies and organizations.

I recently re-read Hollander's (1958) early work on leadership for a review article that I am currently completing. As you know, Hollander argued that leaders build up idiosyncratic credits with followers based on the competence and "signs" of the leader's loyalty to their followers. Over three decades later, Hollander and Offermann (1990) described "self-serving" behavior as one form of leadership action that can "drain idiosyncratic credits" from the leader's bank of loyalty or trust. Again, I do not believe that our differences are as much about definition, as they are about perception. If I agree with your definition of selfishness, it still does not change Hollander and Offermann's conclusion. Leaders *perceived* as being more " self-interested" in an egoistic sense may suffer the loss of loyalty and trust that Hollander and Offermann have referred to in their chapter. I would also argue that the variance in loss is going to be greater or less, depending on the cultural context in which the leader and his or her followers interact and are embedded in over time.

One could argue that visionaries like Bill Gates of Microsoft, through their own egoistic behavior, have demonstrated beyond any reasonable doubt that such behavior can significantly increase the quality of life of people on this planet. Those who believe this position would not see Gates' success and domination of the software market as a loss to humankind. Alternatively, one could also argue that his selfish interests have actually retarded the development of products and services, which could have been avoided if he had taken actions early on for the "good of the group." He has held firm to the idea that opening the "source code" for Microsoft products was not in his or Microsoft's self-interest. Gates felt that taking this approach would be a sacrifice that would put his company at a significant disadvantage in the market. Now, let us contrast his view of software development with a growing competitor of Microsoft, which may represent a case of "altruistic egoism." Linux is a software system that follows an open source code format. Its founder believed that opening the source code to all software programmers would benefit not only the creative development of his software but himself as well. On the surface, his actions could be easily construed as sacrificing his own self-interests for the good of the larger community in that everyone knows the code. Going back to my point about perception, it is interesting that Bill Gates is seen as being on the side of the "dark forces," while Linux is viewed as the "white knight" in the software field, ready to slay the Microsoft dragon. One leader "appears" to place his interests first, while another leader "appears" to place the interests of the community first. Yet, no one really knows either person's intent in terms of the actual strategy that was chosen, but that does not prevent us from making judgments about their intent. My position has been as follows: Where leaders demonstrate self-sacrifice, or clearly delay self-interests to accommodate the group's interest, the signal sent to their followers is generally a more positive one. These behaviors are significant signals of a leader's intent, just as keeping the "source code" secret is one bit of data concerning a leader's selfish intent. How leaders manage these signals and the impact it has on group efficacy, commitment, cohesion, trust, and loyalty are interesting avenues for future research to explore.

Leadership and how it is perceived are all the more difficult to explain as a consequence of the human conditions that were summarized previously. Unfortunately, when we explore leadership in different "real worlds," it is difficult, if not impossible, to explain intent and its consequences by neatly packaging it into an egoistic framework. We could spend time arguing over how we should define truth, or what is good, or what is moral or immoral. However, I think there is little room to argue that leadership is in the "eye of the beholder," and that this beholder oftentimes views self-interested leaders as not being the ideal leader.

Ideals and Idolization

Somehow you came away from my first letter with the idea that I viewed Mother Teresa as my ideal role model. I certainly used her as an example of how one can translate self-sacrifice into loyalty and commitment. She did express ideals that I respect, and I am keenly interested in understanding how they affected her followers in life, and subsequently after her death. However, you make an attribution about me idolizing her, which was incorrect, and appears to be based more on your philosophy than my own.

Let me add to the mix that I, too, admire people who are focused on production, and yet, I am intrigued by those leaders who are willing to delay or give up wealth for some cause they believe in, sacrificing short-term interests for a higher value. However, I do not idolize Mother Teresa. I am firmly against the idolization of leaders, and indeed chose the term *idealized* in our model of leadership to distinguish idealized vs. idolized leaders. The former are those who build people up to be leaders; the latter are those who expect unquestioning followers. I think Mother Teresa is more idealized vs. idolized, at least by me.

Turning to your last points about the military. Private industry is paying more than our government to lure people out of the military, and this is apparently attracting people to leave military careers. If we paid soldiers exactly what they could be paid in private industry, that still might not address the problems we are confronting today with retention. A recent study on the culture of the U.S. military showed that retention rates were related to the culture of a soldier's unit and indirectly to the leadership of that unit.

Soldiers stay in the military because of an emotional attachment, as well as for rational reasons. Their willingness to sacrifice their lives for our country also depends on their emotional attachment to their fellow soldiers. And perhaps they are willing to give up their lives for a higher value that is associated with being loyal to their fellow soldiers, thus substituting a lower value for a higher value. However, you have yet to convince me that giving up one's life "rationally" is not a sacrifice. Yet, this area is worth exploring in terms of pursuing a systematic line of study that examines why people are willing to sacrifice for the good of any group, and what types of changes they will accept, if not embrace, to do so.

In closing, what else can I agree with you on? We cannot simply judge a leader's intent by the actions that have been taken. Perhaps in the leader's mindset she created a movement out of self-interest, but from the followers' perspective, it looked and felt like altruism. Again, from both the leader's and follower's side, it is how their behaviors are perceived and interpreted at the end of the day that seems to really matter in terms of judging leadership. If we can agree on that, then we have a starting point for a very useful line of research inquiry.

Regards,

Bruce

ACKNOWLEDGMENT

Reprinted from *The Leadership Quarterly* 13(2): 169–191; copyright © 2002, with permission from Elsevier.

REFERENCES

Avolio, B. J. 1999. *Full leadership development: building the vital forces in organizations.* Thousand Oaks, CA: Sage Publications.
Bass, B. M. 1998. *Transformational leadership: Industrial, military and educational impact.* Mahwah, NJ: Lawrence Erlbaum and Associates.
Drucker, P. F. 1999. The new pluralism. *Leader to Leader,* Fall: 18–23.

Hollander, E. P. 1958. Conformity, status, and idiosyncrasy credit. *Psychological Review 65*: 117-127.

Hollander, E. P., and L. R. Offermann. 1990. Power and leadership in organizations: Relationships in transition. *American Psychologist 45*: 179–89.

House, R. J., and R. N. Aditya. 1997. The social scientific study of leadership: Quo vadis? *Journal of Management 23*: 409–73.

Johns, G. 1999. A multi-level theory of self-serving behavior in organizations. *Research in Organizational Behavior 21:* 1–38.

Locke, E. A. 2000. *The prime movers: traits of the great wealth creators.* New York: AMACOM.

Locke, E. A., and J. Woiceshyn. 1995. Why businessmen should be honest: The argument from rational egoism. *Journal of Organizational Behavior, 16*: 405–14.

Miller, D. T. 1999. The norm of self-interest. *American Psychologist, 54*: 1053–60.

Peikoff, L. 1991. *Objectivism: the philosophy of Ayn Rand.* New York: Dutton.

Rand, A. 1952. *The fountainhead.* New York: Signet.

Rand, A. 1957. *Atlas shrugged.* New York: Signet.

Rand, A. 1962. The "conflicts" of men's interest. *Objectivist Newsletter, 1*: 32 ff.

Rand, A. 1964. *The virtue of selfishness.* New York: Signet.

Salancik, G. R., and J. R. Meindl, 1984. Corporate attributions as strategic illusions of management control. *Administrative Science Quarterly 29*: 238–54.

Selye, H. 1974. *Stress without distress.* New York: Signet.

Smirich, L., and G. Morgan. 1982. Leadership: the management of meaning. *Journal of Applied Behavioral Science, 18*: 257–73.

Weick, K. 1979. *The social psychology of organizing.* Reading, MA: Addison-Wesley.

Weick, K. E., and K. H. Roberts. 1993. Collective mind in organizations: Heedful interrelating on flight decks. *Administrative Science Quarterly 38*: 357–81.

7

Explaining Ethical
Failures of Leadership

Terry L. Price

INTRODUCTION

One surprising feature of ethical failures of leadership is that, very often, the immorality of the relevant decision, action, or policy was never in doubt (Ludwig and Longenecker, 1993). Unfortunately, this is true across leadership contexts—in public, private, and nonprofit sectors. For example, when Trent Lott waxed nostalgic over our segregationist past, there was little debate about the immorality of his remarks, which ultimately resulted in his resignation as Senate majority leader. Similarly, we hardly needed sophisticated moral theory to determine whether Enron executives were wrong to engage in accounting irregularities in order to inflate profits. Finally, lest we think that high-profile leaders outside of politics and business are immune to straightforward ethical failure, recall that Cardinal Bernard Law was forced to step down as Boston's archbishop under charges that he repeatedly assigned priests involved in child sexual abuse to new parishes and protected them from criminal prosecution.

Accordingly, when an ethical failure of leadership is exposed, we are inclined to look for an *explanation of the leader's behavior*, not an *analysis of the moral status* of what was done, even though much of moral theory is preoccupied with questions of how to determine what morality requires. In an effort to answer these questions, normative theorists work to locate those features of decisions, actions, and policies that make them morally good or morally right. The focus of these ethicists seems to imply that a more complete characterization of ethical success would put leaders in a better position to behave morally. The central question raised by the preceding cases however, seems to be not so much one about *how* leaders should act but, rather, one about *why* they act as they do. *Why* do leaders fail ethically when it is so obvious to the rest of us *how* they should act?

This question has its home in the general area of moral psychology. So located, it is closely related to questions about ethical failure more generally. In fact, one might think that the moral psychology behind ethical failures of leadership is part and parcel of a more basic view of human nature, namely, that our behavior—especially in its immoral varieties—is largely self-interested. The standard argument in moral theory and applied ethics relies on this view of human nature, suggesting that ethical failures are essentially *volitional, not cognitive.* We behave immorally simply because we are moved to do something other than what morality requires, not because we lack access to morality's requirements.

Initially at least, this account seems to fit well with the preceding examples of ethical failures of leadership. We are often inclined to say of morally tainted leaders that they *knew* that what they were doing was morally wrong but, nevertheless, that they were *motivated* to do it anyway. But I want to argue that the volitional account of human immorality will not be sufficient to explain ethical failures of leadership. Simply applying the volitional account to leadership contexts ignores the fact that leadership exaggerates cognitive challenges that can lead to ethical failure. More than most agents, leaders have reason to believe that they are not bound by the requirements of morality. The primary purpose of this chapter is to draw attention to these cognitive challenges and to explain why leaders are particularly susceptible to them.

The second part of the chapter lays out the volitional account of ethical failures of leadership as it is articulated in the work of Dean Ludwig and Clinton Longenecker (1993). These authors appeal to the volitional account to make sense of the fact that "many of the ethics violations we have witnessed in recent years result from a ready willingness to abandon personal principle—not so much a matter of ethics as of virtue and lack of fortitude and courage" (pp. 267–268). The third part of the chapter distinguishes between two kinds of cognitive challenges to moral behavior: mistakes about the *content* of morality and mistakes about its *scope.* This distinction is important because the initial plausibility of the volitional account turns on the weaknesses of only one version of cognitive account, that is, the explanation on which ethically fallen leaders are said to be mistaken about morality's content.

The fourth part of the chapter further defends the cognitive account of ethical failures of leadership by highlighting the exceptions that leaders are inclined to make of themselves, and the last part considers a potential justification for these exceptions.

THE VOLITIONAL ACCOUNT OF ETHICAL FAILURES OF LEADERSHIP

In its most plausible formulation, the volitional account of ethical failure implicitly assumes that much of human behavior is egoistic. On this view of human motivation, morality competes not with ignorance but, rather, with self-interest. The normative force of moral principles thus depends greatly on the extent to which we can reasonably expect that immoral behavior will be found out and, upon being found out, that we will face unwanted consequences for engaging in it. Fortunately, society provides many effective mechanisms for making sure that the demands of self-interest parallel the requirements of morality. It is typically in our interests to conform our behavior to these requirements because, when we do not, others withhold their cooperation or, worse still, work in concert to punish us. Nevertheless, if this view of human motivation is correct, then we will be inclined to behave immorally when there is good reason to think that our interests in behaving morally have run out.

A character in Plato's *Republic* well illustrates the strongest version of this view with the story of the shepherd Gyges.

> The story goes that he was a shepherd in the service of the ruler of Lydia. There was a violent thunderstorm, and an earthquake broke open the ground and created a chasm at the place where he was tending his sheep. Seeing this, he was filled with amazement and went down into it. And there, in addition to many other wonders of which we're told, he saw a hollow bronze horse. There were windowlike openings in it, and, peeping in, he saw a corpse, which seemed to be of more than human size, wearing nothing but a gold ring on its finger. He took the ring and came out of the chasm. He wore the ring at the usual monthly meeting that reported to the king on the state of the flocks. And as he was sitting among the others, he happened to turn the setting of the ring towards himself to the inside of his hand. When he did this, he became invisible to those sitting near him, and they went on talking as if he had gone . . . When he realized this, he at once arranged to become one of the messengers sent to report to the king. And when he arrived there, he seduced the king's wife, attacked the king with her help, killed him, and took over the kingdom. (Plato, trans. 1992, pp. 35–36 [359d–360b])

The point of Plato's interlocutor is that Gyges' behavior does not set him apart from the rest of us: with nothing to fear from behaving immorally, each of us would behave just as Gyges did. For good reason, many readers will be unwilling to accept this strong version of the volitional account. Nevertheless, the argument from egoism has important implications for thinking about the ethical challenges of leadership. The most important, perhaps, is that power can insulate leaders from the contingencies that force self-interest and morality together. That is, individuals in leadership positions can think they have less reason to expect the setbacks to self-interest that most of us associate with immoral behavior. Herein lies one of the moral perils of leadership: leaders, we might say, have too many rings.

A weaker version of volitional account finds insightful expression in Ludwig and Longenecker's (1993) articulation of "the Bathsheba syndrome." These authors draw upon the biblical story of David and Bathsheba to argue that success brings with it formidable motivational challenges. In this story, David seduces Bathsheba, the wife of Uriah, and Bathsheba becomes pregnant with his child. In an attempt to create the impression that Bathsheba is pregnant with Uriah's child, David hastens to have Uriah returned home from battle. To the surprise of David, however, Uriah's loyalty to his fellow combatants makes him unwilling to sleep with Bathsheba. David finally resorts to a more serious breach of faith: David has Uriah sent to the battlefront to guarantee that he will lose his life. Uriah is indeed killed, and upon learning of his death, David takes Bathsheba as his wife. On Ludwig and Longenecker's view, the essential features of David's ethical failing are no different from that of the contemporary ethical failures of leadership. These authors tell us that "David clearly knew the gravity of the violation he was engaging in and clearly knew the penalty if exposed" (p. 266). Not unlike ethically fallen leaders of today, that is, David simply lacked motivation to do what was morally right, even though he well knew what morality required.

Ludwig and Longenecker locate the source of ethical failures of leadership in success itself. On their analysis, the by-products of success can seriously strain a leader's motivational ties to morality. First, successful leadership can make for complacency and loss of strategic focus. Second, it is commonplace for a leader's success to be accompanied by privileged access to information, people, or objects. Third, successful leaders frequently have unrestrained control of organizational resources. Fourth, a leader's success can inflate his or her belief in his or her own ability to control outcomes. In combination, according to the authors, these by-products are especially liable to spawn unethical behavior. They make mention of two such "explosive combination[s]" (p. 269). Complacency frees a leader to act on temptations that privileged access brings with it, and unrestrained control of resources feeds a leader's inflated belief that he or she can conceal his or her actions and their effects when these temptations have gotten the best of the leader. On either combination, then, leaders succumb to challenges that are essentially volitional in nature.

Admittedly, as with all volitional understandings of immoral action, Ludwig and Longenecker's explanation of ethical failures of leadership must draw upon the cognitive considerations surrounding the transgression. In other words, in addition to pointing out the temptations that give rise to ethical failure, the explanation must also appeal to the fact that leaders believe both that immorality is in their interests and that it is within their power to carry out a successful cover-up. Nevertheless, these explanations of ethical failure are best characterized as volitional because the beliefs in question are factual beliefs that become morally problematic only when coupled with the egoistic assumption that their possessor will be motivated to act on them. Volitional understandings of immorality, that is, do not claim that an explanation of unethical behavior will make no appeal to the beliefs of immoral agents, just that mistaken moral beliefs play no part in this explanation.

The egoistic assumptions at the heart of the Bathsheba syndrome come out most clearly in Ludwig and Longenecker's proposed solutions to it. Their ultimate aim is to force morality and self-interest back together again, to get leaders to see that "[e]ven kings who fail to provide ethical leadership are eventually found out" (p. 271). By way of advice to individual leaders, the authors propose strategies for maintaining an accurate view of what constitutes one's self-interest. They suggest, for example, that leaders would do well to "read the papers for constant reminders that the chances of being caught have never been greater" (p. 272). The authors also recommend that leaders anticipate opportunities for immorality by creating conditions under which it will be difficult to act solely upon self-interest. They advise, for instance, that leaders engage in a form of self-binding and surround themselves with "ethical team[s] of managers" (p. 272), much as Homer's Odysseus made use of ropes for his body and wax for his men's ears to fend off the temptations of the sirens' song (Homer, trans. 1963, Book XII, pp. 214–215).

The recommendations that Ludwig and Longenecker make for boards of directors are no different on this score. Since "[d]etection is the primary factor that deters unethical behavior," organizations should "make prudent use of such devices as regularly scheduled audits" and "consider the use of ombudsmen" (p. 272). Here, as with all the recommendations, the goal is to institute *transformative* checks, checks that remake self-interest so that it is expressed in morally acceptable ways. By significantly increasing the chances that unethical behavior will be detected, the purpose of these checks is to guarantee that it is no longer in a leader's self-interest to behave immorally. The under-lying assumption behind all these solutions, then, is that the problems themselves are primarily egoistic in nature. Given that self-interest routinely drives ethical failures of leadership, egoistic solutions are necessary to make certain that leaders perceive their self-interest as being bound up with the requirements of morality.

It can hardly be disputed that leaders sometimes fail ethically because they are willing to sacrifice morality for self-interest. Ludwig and Longenecker are to be commended for reminding us of the temptations that leadership brings with it and, in particular, that leadership often provides opportunities for thinking that acting on these temptations might make the sacrifice of morality worthwhile. My suspicion, how-ever is that the egoistic assumptions at the heart of this view do not do justice to the moral psychology of leaders. For the volitional account assumes that leadership does little more than alter the contingencies associated with normal human motivation. In other words, it assumes that leadership does not affect changes in the way that leaders think about morality. On this assumption, the ethical challenges of leadership are no different in kind from the motivational challenges that we all face. It is just that leaders must face them on a much grander scale because the circumstances of success often ease the tensions between self-interest and immorality. But I want to propose that there is some-thing cognitive about the ethical failures of leadership. The argument for this claim turns on showing that there is a plausible alternative to the volitional account.

THE COGNITIVE ACCOUNT OF ETHICAL FAILURES OF LEADERSHIP

Much of the strength of the volitional account rests on the apparent weaknesses of the cognitive account of ethical failures of leadership. Plainly stated, since leaders typically can be expected to know the moral status of their behavior, it is hard to see to what we might appeal—aside from motivation—to explain those instances in which they fail ethically. This inference assumes, though, that all relevant cognitive challenges to moral behavior are connected to mistakes about what kinds of *behavior* are required by morality. On a first reading, this assumption seems acceptable enough. After all, it is a small step from knowing that a particular behavior is morally required to knowing what one ought to do. Here, however, I draw attention to a second kind of cognitive challenge to moral behavior, one to which leaders are particularly susceptible. On this line of argument, we cannot infer from the fact that a leader knows what behaviors are required by morality that he or she is not morally mistaken in a way that vindicates the cognitive account of ethical failures of leadership.

Cognitive mistakes of morality come in two basic varieties: mistakes about morality's *content* and mistakes about its *scope*. Mistakes of content are indexed to beliefs about the moral status of *actions*, most commonly, to beliefs about what kinds of actions are morally right or morally good. For instance, a leader might mistakenly believe that lying is a morally permissible means of getting follower compliance or that revenge for disloyalty is morally good. Content mistakes can also be indexed to failures to see why these actions are wrong, that is, to ignorance of what features make them wrong. In contrast, mistakes of scope are indexed to beliefs about the moral status of *individuals*, specifically, to beliefs about their place within the moral community and the extent to which these individuals are subject to the rights and responsibilities that membership implies. Scope mistakes are thus errors about the application of morality's strictures. In their most straightforward form, questions of scope endeavor to fix the domain of individuals to whom moral obligations are owed. By way of example, a central scope question for the CEO of Walmart is whether his company has any moral obligations to small, local stores that are often put out of business when Walmart enters a community, in addition, that is, to the moral obligations that it has to stockholders, employees, and customers.

Ethicists and philosophers spend a lot of time thinking about questions of moral content. This alone should give us reason to question the ascendancy of the volitional account of ethical failures of leadership. If morality is as difficult as these thinkers make it out to be, then it would seem to follow that people can behave immorally because they are sometimes ignorant of what actions are morally right or good. That said, it is worth noting that much of our history's most morally reprehensible behavior has been connected to questions about the scope of morality, not its content. Here we need only reflect upon the institution of slavery in the United States, the treatment of Jews (and others) in Nazi Germany, and the policy of apartheid in South Africa. We might also think about our own society's treatment of women. Even Trent Lott's racially offensive remarks can be understood in terms of a mistake about morality's scope. Suffice it to say that we have a long history of ignoring the moral status of particular groups of individuals in our society.

For our purposes, the primary point of relevance for these examples is that mistakes about the scope of morality's requirements make for a second way—in addition, that is, to mistakes of content—in which ethical failures can be grounded in how we *think* about morality. The most commonplace scope mistakes are represented by the extension of morality's *protections* to particular individuals and not to others. But

questions about the scope of morality are not exhausted by this particular concern. In a less straightforward, but equally significant, form,
scope questions endeavor to fix the domain of individuals who have
these obligations in the first place. Scope mistakes, that is, can also take
the form of cognitive errors about which individuals are *bound* by its
requirements (Hampton, 1989). An individual of moderate income, for
instance, might mistakenly believe that he, unlike the wealthy, is not
subject to a moral requirement to help the poor. It is this latter kind of
mistake about the scope of morality that is particularly relevant for
understanding of ethical failures of leadership.

As an impetus to my argument for this claim, let us reconsider
Ludwig and Longenecker's (1993) rejection of a cognitive understanding of David's ethical failure. The authors claim that "David clearly
knew the gravity of the violation he was engaging in . . ." (p. 266) and
that it was "the prophet Nathan (who was in this case the equivalent of
a modern day whistle-blower) who led David to realize that his cover-
up had been a failure" (p. 271). Since David knew that what he was
doing was wrong, Nathan's role was simply to convey to David that he
had been found out and to expose his wrongs to all of Israel. It is
significant, though, that the biblical text itself gives a much larger role
to Nathan.

> And the Lord sent Nathan to David. He came to him, and said to him,
> "There were two men in a certain city, the one rich and the other poor. The
> rich man had very many flocks and herds; but the poor man had nothing
> but one little ewe lamb, which he had bought. And he brought it up, and
> it grew up with him and with his children; it used to eat of his morsel, and
> drink from his cup, and lie in his bosom, and it was like a daughter to him.
> Now there came a traveler to the rich man, and he was unwilling to take
> one of his own flock or herd to prepare for the wayfarer who had come to
> him, but he took the poor man's lamb, and prepared it for the man who
> had come to him." Then David's anger was greatly kindled against the
> man; and he said to Nathan, "As the Lord lives, the man who has done
> this deserves to die; and he shall restore the lamb fourfold, because he did
> this thing, and because he had no pity." Nathan said to David, "You are
> that man." (*New Oxford Annotated Bible,* 2 Samuel 12:1–7)

To be sure, Nathan does inform David that his wrongs have been
discovered. But this passage reveals an additional task for Nathan.
What exactly was his role?

The answer to this question must focus on the purpose behind
Nathan's parable. Why, for example, does he appeal to the wrongs of
another to make his point? My claim is that the purpose of Nathan's
parable is educative: The story addresses peculiar cognitive challenges
to ethical leadership. In the end, David was mistaken about the scope

of morality, and this particular cognitive challenge comes to bear on our understanding of his behavior. The main argument for this claim is that the parable is out of place on alternative analyses of David's ethical failure. On the assumption that David's moral challenge was volitional and that Nathan's task was essentially that of a whistle-blower, the parable is unnecessary to the task set for Nathan. If David knows what morality demands of him, then he does not require a story from Nathan to get him to see its force. The volitional account thus makes Nathan's parable redundant since this explanation rests on the assumption that David already knew what the parable conveys.

Nathan's story is similarly unmotivated on the view that David was mistaken about the content of morality. This cognitive understanding of David's ethical failure makes the parable not redundant but, nonetheless, unhelpful, for the parable makes moral sense to David only if he recognizes that it is generally wrong for the privileged to take advantage of the less privileged. Put another way, if Nathan's story is to have any purchase with David, we must assume that David was not mistaken about the general moral status of the actions attributed to the rich man. This means that David must have had some basic understanding of the content of the relevant moral requirements. The parable is educative in character, then, in precisely this sense: it was meant to show David the universality of the general prohibitions that he already accepts. David, it seems, failed to see that morality's requirements also applied to him. The purpose of the parable was to teach him that he too is bound by morality, that success did not remove him from its scope.

What should we make of the fact that David instigated an intricate scheme to cover up his actions? Doesn't this fact imply that David knew that what he was doing was wrong? We should first note that David's scheme implies only that he believed that others—in particular, Uriah—would object to his seduction of Bathsheba. While this belief may be relevant to an assessment of David's culpability for his ignorance (Smith, 1983), it would be a mistake to infer from David's awareness of potential objections to his behavior that he himself accepted that what he was doing was wrong. Here, the inference is no more valid than the argument for the claim that "closet" racists really know that their views are wrong after all. Notice, too, that children are prone to cover-ups of immoral behavior. Still, we generally reject the view that they have a proper understanding of morality's requirements. The cognitive predicaments of childhood come to bear on our attributions of responsibility to them, and this is true regardless of whether they are able to apply the labels of morality with a good degree of success. My suggestion is that David's cognitive predicament was importantly similar to that faced by such individuals: Children and some adults have yet to see what morality requires; David had lost sight of it.

A second point of response on behalf of the cognitive account appeals to what David must have believed about the nature of morality. One belief that we can safely attribute to David is that his actions could not be hidden from God, who was for David the source of morality's authority. Given David's commitment to this view of morality, his cover-up cannot be understood as an effort to evade the authority of moral requirements that he took to be binding. Again, moral judgment for David was essentially judgment from God. So locating the authority behind David's morality therefore undermines the plausibility of Ludwig and Longenecker's explanation of his ethical failure. Unlike the successes of leaders not committed to theologically based moralities, David's success could not have made him any more able to circumvent authentic moral judgment. As a consequence, we cannot accept a view on which it is assumed that David believed that he could get away with behavior that was immoral before God. A more plausible explanation of David's ethical failure, then, appeals to the distinction between the content and the scope of a moral requirement. Although David believed that what he did was generally wrong, he did not believe that this prohibition applied to him.

THE MORAL PSYCHOLOGY OF EXCEPTION MAKING

My argument to this point, of course, is not intended as an exercise in biblical exegesis. Rather, it is offered as an alternative explanation for the fact that leaders are particularly susceptible to ethical failure. According to the account on offer, ethical failures of leadership are closely connected to mistaken beliefs about morality's scope. Leadership induces and maintains a leader's belief that he is somehow excepted from moral requirements that apply to the rest of us. The purpose of this part of the chapter is to begin to fill out the cognitive account of ethical failures of leadership. In particular, it aims to underscore the peculiar features of leadership that effect this cognitive transformation. My claim is that the way we think about leadership is bound up with the notion of justification. It is this conceptual link that structures the moral psychology of exception making, sometimes with ethical failure as a result.

To say that an individual's action was *justified* is to say that he did what is right or, at least, permissible. By way of example, if an employee misses a staff meeting because only she can complete a time-sensitive task that has materialized at the last minute, then we say that her absence was justified because what she did was appropriate to the circumstances. The notion of justification differs from the notion of excuse in the following way. To say that an individual's action was excused means that even though the behavior in question is inappropriate, we do not hold the individual accountable because of the presence of responsibility-undermining factors. If the employee missed the meeting, say, because she had been inadvertently locked in her office, then we say that her absence is excused because it was due to factors beyond her control. Although she did what she should not have done, she is not to blame for her inappropriate behavior.

The distinction between justification and excuse thus marks two basic ways in which individuals can elude attributions of blameworthiness for behavior that is typically subject to disapprobation. In the case of justified behavior, the actor is not bound by a requirement that normally applies because this requirement has been undercut by an alternative one that better suits the circumstances. This means that the actor's behavior falls outside of the scope of the requirement. With respect to excused behavior, the actor is no less bound by the requirement than any of the rest of us. But, in this case, the individual eludes an attribution of blameworthiness because we cannot reasonably expect satisfaction of the requirement in the circumstances, not, that is, because the requirement itself has been undercut (Price, 1993). For our purposes, this distinction is important because it lends itself to an accurate understanding of the moral psychology of exception making.

Leadership purportedly brings with it justification for doing a myriad of things that others are not permitted to do. This is just to say that a leader's position often supports the assumption that its occupant is removed from the scope of requirements that apply in full force to the rest of us. To take a recent, tragic example in New York City, "Councilman James E. Davis was shot to death on a City Hall balcony by a political rival" as a result of a policy according to which "elected officials did not have to walk through [metal] detectors" (Hu, 2003, p. B3). A more ordinary example is that leaders routinely give little notice to standard expectations of promptness. Here, of course, the idea is that leaders are justified in being late because the requirements of promptness are subordinate in force to the other requirements to which leaders are subject. Simply put, leaders sometimes have more important matters to which they must attend. As a consequence, the inclination is to say that their behavior is justified in just these cases.

When leaders elude an attribution of blameworthiness in this way, it is not quite right to classify what they have done as excused because the presence of legitimating reasons for their behavior implies that the relevant requirement fails to apply to them in the circumstances. In other words, in these particular cases, the claim is that they have done what is permissible or, more strongly, required of them by their positions of leadership. There is a sense, then, in which leadership has removed them from the scope of the requirement. If leaders are similarly removed from the scope of other normally applicable requirements, then this feature of leadership makes for a formidable cognitive task. Explicitly stated, leaders must differentiate between those requirements that apply to them and those with respect to which a deviation is justified. Ethical failure occurs, then, when leaders pay no heed to the fact that their behavior is well within the scope of a requirement that applies to the rest of us.

It was just this kind of disregard that made Vaclav Havel, then president of the Czech Republic, vulnerable to criticism for "driving [a model car] about 100 miles an hour, far above the posted speed limit" (Erlanger, 1999, p. A12). Similarly, before becoming governor of Massachusetts, Lieutenant Governor Jane Swift went before the state Ethics Commission for using a state police helicopter to travel home for Thanksgiving and for using "staff members to take in her dry-cleaning and watch 'adorable' Elizabeth [Swift's daughter] in the office" (*Economist*, 2000, p. 33). Justifying this behavior by appeal to her leadership position, she said, "I have stated on numerous occasions that I face many of the same challenges as other working parents but I also have some differences because of my schedule"(Rezendes, 2000, p. A1). A more serious case of exception making is the recent Bush administration decision to show pictures of the dead bodies of former Iraqi President Saddam Hussein's sons, Odai and Qusai. Defense Secretary Rumsfeld justified the decision this way: "It is not a practice that the United States engages in on a normal basis . . . I honestly believe that these two are particularly bad characters, and that it's important for the Iraqi people to see them, to know they're gone, to know they're dead and to know they're not coming back" (Associated Press, 2003).

Unfortunately, negotiating these scope questions in an effort to avoid ethical failure is not an easy task, especially in environments in which the justificatory force of leadership is at its strongest. Generally, when there are great disparities between what is required of leaders and what is required of others, we might well expect leaders to come to see themselves as outside the scope of morality altogether. It should come as no surprise to us, I think, that the backdrop for David's ethical failing was an environment apparently rich in such disparities. Nathan reminds David, for example, that God "'gave [him his] master's house, and [his] master's wives into [his] bosom, and gave [him] the house of Israel and of Judah; and if this were too little, [God] would add to [him] as much more'" (*New Oxford Annotated Bible*, 2 Samuel 12:8). With this consideration to mind, there is reason to suspect that indulgence might have been part of the cause of David's ethical failure, not its solution. To continue the argument, notice that David's punishment was no different in this respect: "divine judgment fell upon the child [born to

David by Bathsheba], according to the ideas of the day, *as a special favor to David"* (*New Oxford Annotated Bible*, p. 390, emphasis mine). The justificatory force of leadership in David's particular circumstances, it seems, aggravated the cognitive challenges to which he was exposed as a leader of the Hebrew people.

The challenge for leadership ethicists, then, is to clarify and to give precision to the justificatory force of leadership. Leaders are excepted from the scope of normally applicable moral requirements only on the condition that there is some reason or set of reasons that legitimates the exception. The practical version of this challenge, of course, is to create and sustain an environment in which the justificatory force of leadership cannot be reduced to a set of assumptions that simply accompany a leader's position. Perhaps the most important feature of this model environment is the expectation that leaders make explicit appeal to the reasons that legitimate deviations from the moral requirements by which the rest of us are bound. This expectation is one that groups, organizations, and societies must make of leaders and that leaders must make of themselves, if, that is, we are to accommodate the cognitive challenges that leadership brings with it.

At the very least, clarifying the justificatory force of leadership in this way would entail an exacting examination of the powers and privileges of leadership. As I have argued, the greatest threat embodied in these powers and privileges comes from their contributions to the moral psychology of exception making. An appeal to the cognitive explanation of ethical failures of leadership thus draws our attention to a prima facie reason against the exceptions we make for leaders, a reason that stands to be outweighed by legitimating reasons for these exceptions. Interestingly enough, a normative analysis of the powers and privileges of leadership involves precisely the kind of moral theorizing that initially seemed irrelevant to our understanding of ethical failures of leadership. In other words, we must consider the reasons that potentially legitimate exception-making behavior by leaders. I suggest that the standard legitimating reasons appeal to normative expectations about the importance of achieving collective goals.

THE JUSTIFICATORY FORCE OF LEADERSHIP

Joanne Ciulla was the first to note that even our definitions of leadership have always embodied normative expectations (1998a). However, she argues that scholars who advance these definitions have been "sloppy about the language they use to describe and prescribe" (1998a, p. 13). Descriptive claims are appropriate to an articulation of "technically good or effective" leadership, but prescriptive claims must be reserved for "morally good" leadership (Ciulla, 1998a, p. 13). The temptation, of course, is to try to push the two together.

> Are leaders more effective when they are nice to people, or are leaders more effective when they use certain techniques for structuring and ordering tasks? One would hope that the answer is both, but that answer is not conclusive in the studies that have taken place over the last three decades. The interesting question is What if this sort of research shows that you don't have to be kind and considerate to other people to run a country or a profitable organization? Would scholars and practitioners draw an ought from the is of this research? (Ciulla, 1998a, p. 14)

Here, Ciulla is concerned with the *ought* of morality, and she is correct to criticize leadership scholars who draw conclusions about what one morally ought to do from nonmoral premises about effectiveness. But it is not quite right to say that nonmoral premises about effectiveness are merely descriptive. Although attributions of "technically good" or effective leadership are not fundamentally moral claims, they are nonetheless normative claims. These claims attach to leaders who, in a very important way, do what they *ought* to do: realize collective goals they have set out to achieve with followers.

Ciulla's contention that "definitions of leadership have normative implications" (1998a, p. 13) is more to the point, then, than she seems to realize. In addition to its moral norms, leadership gives rise to norms of effectiveness. These norms embody expectations that leaders will pursue goals that privilege group interests. Followers commonly expect leaders to put their needs first, and most leaders expect no less of themselves. Unfortunately, this connection between leadership and effectiveness also has its moral downside. As Ciulla puts it, "The traits that make corporate America admire Jack Welch are the ones that contribute most to moral amnesia, such as intense focus on reaching the next quarter's corporate goals" (1998b, p. 102). In other words, a leader's commitment to achieving collective goals can promote ethical failures of leadership in the same way that an individual's belief about the importance of his or her personal commitments can be an impetus to immoral behavior.

The commitment that leaders must have to group interests also explains why strongly impartialist ethical theories such as utilitarianism threaten to undermine the ordinary exercise of leadership. The ordinary exercise of leadership gives special attention to these interests, sometimes to the exclusion of serious concern for the interests of outsiders. Some leaders take these particularistic expectations on their behavior to have extraordinary normative force. For instance, in an effort to protect American officials and military personnel, the Bush administration has argued for considerable exceptions to the recently ratified International Criminal Court. Other leaders conform their behavior to these expectations by simply redefining group membership. Under this description we can place the CEO who defends the claim that he or she is "morally justified by underscoring that the downsizing was necessary for the organization's survival and for the benefit of the remaining employees and other stakeholders" (Bass and Steidlmeier, 1999, p. 204). Not all leaders readily engage in this kind of redefinition, but most would be hardly recognizable if they put the interests of outsiders on a par with the interests of the group.

The potential for conflict between this normative feature of leadership and the demands of morality means that an appeal to a leader's self-interest is not sufficient to fill out an account of ethical failures of leadership. Our understanding of such failures must also attend to the conflict between norms of effectiveness and moral norms, as this conflict gets played out in leadership behavior. That is, only by attending to normative expectations that leaders privilege group interests can we make sense of the exceptions that we allow them and that they allow themselves. These normative expectations on their behavior are well articulated in Michael Walzer's argument that a political leader's "decision to run [is] a commitment (to all of us who think the election important) to try to win, that is, to do within rational limits whatever is necessary to win" (1973, p. 165). But the type of justification that Walzer has in mind is by no means limited to politics. Leaders across sectors use norms of effectiveness to justify exceptions to moral requirements so that they can pursue their goals, goals that ultimately represent our interests.

Justification in this particular sense means that what the leader did was permissible according to values that reflect the interests of the group or, more strongly, was required by these values. The justification appeals directly to these values in order to argue that the circumstances in which a leader deviated from a moral requirement are relevantly different from the circumstances in which this requirement typically applies. To be sure, the force of the justification depends on, among other things, just how exceptional we think his or her circumstances really are. It may also depend on the truth of the claim that only he or she has what it takes to get the job done, in effect, that he himself, she herself is exceptional. However, this claim is not difficult to establish for many leaders, since it is the fact that they are set apart from followers by virtue of their superior experience, motivation, and skills that puts them in positions of leadership in the first place.

In the end, the exceptions we make for leaders may be an integral part of the relationship between leaders and followers. E. P. Hollander's seminal work on social exchange holds that an emergent leader "achieves status (in the form of idiosyncrasy credits) by fulfilling common expectancies and demonstrating task competencies" and that "(a)s he continues to amass these credits he may eventually reach a threshold which permits deviation and innovation, insofar as this is perceived by others to be in the group's interests" (1964, p. 159). Given the perceived permissibility of these exceptions, it should come as little surprise to us that leaders sometimes make exceptions for themselves when it comes to moral requirements. One consequence of this kind of normative fluidity is that the justificatory force of leadership induces and maintains a leader's belief that he or she is removed from the scope of morality. Although the leader recognizes the general force of moral requirements as they are applied to others, he or she may fail to see that these requirements apply to him or her as well.

The problem for such leaders, then, is not so much that they need something akin to moral imagination to "project alternative ways to frame experience and thus broaden, evaluate, and even change [their] moral point of view" (Werhane, 1999, p. 90). After all, they may be perfectly willing to use the appropriate ethical perspective to apply moral requirements to followers as well as to other leaders. For these cases at least, it will not be cognitively sufficient for ethical leadership "to get a distance from a particular point of view or the point of view of one's colleagues, one's constituents, and/or the institutional or regulatory framework in which one is operating" (Werhane, 1998, p. 88). Sometimes distance is the last thing that leaders need. Even one who "can disengage oneself from the context of specific decisions, from one's particular 'movie'" (Werhane, 1999, p. 62) and find the right "script" or mental model to frame a moral challenge still can be susceptible to cognitive errors that result in ethical failure. Such individuals may simply fail to put themselves in the lens of the camera (Wicklund and Duval, 1971).

Whatever the normative expectations on leaders, they must recognize that the justificatory force of leadership often runs out when it comes up against moral requirements. If the pursuit of goals that represent the interests of the group means that leaders need to deny legitimate moral demands that might be made by outsiders or by individual followers themselves, then—noble though their goals may be—leaders should defer to these demands. Conformity to moral requirements is essential for protecting the interests of outsiders because their interests often fail to get incorporated into the values of leaders. It can be equally important to the followers, though, especially on theories of leadership that recommend that leaders work from the perspective of values that followers might reject. So if leaders are to avoid ethical failure, they will sometimes have to defy normative pressures to privilege group interests. Even though these pressures are associated with leadership itself, they often fail to justify the exceptions that leaders make of themselves (Price, 2003).

ACKNOWLEDGMENTS

Reprinted with permission from Emerald Publishing Limited, www.emeraldinsight.com.

I wish to thank Joanne Ciulla, Douglas Hicks, John Rosenblum, Lori Speagle, Ronald Thiemann, and students in my fall 1999 Ethics and Leadership course for helpful comments and conversations on earlier versions of this chapter. Thanks are also due to Cassie King, Angela Mims, and Elizabeth Peiffer for their valuable research assistance.

REFERENCES

Burns, R. Associated Press. July 24, 2003. Rumsfeld says American forces had no chance of taking Saddam's sons alive.

Bass, B., and Steidlmeier, P. 1999. Ethics, character, and authentic transformational leadership behavior. *The Leadership Quarterly, 10:* 181–217.

Ciulla, J. 1998a. Leadership ethics: Mapping the territory. In *Ethics, the heart of leadership,* edited by J. Ciulla. Westport, CT: Praeger.

Ciulla, J. 1998b. Imagination, fantasy, wishful thinking and truth. *Business Ethics Quarterly Special Issue:* 99–107.

Economist. 2000. Ms Swift's dilemma. 29 January, p. 33.

Erlanger, S. November 4, 1999. Havel finds his role turning from Czech hero to has-been. *The New York Times,* pp. A1, A12.

Hampton, J. 1989. The nature of immorality. *Social Philosophy and Policy* 7(1): 22–44.

Hollander, E. P. 1964. *Leaders, groups, and influence.* New York: Oxford University Press.

Homer. *The Odyssey* (R. Fitzgerald, Trans.). Garden City, NJ: Anchor Books. (Original work composed circa 8th–7th centuries B.C.E.)

Hu, W. July 26, 2003. Bloomberg says he has imposed security at city hall. *The New York Times,* p. B3.

Ludwig, D. C., and C. O. Longenecker. 1993. The Bathsheba syndrome: The ethical failure of successful leaders. *Journal of Business Ethics 12,* 265–73.

New Oxford Annotated Bible. 1977. Edited by H. G. May and B. M. Metzgar. New York: Oxford University Press.

Plato. 1992. *Republic* (G. M. A. Grube, trans., and C. D. C. Reeve, ed.). Indianapolis: Hackett. (Original work written circa 380 B.C.E.)

Price, T. 1993. Faultless mistake of fact: Justification or excuse? *Criminal Justice Ethics 12(2):* 14–28.

Price, T. 2003. The ethics of authentic transformational leadership. *Leadership Quarterly14:* 67–81.

Rezendes, M. January 6, 2000. Swift defends aides' help in personal life. *Boston Globe,* p. A1.

Smith, H. 1983. Culpable ignorance. *Philosophical Review 92:* 543–72.

Walzer, M. 1973. Political action: The problem of dirty hands. *Philosophy and Public Affairs 2:* 160–80.

Werhane, P. H. 1998. Moral imagination and the search for ethical decision-making in management. *Business Ethics Quarterly Special Issue:* 75–98.

Werhane, P. H. 1999. *Moral imagination and management decision-making.* Oxford: Oxford University Press.

Wicklund, R., and S. Duval. 1971. Opinion change and performance facilitation as a result of objective self-awareness. *Journal of Experimental Social Psychology, 7:* 319–42.

Part IV

Puzzles and Perils
of Transformational
Leadership

8

The Trouble with Transformational Leadership: Toward a Federalist Ethic for Organizations

Michael Keeley

After the American War of Independence, a variety of local conflicts broke out within the loosely united states. New York taxed ships bound for New Jersey, which retaliated by levying lighthouse fees. Maryland fishermen fought Virginians over oysters taken from Chesapeake Bay. Moneyless farmers in Massachusetts banded together to stop courts from convening and sending debtors to prison. Such events brought state delegates to Philadelphia in the summer of 1787 to plan a new organization: a federal government to coordinate their joint affairs and protect their individual rights. The resulting plan, the Constitution of the United States, was shaped in large part by James Madison—who set the stage for the Philadelphia convention with a speech about a classic organizational problem.

Madison told the delegates that all societies were divided into different interest groups, or factions: "rich and poor, debtors and creditors, the landed, the manufacturing, the commercial interests, the inhabitants of this district, or that district, the followers of this political leader or that political leader, the disciples of this religious sect or that religious sect" (June 6, 1787; quoted in Padover, 1953:17–18). Madison went on to observe that throughout history different factions have tried to take advantage of one another: "In Greece and Rome the rich and poor, the creditors and debtors, as well as the patricians and plebeians alternately oppressed each other with equal unmercifulness. . . . We have seen the mere distinction of color made in the most enlightened period of time, a ground of the most oppressive dominion ever exercised by man over man." Madison concluded that a key problem in designing a system of government was how to manage factional tensions, given the readiness of groups to pursue their own interests at others' expense.

Two hundred years later, this is still a key problem in the management of governments, corporations, and organizations of all sorts. The general issue is how to deal with the diverse interests that are prevalent in any complex social system: how, for example, to reconcile the expectations of various lobbies, lawmakers, taxpayers, and other constituents of public agencies; how to satisfy the frequently competing claims of investors, employees, customers, dealers, and other stakeholders of private firms; how, more specifically, to control in-fighting among corporate divisions, to gain union cooperation in meeting foreign competition, to contain executive salaries and perks, to keep insiders from exploiting privileged information, and so on.

Lately, writers on management have voiced real concern about such things. In both popular and academic reports, a common complaint is that many of our organizations are going to ruin because those in charge have let private interests (their own included) run amok. Zaleznik (1989:11), for instance, contends that "business in America has lost its way" due to mediocre management, whose major fault has been complicity in self-serving organizational politics as opposed to productive work. John Gardner (1990: 94–95) adopts a Madisonian perspective and sees "the mischiefs of faction" throughout the fabric of American society, which is at best "loosely knit, at worst completely unraveled"; to Gardner, "it is a mystery that [this society] works at all," as group after group pursues parochial aims and grievances in a "war of the parts against the whole." From a global standpoint, Bennis and Nanus (1985: 2) argue that "a chronic crisis of governance—that is, the pervasive incapacity of organizations to cope with the expectations of their constituents—is now an overwhelming factor worldwide."

What is interesting about recent attempts to deal with the problem of faction is that these writers, and many others, offer a cure that Madison in 1787 considered worse than the disease. The suggested remedy is a type of *leadership* that transforms self-interest and unites social systems around common purposes (often termed *transformational* leadership). So opposed was Madison to this prescription that he insisted on Constitutional devices to counteract it in the American system of government. The American experiment was to be a government of *laws*, not of men or women or charismatic leaders.

Perhaps Madison was shortsighted; perhaps his concerns have little applicability to nongovernmental organizations; perhaps they are no longer relevant at all. But possibly he recognized something important that has been overlooked by modern leadership theorists. The purpose of this chapter is to compare Madison's views and emerging theories of leadership, especially as these bear on the problem of controlling self-interested organizational behavior.

TRANSFORMATIONAL VERSUS TRANSACTIONAL LEADERSHIP

Much of the current interest in transformational leadership stems from a study of governmental leaders by political scientist-historian James MacGregor Burns (1978). Burns differentiates two sorts of leadership: *transactional* and *transforming*. The more common, he notes, is transactional leadership. This involves the exchange of incentives by leaders for support from followers—in politics, for instance, jobs for votes, or subsidies for campaign contributions. The object of such leadership is agreement on a course of action that satisfies the immediate, separate purposes of both leaders and followers.

Transforming leadership, in contrast, aims beyond the satisfaction of immediate needs. According to Burns (1978: 4), "the transforming leader looks for potential motives in followers, seeks to satisfy higher needs, and engages the full person of the follower." Here, the object is to turn individuals' attention toward larger causes (political reform, revolution, national defense, etc.), thereby converting self-interest into collective concerns. The distinguishing feature of transforming leadership is a common goal; the purposes of leader and followers, "which might have started out as separate but related, as in the case of transactional leadership, become fused" (Burns, 1978: 20).

Burns goes on to develop the basic normative theme of the paradigm: Transforming leadership is generally superior to transactional—indeed, the latter is hardly leadership at all. For Burns, transforming leadership is motivating, uplifting, and ultimately "*moral* in that it raises the level of human conduct and ethical aspiration of both leader and led" (1978: 20). A textbook example is Gandhi's elevation of the aspirations and life chances of millions of Indians who followed him toward independence. Transactional leadership, on the other hand, is characterized as immobilizing, self-absorbing, and eventually manipulative in that it seeks control over followers by catering to their lowest needs. Burns' examples of transactional figures include Tammany Hall bosses bent on trading political favors for preservation of the status quo. In Burns' view, transactional politicians are questionable "leaders" because they focus on mutually tolerable behavior, rather than jointly held goals—on means, rather than ends—and "leadership is nothing if not linked to collective purpose" (Burns, 1978: 3).

This line of analysis has been extended to organizations by a number of theorists. Bass (1985) finds elements of transactional leadership at the root of popular organizational theories (such as exchange, expectancy, and path-goal models) and common management practices (such as contingent reinforcement and management-by-exception). These theories and practices imply that organizations consist of agreements between managers and subordinates to fulfill specific obligations for mutual advantage; they further imply that leaders should make these agreements even more specific in order to increase subordinates' satisfaction and performance. Bass argues, however, that any satisfaction or performance gains from transactional leadership are apt to be small. He claims that much larger effects are produced by "transformational" leaders, as suggested by Burns.

THE VISION THING

Bass builds on Burns' framework by identifying three main components of transformational leadership. The first and most important component, *charisma*, is displayed by leaders "to whom followers form deep emotional attachments and who in turn inspire their followers to transcend their own interests for superordinate goals" (Bass, 1985: 31). The second component, *individualized consideration*, is shown by leaders who mentor and enhance the confidence of followers. The final component, *intellectual stimulation*, occurs as leaders arouse awareness of shared problems and foster visions of new possibilities.

Bass associates these three aspects of transforming leadership with extraordinary levels of effort and high degrees of organizational effectiveness. While he stops short of insisting that transformational administrators are always more moral than transactional types, he follows Burns in portraying the former as true *leaders* who raise attitudes and behavior to a "higher plane" of maturity, the latter as mere *managers* mired in "compromise, intrigue, and control." According to Bass (1985: 187), transactional managers act like "everyone has a price; it is just a matter of establishing it;" whereas transformational leaders motivate individuals to put aside selfish aims for the sake of some greater, common good.

Other theorists have concentrated on particular features of transformational leadership. Conger and Kanungo (1988), for instance, try to give a more precise account of charisma as a dimension of leader behavior. The authors describe charismatic transformation as a three-stage process in which leaders, first, identify deficiencies in the status quo, second, formulate and articulate a vision of ideal goals that highlight present deficiencies and, third, devise innovative means of achieving the vision. Throughout this process, charismatic leaders exhibit a variety of distinctive behaviors: They actively search out existing or potential needs for change, set bold (even utopian) goals, and employ unconventional or countercultural tactics. They build enthusiasm for their vision through symbols, rhetoric, and other forms of impression management. Finally, they set examples by performing heroic deeds involving self-sacrifice and personal risk (a consummate act being Lee Iacocca's taking charge of troubled Chrysler and reducing his first year's salary to $1). Conger and Kanungo hypothesize that these charismatic behaviors result in high emotional attachment of followers to leaders, high commitment to shared goals, and high task performance.

ADMINISTRATIVE IMPLICATIONS

Among students of transformational leadership, there is hardly consensus on all issues, but there does seem to be broad agreement on the following basic ideas. It is a fact of organizational life that participants get preoccupied with their own aims and interests. This has certain negative consequences, such as unproductive conflict and depletion of resources. To avoid these consequences, it is necessary to unify organizational members by refocusing their attention on collective goals. This is no job for the faint of heart. Extraordinary leaders are required to transform members' self-interested tendencies—leaders who can create exciting visions, communicate these in compelling ways, and energize others to achieve them, despite personal costs. Bass (1990: 21) summarizes the administrative ideal:

> Superior leadership performance—transformational leadership—occurs when leaders broaden and elevate the interests of their employees, when they generate awareness and acceptance of the purposes and mission of the group, and when they stir their employees to look beyond their own self-interest for the good of the group.

The policy implication is that "transformational leadership should be encouraged" (Bass, 1990: 25). Bass supplies examples. At the individual level, factors associated with transformational leadership "should be incorporated into managerial assessment, selection, placement, and guidance programs." At the organizational level, institutional constraints on managerial behavior should be reduced to allow transformational leaders more freedom of action: "Organizational policy needs to support an understanding and appreciation of the maverick who is willing to take unpopular positions, who knows when to reject the conventional wisdom, and who takes reasonable risks" (Bass, 1990: 26).

Proponents of transformational leadership suggest that, without it, organizations are just marketplaces for self-serving transactions, subject to drift and disintegration. With no leaders to transform them, corporations become disabled by bureaucracy and mediocrity, since positions of authority fall to transactional managers who simply *muddle through*, much like their governmental counterparts described by Burns (1978: 405):

> [They] grope along, operating "by feel and by feedback." They concentrate on method, technique, and mechanisms rather than on broader ends or purposes. They protect, sometimes at heavy cost to overall goals, the maintenance and survival of their organization because they are exposed daily to the claims of persons immediately sheltered by that organization. They extrude red tape even as they struggle with it. They transact more than they administer, compromise more than they command, institutionalize more than they initiate. They fragment and morselize policy issues in order to better cope with them, seeking to limit their alternatives, to delegate thorny problems "down the line," to accept vague and inconsistent goals, to adapt and survive. Thus they exemplify the "satisficing" model, as economists call it, far more than the "maximizing" one.

Who would want to settle for leaders of this type? Who would *not* find transformational leadership more interesting to study and more deserving of encouragement? Possibly, James Madison.

THE FRAMERS' VISION AND THE CHIEF EXECUTIVE OF THE CONVENTION

Many of the governmental practices that bother leadership theorists, such as James MacGregor Burns, are the legacy of Madison and the other framers of the United States Constitution. Burns, in particular, has very grudging respect for this legacy. In an earlier (1963) work, he characterized the American political process as *The Deadlock of Democracy*, an allusion to "the system of checks and balances and interlocked gears of government that requires the consensus of many groups and leaders before the nation can act" (1963: 6). Burns states that this system exacts a "heavy price of delay and devitalization" and that it was "designed for deadlock and inaction" from the start—by Madison and those delegates to the Constitutional Convention who shared his fear of strong leadership.

The framers' implicit theories of leadership, however, were far from naive; and their explicit plan of government, with all its interlocking checks and balances, was not irrational. The framers were people of practical affairs—planters, lawyers, traders, above all politicians—and so, perhaps, transactional leaders in Burns' terms. Yet they were also educated people, who were aware of the heights to which leaders could aspire in the ideal world of political theory. They obviously had never read John Gardner, or used the jargon of transformational leadership. But they read similarly inclined writers, like Plato; they knew of related protagonists, like philosopher-kings. And they rejected the lot.

What's more, the framers shied away from transformational leadership knowing, firsthand, maybe the finest example of it. At their meeting in Philadelphia, they drafted their plan of divided government under the supervision of one of the most revered leaders in history. Look for a moment at the background of the convention's chief executive.

The unanimous choice to preside over the Constitutional Convention was George Washington—father of the country, symbol of virtue, and a larger-than-life monument even in 1787 (Cunliffe, 1982). Much of Washington's fame stemmed from his ability to transform a fractious lot of rebels into a victorious army in the American War of Independence. No small feat: Rank-and-file Americans were not eager to risk *their* lives and fortunes fighting for the sacred honor of Congress. Volunteers from some states wanted nothing to do with militia from others. Farmers and merchants were reluctant to take Continental currency and provide food or supplies to Washington's forces. His staff included quarrelsome, treasonous, and just useless officers. (While short of good officers, for instance, Washington had a surplus of unemployed European officers sent by friends abroad; Morison notes that, "since Americans disliked serving under foreigners, there was nothing for most of them to do except serve on Washington's staff, and tell him in French, German, or Polish as the case might be, that his army was lousy," 1965: 230.)

Washington's army lost most of the battles, yet somehow won the war. Flexner's (1967) account of Washington's behavior as Commander in Chief describes a transformational leader in every sense of the term. From the outset, Washington displayed heroic acts. Upon accepting command of the Continental Army, he informed Congress that he would take no salary, a selfless and inspiring gesture in an age when it was customary for military officers to enrich themselves at public expense. (Two centuries later, Iacocca's deferral of compensation at Chrysler seems cheap by comparison.) Throughout the war, shortages of money and equipment drove Washington to devise unconventional means of motivating his troops. British and other professional soldiers of the time were paid to carry out orders without concern for what the struggle was all about—European kings and generals did not want their armies thinking about which way to point their weapons! Lacking the funds to employ such compliant professionals, Washington united and motivated a bunch of rugged individualists by refocusing their attention on higher ends: "Washington labored to inspire his soldiery with confidence in the value and the nobility of the cause" (Flexner, 1967: 542-543). This military innovation—encouragement of combat by appeals to nationalism—transformed not only the Continental Army, but the very nature of modern warfare.[1]

Such was the man selected to serve as president of the Constitutional Convention. If ever there existed a role model of transformational leadership, here it was right in the midst of the delegates as they went about designing a system of government.

What's interesting is that the framers recognized and appreciated individual greatness—but they refused to count on it. Despite the pressing social problems that brought them together, they decided *not* to bet their future, and ours, on model leaders like George Washington. Rather, they chose to protect us from the misdeeds of scoundrels and the frailties of ordinary men and women. The fates of nations whose political systems are more open to strong leadership (say, China or the former Soviet Union) suggest that the choice was a fortunate one. The historical record suggests it was also an *informed* choice.

MADISON'S PLAN

Madison's analysis of the issues is the most famous. Recall his opening point that all societies are divided into different interest groups or factions: rich and poor, debtors and creditors, inhabitants of various regions, disciples of one religion or another, followers of this leader or that, and parties to all sorts of commercial dealings. These factions tend to pursue their own welfare at others' expense, resulting in conflict. Unless managed in some way, conflicts get settled by force: policies are made by those with the most power at the time. This leads, ultimately, to injustice and instability. How, then, to manage factional conflict and minimize its potential for harm?

In *Federalist* No. 10, Madison examines alternative strategies. According to Madison, there are two ways of curing the mischiefs of faction: one, by removing its causes; the other, by controlling its effects. There are, in turn, two ways of removing the causes of faction: the first, by suppressing the freedom of persons to advance their own interests; the second, by persuading persons to share the same interests.

Madison questions both methods of avoiding the causes of faction. The first, denying personal freedom, he considers unwise. It stifles initiative, destroys political life, and is even worse for individuals than the condition it is meant to remedy. The second, inducing common interests, Madison considers impractical. Although some people may share some interests for some time (for instance, the coalition of militants who waged the American War of Independence), commonality of purpose is fragile at best (as shown after the war, when those who fought and wound up impoverished turned against those who profited). Madison argues that, if nothing else, the varying abilities and fortunes of individuals will divide them into haves and have-nots, whose interests diverge in matters of social policy. He adds that "different leaders ambitiously contending for pre-eminence and power" will be more apt to inflame and exploit such societal divisions than to reconcile them. Madison, therefore, opts to control the effects of faction, instead of its causes. He proposes to use government to help factions check and balance one another, thus limiting the capacity of the strong to take advantage of the weak.

In sum, the framers' task was to "enable the government to control the governed; and in the next place oblige it to control itself" (*Federalist* No. 51: 322). The trick was to preclude tyranny, which Madison equates with the accumulation of power in the same hands—whether few or many, whether self-designated or elected. Consolidation of power or tyranny, he says, cannot be prevented by formal, legal restrictions, by mere "parchment barriers," but only by "rival and opposite interests." So the framers set about dividing power, devising checks and balances. Power was first divided between "two distinct governments," state and federal, which vie to control one another. Within each government, power was then subdivided among "distinct and separate departments," which have wills of their own, stemming from the desires of member-officials to maintain or enlarge their personal authority. Madison comments,

> Ambition must be made to counteract ambition. The interest of the man must be connected with the constitutional rights of the place. It may be a reflection on human nature that such devices should be necessary to control the abuses of government. But what is government itself but the greatest of all reflections on human nature? If men were angels, no government would be necessary. (*Federalist* No. 51: 322)

Further divisions were created, Madison continues, since "it is not possible to give each department an equal power of self-defense" against encroachments by others. (Because Congress was considered likely to dominate, for example, federal legislative power was divided again between two houses.) Still other checks and balances, such as an executive veto, were added as backup devices for preserving, in practice, the departmental independence prescribed on paper.

This compounding of separations has seemed excessive to some critics (e.g., Dahl, 1956; Burns, 1963; Sundquist, 1986), who complain that it weakens national resolve, hampers unified action, or thwarts majority wishes. But Madison and the framers accepted consequences of this sort to avoid more serious ones. Their constitutional system was arranged to protect individuals in minority factions from being bull-dozed by members of majority factions bent on pursuing some alleged common goal. In this regard, the framers—and Madison especially—showed insights into social behavior and ethics that elude modern advocates of transformational leadership.

MADISONIAN AND TRANSFORMATIONAL LEADERSHIP MODELS COMPARED

To better appreciate Madison's approach, compare his views of human nature with the motivational assumptions of transformational leadership as outlined by Burns (1978). Like Madison, Burns begins with conflict, which provides the "seedbed" of leadership: "Every person, group, and society has latent tension and hostility. . . . Leadership acts as an inciting and triggering force in the conversion of conflicting demands, values, and goals into significant behavior" (Burns, 1978: 38). In this process, leaders can appeal to a variety of motives for coopera-tion. The type of motive triggered is critical, argues Burns. Here he invokes a theory of psychological development borrowed, in part, from Freud, Maslow, Kohlberg, and others—which, all together, looks a lot like Herzberg's (1966) two-factor theory of motivation.

Burns differentiates "lower" needs, such as physical survival and economic security (similar to Herzberg's hygiene factors), from "higher" needs, such as moral purpose and "participation in a collective life larger than one's personal existence" (similar to Herzberg's motiva-tors). The lower needs are addressed by transactional leaders, who may at best defuse conflict by meeting the parochial demands of their differ-ent constituents. The higher, more "authentic" needs are engaged by transforming leaders who can refocus attention—with much greater effect—on common goals that have transcendent value. The greater the goal, the greater the energizing force: "the leader who commands compelling causes has an extraordinary potential influence over follow-ers. Followers armed by moral inspiration, mobilized and purposeful, become zealots and leaders in their own right" (Burns, 1978: 34).

Madison could have accepted most of this; he was certainly not ignorant of the transforming potential of leadership. But he thought beyond it, to the problems that zealots—armed by moral inspiration, mobilized and purposeful—might create for persons who disagreed with them. Madison concentrated on a fact about human motivation that proves troublesome for transformational-leadership theories: Not everyone is attracted to the same goals or leaders. This fact has been well established by research on both motivation and leadership. Not all workers, for example, are motivated as Herzberg and Burns suggest; some (especially academics and other professionals) do appear to be driven by "higher" needs and transcendent goals, but others seem to prefer fulfillment of the bread-and-butter flavor (Schein, 1980; Steers and Porter, 1987). With respect to leadership, even champions of the transformational approach acknowledge the fact of individual differences, that "some employees may not react well to a leader even though most view the leader in a positive way and as transformational" (Avolio, Waldman, and Yammarino, 1991: 15). To Madison, such individual differences make all the difference in the world.

Madison reminds us that, because people differ, minority ideas about the value of particular goals and interests are likely to exist within large social groups—even where leaders are able to transform many individual views into a majority vision. In a letter to Thomas Jefferson soon after the Constitutional Convention, Madison wrote that popular theories supposed "that the people composing the Society enjoy not only an equality of political rights; but that they have all precisely the same interests, and the same feelings in every respect" (October 24, 1787; in Padover, 1953: 40–41). Were this really the case, Madison noted, "the interest of the majority would be that of the minority also; [public policy] decisions could only turn on mere opinion concerning the good of the whole, of which the major voice would be the safest criterion." But, he points out to Jefferson, "no society ever did or can consist of so homogeneous a mass of Citizens." Madison cites his famous examples of different economic interests (rich and poor, farmers and merchants, etc.) and differences of belief (political, religious, and so forth), emphasizing that these persistent distinctions matter very much to ordinary people if not to social theorists. "However erroneous or ridiculous these grounds of dissension and faction may appear to the enlightened Statesman or the benevolent philosopher," Madison says, "the bulk of mankind who are neither Statesmen nor Philosophers, will continue to view them in a different light. It remains then to be enquired whether a majority having any common interest, or feeling any common passion, will find sufficient motives to restrain them from oppressing the minority."

Here we come to the crux of things. If not all social participants have the same goals, if transformational leaders are not able to persuade *everyone* to voluntarily accept a common vision, what is the likely status of people who prefer their own goals and visions? Judging from the rhetoric of management experts like Bennis (1989), who complain of individuals marching stubbornly to their own drummers, or communitarian writers like Etzioni (1988), who sound alarms about persons selfishly asserting their rights against society, it may be perilous indeed. Nonconformists have been targeted for criticism by leadership theorists since Plato (see his *Republic*), and many have been subjected to *real* injury by historical leaders with single-minded majorities on their side. (A brutal illustration is the persecution of Chinese dissidents in the Cultural Revolution inspired by Mao Zedong, one of James MacGregor Burns' transforming heroes.)

Madison posed to Jefferson: What if two persons share an interest that is disagreeable to a third; would the rights of the third be secure if decisions were left to a majority of the group? "Will two thousand individuals be less apt to oppress one thousand or two hundred thousand one hundred thousand?" (October 24, 1787; in Padover, 1953: 41) What, after all, will stop majorities from taking advantage of anyone who opposes them? Madison considers possible restraints, such as concern for the public good, fear of negative public opinion, and personal moral standards. He rejects each as ineffective: The public good is no use, since majorities (and their leaders) define it for themselves. Similarly, public opinion supports their actions, by definition. And personal morality falls victim to groupthink:

> The conduct of every popular Assembly, acting on oath, the strongest of religious ties, shews that individuals join without remorse in acts against which their consciences would revolt, if proposed to them separately in their closets. (p.42)

The conclusion drawn by Madison is a flat-out repudiation of transformational leadership. He reasons that, if differences in individual interests exist within society, and if a majority united by a common interest cannot be restrained from harming minorities, then the only way to prevent harm is to keep majorities from uniting around common interests—the *reverse* of what transformational leaders are supposed to do. In other words, unless leaders are able to transform everyone and create absolute unanimity of interests (a very special case), transformational leadership produces simply a majority will that represents the interests of the strongest faction. Sometimes this will is on the side of good—as in Gandhi's case. Sometimes it is on the side of evil—as in Hitler's. In any case, might is an arbitrary guide to right, as Madison clearly understood.

This, then, is why the Madisonian system of government divides power and purpose, why it frustrates majority wishes, and why it checks leadership in the pursuit of "collective" goals. It was designed to work this way to protect the basic interests of the weak from the self-interest of the strong. Without such protection, any response to the problem of faction is no solution: social life can remain as imagined by Burns and others who would transform it—dog eat dog.

ORGANIZATIONAL IMPLICATIONS

Warren Bennis, a veteran observer of organizational leadership, sounds a familiar theme. Asking *Why Leaders Can't Lead* (1989: 40), Bennis points to increasing selfishness in American society and organizations. He notes that "everyone insists on having his or her own way now," from young urban professionals, to corporate executives, to the president of the United States. The trouble is that there is no agreement or commitment to the public good, no common vision, no mutual purpose:

> As the world has divided into factions, so has America, and so consensus is harder and harder to come by. Each faction marches stubbornly to its own drummer, has its own priorities and agenda, and has nothing in common with any other faction—except the unbridled desire to triumph over all the others. The Peruvians call this *arribismo*. It means, "You've got yours, Jack, and now I'm going to get mine." It means "making it," carried to the *n*th power. This fragmentation and fracturing of the common accord occurred for good reason, because, in America, those on top have traditionally tried to keep everyone else down, but it makes leadership a chancy undertaking at any level (Bennis, 1989: 144).

Bennis' solution: "People in authority must develop the vision and authority to call the shots" (p. 154).

Huh? Entrust those greedy individuals on top with even greater power to pursue "the common good" as they envision it? In fairness to Bennis, there's a bit more to his argument; but it's difficult, in theory, to get from selfish public and corporate officials to selfless transformational leadership—perhaps even harder, in practice. Madison foresaw this. Moreover, his view is just as applicable to "private" organizations as governmental ones, since the same problems arise in their design. Among the most fundamental are problems of controlling factions and ambitious leaders.

THREATS POSED BY LEADERS

Madison suggests to us that, in any kind of social system, inspired leadership can do as much harm as good. Lately, journalists and insiders have documented ample damage done by corporate folk heroes once hailed as transformational leaders (such as F. Ross Johnson, who led barbarians to the gate at RJR Nabisco: Burrough and Helyar, 1990). Some advocates of transformational leadership allow that there is a "dark side," that the risks can be as large as the promises (Howell and Avolio, 1992). Yukl (1989) remarks that history is full of charismatic leaders who caused death, destruction, and misery or who ruled over firms like tyrants and egomaniacs. However, Madison remains exceptional in taking the matter seriously.

In proposing social structures that would impact people's daily lives, Madison recognized a responsibility to build in protections against abuses of power. Contemporary leadership theorists are more inclined to shrug off the issue—and to depict protective devices (i.e., checks and balances and right-conferring rules) as bureaucratic hindrances that reduce the autonomy and transforming potential of leaders. Bass (1990: 24–25), for example, grants that some transformational leaders have "authoritarian tendencies," that "some fulfill grandiose dreams at the expense of their followers"; yet, he still prescribes more "flexible" organizational structures to encourage determined leadership. Others offer timid advice to treat transformational leadership with caution. Roberts and Bradley (1988) compare charisma to an unpredictable genie in a bottle; they ask whether it should be set free to transform organizations; then, they leave the question hanging. Howell and Avolio (1992) go a bit further and urge top managers to screen corporate leaders more carefully to weed out unethical charismatics; but they fail to indicate just what to screen for, how to control those doing the screening, or what to do about opportunists who slip through the net. Howell and Avolio hold out a lot of hope for voluntary ethical codes and executives who function as positive role models. Although such things are not necessarily worthless, Madison knew enough not to rely on them. He felt that flesh-and-blood persons who might suffer from misconduct by public officials deserved better than parchment barriers and hypothetical defenses. Persons vulnerable to corporate officials do too.

But Madison's challenge goes far beyond showing the dangers of charismatic leaders, or the moral obligation to control them. It cuts to the very heart of transformational leadership theories, to the value of collective goals. Individuals are at risk, Madison argues, not only from self-interested leaders but from self-interested majorities acting in the name of some "common purpose." In modern organizations, no less than in the colonial assemblies of Madison's experiences, focused groups can act in ways that their members would not dream of, alone in their closets.

THREATS POSED BY FACTIONS

Grenier (1988) tells a relevant story of a company named (*really*) Ethicon. A suture-making subsidiary of Johnson & Johnson, Ethicon built an innovative plant in New Mexico that was designed to "de-bureaucratize" the work environment: Jobs were organized around teams—quality circles—in a flexible, participative organizational structure. "The designers of the Ethicon work environment were trying to present a new vision of work in contemporary America, a vision of unity, cooperation, purpose, and inspiration" (Grenier, 1988: xiii).

Grenier studied teams in operation and found some grim facts behind the vision. In Ethicon's explanation of quality-circles to employees, "the concept was likened to a sports team, where all participants worked together for a common goal and had a voice in how that goal would be reached" (Grenier, 1988: 26). In theory, company supervisors (the team coaches) served as *facilitators* of communication, while workers discussed means of achieving production goals, including decisions about hiring, firing, evaluating, and disciplining other team members. In reality, "many workers referred to the team system as the 'rat system,'" because it pitted workers against one another to root out "counterproductive behavior." Counterproductive behavior turned out to be any expression of discontent with Ethicon or support for the Amalgamated Clothing and Textile Workers Union, which began an organizing campaign soon after the plant opened. A key issue among union supporters was their low wage in New Mexico, compared to company workers elsewhere. For Ethicon, the lower wage was a reason for locating in New Mexico in the first place, and a reason for trying to stay nonunion.

From the start, Grenier reports, management carefully screened employees to select "team players" and exclude union sympathizers. A subsequent strategy used teams to control workers who developed pro-union attitudes. The team strategy relied on peer pressure "to deprive the pro-union employees of status and identify them as losers" (Ethicon psychologist, quoted in Grenier, 1988: 90). Facilitators were trained not only to bring "negative attitudes" to the group's attention in team meetings, but to encourage the anti-union majority to denounce their pro-union colleagues (with remarks like, "If you're not happy with the company, why don't you resign? If it were up to me I'd fire you" p. 77). Workers singled out for public censure compared the feeling to being attacked by a pack of wolves, and some union activists were, indeed, fired. According to Grenier, such things went on because facilitators won approval from management, team members in turn won recognition from facilitators, and new hires won acceptance from the group by showing support for the company. Seeing the fate of "losers," the majority of workers just conformed. "The issue was who had the power to do more for the workers, and management had convinced most of the workers that management could do more, good and bad, than the union" (Grenier, 1988: 147).

In the end, the pro-union minority lost the election (141 to 71). The victors gloated. And their opponents filed unfair-labor-practice charges (some of which were later settled in favor of union supporters discharged or denied jobs during the campaign).

The moral of the story is that Ethicon's efforts to achieve unity of purpose produced, instead, a sharply divided workforce motivated by fear. Ethicon's approach was to eliminate the causes of faction (a) by enlisting persons to share the same interests and (b) by suppressing dissent among those who failed to go along, the very cures that Madison said were worse than the disease. And the result, as Madison might have predicted, was not the peaceful absence of conflict, but a bitter truce between the victorious majority and a resentful, powerless minority.

RIGHTS VERSUS GOALS
IN ORGANIZATIONAL THEORY

Many ordinary people might agree wholeheartedly with proposals to secure basic individual interests and freedoms against infringement in the workplace. Many might welcome, for example, guarantees of rights to due process in termination decisions (rights that tenured faculty members, of both public and private institutions, take for granted). Leadership theorists, on the other hand, express much less enthusiasm about protecting individual rights that could conflict with organizational goals. Things like freedom in the factory, unions, and constitutional checks on corporate policies are not generally what theorists have in mind when speaking of worker "empowerment." In the leadership literature, the meaning of the term is more like the interpretation at Ethicon–New Mexico: a Hegelian notion of freedom to serve the goals of the organization. (For a classic statement of this position, see Selznick, 1957; for a more recent version, see Kanungo, 1992.[2]) Reich's idea of empowering workers to seek their own goals in organizations is apt to seem a little too, well, *free*. In such ethical matters, however, the opinions of Reich, Madison, and ordinary people may be better guides than traditional theories of organization.

Organizational theorists have historically found individual rights and freedoms less appealing than collective goals, not only in organizations but in society at large. On the heels of the American and French Revolutions, a pioneering organizational theorist, Henri de Saint-Simon, criticized Madisonian tendencies in the French Constitution:

[Lack of collective purpose] is the great gap in the Charter. It begins, as do all the constitutions dreamed up since 1789, by putting forward the rights of Frenchmen, which can only be clearly determined when the purpose of society is established in a positive way, since the rights of every associate can only be based upon the abilities which he possesses and which contribute toward the common goal. (1821: 167)

It cannot too often be repeated that society needs an active goal, for without this there would be no political system. . . . The maintenance of individual freedom cannot be the goal. . . . People do not band together to be free. Savages join together to hunt, to wage war, but certainly not to win liberty. . . . (1821: 158)

Saint-Simon was wrong, and Madisonian thinking prevailed in the reformation of many Western governments. Two hundred years of political history have shown that people *do* join together in societies to advance personal freedom and individual rights. People have joined organizations (especially labor organizations) for similar reasons.

Social theorists have remained uncomfortable about all this. Auguste Comte (1851–54: 368), Saint-Simon's disciple and the founder of modern sociology, challenged workers to consider themselves servants of society and its goals rather than "insisting on the possession of what metaphysicians call political rights, and engaging in useless discussions about the distribution of power." Later, Henri Fayol (1916: 60), who laid much of the groundwork for a theory of management, expressed dismay that individuals refused to subordinate their interests to a common goal, either of business or nation: "ignorance, ambition, selfishness, laziness, weakness and all human passions tend to cause the general interest to be lost sight of in favor of individual interest and a perpetual struggle has to be waged against them." More recently, Henry Mintzberg, a prominent organizational theorist, has likened organizations without common goals to "a bucket of crabs, each clawing at the others to come out on top," (1983: 421) just as in society at large, where pulling toward private ends (a pluralist "political arena") "will be found in the breakdown of any form of government, under conditions typically described as anarchy or revolution" (1983: 462).

Some have tried to argue that "organization[s] would not exist if it were not for some common purpose" (Hall, 1977: 83). Since they do exist, organizations must have the glue—or goals. This "goal paradigm" is still found in mainstream textbooks on organization (e.g., Daft, 1986), but it has prompted growing criticism in more analytical works (e.g., Cyert and March, 1963; Silverman, 1970; Georgiou, 1973; Keeley, 1980; Weick, 1985). The main objection is that it is easy to talk about common, organizational goals in the abstract, yet difficult to find them in the real world. Certainly, organizations produce real, objective *consequences* (e.g., profits, deficits, wages, pollutants, all kinds of goods and costs). However, participants frequently disagree about the value of these consequences, about which of them are actual *goals* of the organization. In a firm, for instance, owners might view profits as goals, and wages as costs; workers might view wages as goals, and profits as costs; others might view both profits and wages as goals (say, top managers), or costs (say, consumers). It seems that people participate in organizations for a variety of purposes. It seems arbitrary to take some participants' purposes, or goals *for* an organization, to represent goals *of* the organization as a whole. And, for the most part, it seems that organizations look little like the organic, goal-seeking entities of management folklore.

Operational difficulties in identifying organizational goals are disappointing but not quite fatal for the goal paradigm. Theorists have developed a second line of defense, which interprets goal diversity not as evidence of a bad paradigm but bad organizations. In other words, if organizations don't in fact have common goals, then they lack the glue that holds social systems together. And thus, *of course*, they don't resemble functionally integrated organisms but, rather, *disintegrating* "buckets of crabs" or "houses divided against themselves" (Mintzberg, 1983), wars of parts against the whole (Gardner, 1990), fragmented and fractured communities of You've-got-yours-Now-where's-mine egoists (Bennis, 1989), etc. As we've seen, the implication of these images is that social systems without common goals are falling apart and need something like a transformational leader or spirit of community, to supply the missing glue of collective purpose.

What we can learn from Madison, on the other hand, is that no such purpose or glue is necessary. For two centuries, his system of competitive federalism has held together, as a system of *laws*, not of leaders or public purposes. To this day, it works better than suggested by the disparaging images of transformational-leadership theorists. For instance, Burns' (1978) depiction of pluralist public agencies as pork barrels tended by transactional bureaucrats—who muddle along, spewing red tape, passing the buck, and dragging the system down with them—just doesn't square with the facts (Wilson, 1989). Despite sensational reports of government waste, public bureaucracies such as the Social Security Administration have served clients with fairness and efficiency (relative to resources: see Mashaw, 1983; Goodsell, 1983). Despite media criticism of governmental gridlock, divided government has enacted decent legislation, such as the Americans with Disabilities Act and the Civil Rights Act of 1991 (Mayhew, 1991). As Lindblom (1965) has stressed, Madisonian government works not because participants agree on goals, but because they can agree on specific activities (as in acts of legislation) that address their different goals. So, too, in "private" organizations, like corporations, the glue that holds them together need not be consensus on ends but can be simply consent to means—agreement on rules, rights, and responsibilities that serve the separate interests of their participants.

Some organizational theorists have appreciated the point and concluded that organizations generally look neither like social organisms nor asocial free-for-alls, but more like political coalitions (Cyert and March, 1963) or markets (Pfeffer and Salancik, 1978), sets of contracts (Keeley, 1988) or stakeholders (Freeman and Gilbert, 1988). Empirically, models of this sort more fairly reflect the possibility that in organizations, as in society, participants may be less concerned with collective goals than individual rights (for example, contractual rights to a paycheck or return on investment, legal rights to equal opportunity or workers' compensation, moral rights to information about the risks of products or services). Madison's model indicates why these participant concerns are appropriate ethically.

The fundamental issue is that notions of a "common goal," "general interest," "public good," and so forth are *theoretical* concepts (every bit as metaphysical as natural rights). Any *real* social consequence used to operationalize these theoretical terms is apt to impact persons in different, often arbitrary, ways. That's why participants find it hard to agree on "organizational goals." Collective consequences like profits, wages, and even organizational survival, may greatly benefit some participants (e.g., employees of tobacco firms) but ultimately disadvantage others (e.g., tobacco customers who develop smoking-related illnesses). Even participants who share an interest in a particular organizational consequence may be affected very differently by it: Employees with a joint interest in higher wages may care less about an organization's overall salary pool, which could be distributed capriciously, than about *Who gets what?*

Organizations and their leaders can deal with distributional concerns either by seeking fairness of outcomes to individuals (a Madisonian strategy), or by changing the subject. In the tradition of Saint-Simon, transformational leadership aims to get people's thoughts *off* distributional questions and refocus them on common goals, or communal interests. This may sound moral to James MacGregor Burns and like-minded theorists (as well as some critics: Rost, 1991). But the ethical justification for diverting attention from individual to communal interests is unclear, given the hypothetical nature of the latter. If the operational consequences taken to represent collective ends are, in fact, weighted in favor of *some persons*' interests, it seems deceptive to win other persons' support by calling these weighted—perhaps biased—consequences, *common goals*, *goods*, *interests*, etc. Many people are quick to perceive such deception (as demonstrated in public ridicule of trickle-down economics). Other people are more trusting and vulnerable (as shown by supporters of televangelists' visions). In any event, reliance on extraordinary leaders to define collective purposes just papers over the problem of faction and, as Madison saw, puts participants at risk of manipulation, or worse.

In sum, contrary to the claims of theorists like Burns, common goals are no more imperative ethically than they are empirically. As Madison realized, people can still care for one another, if not for some alleged common good. As he explained in *Federalist* No. 10, factional mischief does not follow directly from diversity of interests; rather, it occurs when some people try to impose their interests on others. In other words, the problem of faction is not that individuals pursue separate interests, but that some are stronger, smarter, or richer than the rest and may use their power to take unfair advantage of other persons. Thus, Madison proposed a safer way to prevent factional mischief than transforming individuals and eliminating diversity of interests. His solution was to deter advantage-taking: to devise an impartial system of rules, checks, and balances that can accommodate personal ambitions while protecting each person's basic interests from impairment by others—especially leaders who function in the name of the community.

CONCLUSION

Let me conclude by illustrating what difference a madisonian perspective might make in a familiar kind of organization. The views of Saint-Simon, Mintzberg, Burns, and later leadership theorists are typified by Bennis (1977) in a classic article about his experiences as president of the University of Cincinnati. Wondering "Where have all the leaders gone?", Bennis sees factional misbehavior all about him. The university, he writes, "has blunted and diffused its main purposes" (p. 7) through a proliferation of interest groups. It is besieged by "external" constituencies, such as alumni, parents, and lawmakers. It is "fragmented" by internal pressure groups of all sorts:

> We have a coalition of women's groups, a gay society, black organizations for both students and faculty, a veterans' group, a continuing education group for women, a handicapped group, a faculty council on Jewish affairs, a faculty union organized by the American Association of University Professors, an organization for those staff members who are neither faculty nor administrators, an organization of middle-management staff members, an association of women administrators, a small, elite group of graduate fellows. (p. 8)

These groups, Bennis complains, go their own separate ways, marking the end of community.

Like Bennis, many of us work in complex universities with diverse aims, interest groups, and external dependencies. However, unlike Bennis, few might find such diversity objectionable. What, exactly, is *wrong* with women's groups or black groups or disabled groups or staff associations or other groups that flourish on our campuses?

Why do differences among these groups—in viewpoints, interests, and goals *for* the university—make us less a community, or just a bucket of crabs?

By invoking the ritual formula that organizations *should* have common purposes, and by painting organizations without them as snakepits, theorists perpetuate the illusion that there is something perverse about people who behave differently. Bennis, for example, portrays participants who assert their legal rights in universities as "belly-achers" who take advantage of the system, waste the organization's time and money in court, and prevent the proper authorities (especially presidents, like himself) from exercising real leadership. He is critical of persons who bring suits for injuries, malpractice, civil rights violations, or who are just "fed up with being ignored, neglected, excluded, denied, subordinated" (1977: 8). To counter those who might be tempted to file complaints under consumer protection laws, he adds:

> At my own and many other universities . . . , we are now in the process of rewriting our catalogs so carefully that it will be virtually impossible for any student (read: consumer) to claim that we haven't fulfilled our end of the bargain. At the same time, because we have to be so careful, we can never express our hopes, our dreams, and our bold ideas of what a university could provide for the prospective student. (pp. 13–14)

This is the rub, then. Leaders can't do what they want, because constituents have bold ideas of their own about what the organization should provide in return for their cooperation, and because "the courts are substituting their judgments for the expertise of the institution" (p. 10). "Time was," Bennis says wistfully, "when the leader could decide—period. A Henry Ford, an Andrew Carnegie, a Nicholas Murray Butler could issue a ukase—and all would automatically obey" (p. 7). But no longer, thanks to government, unions, lawyers, and their recalcitrant clients.

Thanks, also, to Madison and the framers. Were it not for the system of law they set in motion, individuals in harm's way of organizations might have little recourse at all. Bennis evokes a timeless undercurrent of leadership theory that Madison struggled against in 1787: a longing for "the philosophical race of kings wished for by Plato" (*Federalist*, No. 49: p. 315). Leaders, in this view, are to fabricate a vision of collective purpose—if necessary, a unifying myth. Followers are to put aside personal interests in its pursuit. (Madison, no doubt, read Plato's parable of the poor carpenter who fell ill and was advised by a doctor to look after himself for a time before carrying out his assigned duties to the community; Plato remarks that the worker must be inspired to ignore such advice, to "go back to his normal routine, and either regain his health and get on with his job, or, if his constitution won't stand it, die and be rid of his troubles" (*Republic*, p. 406). Modern theorists are more sensitive to personal entitlements than the ancient Greeks, but the very concept of transformational leadership implies that individual interests are less legitimate than collective ends. Why else would they require transformation? Accordingly, participants who do not subordinate their interests to "organizational" goals, as envisioned by leaders or majorities, are disparaged, even when their expectations seem quite reasonable. In a university, for instance, what is so *unreasonable* about students expecting to be treated like consumers? Or expecting accurate information in a college catalog? Or expecting the university to fulfill *its* end of the bargain? It is nonsense to suggest that leaders cannot meet such basic expectations and still express *their* hopes and dreams. And it is presumptuous to suppose that these expectations are less valid than the visions of people in power.

In a recent study of academic leadership, Birnbaum (1992) responds appropriately to Bennis' (1977) plaintive question, Where have all the great leaders of the past gone? "They are dead," says Birnbaum, "along with the simpler times in which formal leaders could wield unbridled power to get what they wanted. In today's world of greater participation, shared influence, conflicting constituencies, and assorted other complexities, heeding the current vogue of calls for charismatic presidents who can transform their institutions would be more likely to lead to campus disruption than to constructive change" (pp. xii–xiii). Birnbaum's conclusions are based on a five-year longitudinal study of how college and university presidents exercise leadership. His research challenges a number of myths about effective leaders.

Myth 1—Presidents need to create a vision for their organization that transcends individual interests. Birnbaum found otherwise. Successful leaders and acceptable visions reflected the diverse interests of constituents rather than the leader's goals for the institution. One effective president advised: "do a lot of listening. And when you do that, solicit the dreams and hopes from the people. Tell the people the good things you are finding. And in three to six months, take these things and report them as the things you would like to see happen" (1992: 26).

Myth 2—Presidents should be transformational leaders. Birnbaum discovered that transformational leadership, which changes participants' values and goals for the organization, is abnormal in universities. "Good leaders," he reports, "help change their institutions, not through transformation and the articulation of new goals or values, but through transactions that emphasize values already in place and move the institution toward attaining them" (1992: 30). Transformational efforts to initiate grand schemes "inflict leadership" on constituencies and cause more factional strife than they resolve.

Myth 3—Charisma is an important aspect of leadership. Birnbaum found only a few institutions where presidential charisma helped rather than hindered the organization. He proposes that charisma has more to do with impression management than the hard work of running an institution. It allows presidents to substitute glitz for substance, and it encourages both leaders and followers to act on faith, as opposed to an understanding of the situation. Most important, reliance on presidential charisma tends to diminish the authority of other decision makers and weakens the formal administrative structure of the university. The focus on a leader's persona diverts attention from the long-term job of building an "institutional infrastructure" of mutually accepted practices, rights, and responsibilities.

Birnbaum (a former college president himself) views the support of multiple constituencies as central to presidential effectiveness. His data indicate that the kind of imperial presidency suggested by Bennis is *not* effective. Among institutions studied, a primary cause of presidential failure was unilateral action that furthered presidential goals but was perceived to violate constituents' (particularly faculty) rights. In contrast, effective academic leaders in Birnbaum's sample seem downright Madisonian. The president of one successful institution described his college as "a political system: a 'pluralistic democracy,' with himself as a 'governor,' " which meant treating faculty, union leaders, and other administrators as colleagues, instead of subordinates (Birnbaum, 1992: 127). In general, successful academic leaders respected diversity (appreciating, not deprecating, different values) . They respected participants' own goals for the institution (building on them, vs. correcting them). They respected individuals' right-claims (placing the needs of people before system requirements). And they respected shared leadership (dispersing power, not just decentralizing it). All clearly madisonian priorities.

There is a final point. I suspect that most of us work in universities with *some* Madisonian characteristics, whether top administrators encourage them or not. It is interesting that academic professionals create and seek employment in organizations with such institutionalized checks and balances as self-supporting departments, faculty senates, unions, tenure policies, grievance processes, and committees representing every interest imaginable. If this sort of federalist system is what we choose for ourselves, if we claim academic freedom as our right, why should we prescribe any less freedom for others?

NOTES

1. Washington's inspirational effect on his compatriots is well illustrated by an incident at the close of the war. As hostilities with Britain diminished, so did cooperation between the states with regard to honoring war debts. American soldiers were owed years of back pay; officers had been promised pensions if they served for the duration; and now state representatives were reluctant to pay the bill, hoping the army would just go home. The army instead grew resentful at the lack of public gratitude for members' sacrifices in the cause of independence. A mass meeting of officers was called to discuss ways of securing their rights. Proposed actions included refusing to lay down arms or disband, marching on Congress, and even forming a military community in unsettled land. Some officers wanted Washington to lead the movement against civil authorities, but he appeared at their meeting and argued for restraint. His audience remained unpersuaded until Washington pulled from his pocket a piece of paper, a conciliatory letter from Congress. Flexner (1967: 507) describes the scene:

> The officers stirred impatiently in their seats, and then suddenly every heart missed a beat. Something was the matter with His Excellency. He seemed unable to read the paper. He paused in bewilderment. He fumbled in his waistcoat pocket. And then he pulled out something that only his intimates had seen him wear. A pair of glasses. With infinite sweetness and melancholy, he explained, "Gentlemen, you will permit me to put on my spectacles, for I have not only grown grey but almost blind in the service of my country."

With tough veterans moved to tears, Washington read the letter and left. Passions cooled, officers drifted off, and plans for insurrection were abandoned.

2. Selznick believes that leaders should motivate followers to think for themselves—so long as this contributes to institutional survival and integrity. Similarly, Kanungo tends to equate empowerment with motivation. He rejects notions of empowerment as sharing power or resources. He prefers a view of empowerment as "enabling," which "heightens the motivation for task accomplishment" (p. 418). So conceived, "the behavioral effects of empowerment . . . results [sic] in workers both initiating and persevering in work behavior."

REFERENCES

Avolio, Bruce J., David A. Waldman, and Francis J. Yammarino. 1991. Leading in the 1990s: The four Is of transformational leadership. *Journal of European Industrial Training*, 15: 9–16.

Bass, Bernard M. 1985. *Leadership and performance beyond expectations*. New York: Free Press.

Bass, Bernard M. 1990. From transactional to transformational leadership: Learning to share the vision. *Organizational Dynamics* 18: 19–31.

Bennis, Warren. 1977. Where have all the leaders gone? *Technology Review* 79: 3–12. Reprinted in *Contemporary issues in leadership*, 2d ed. 1989a, edited by William E. Rosenbach and Robert L. Taylor. Boulder, CO: Westview Press.

Bennis, Warren. 1989. *Why leaders can't lead*. San Francisco: Jossey-Bass, 1989b.
Bennis, Warren, and Burt Nanus. 1985. *Leaders: The strategies for taking charge*. New York: Harper & Row.
Birnbaum, Robert. 1992. *How academic leadership works*. San Francisco: Jossey-Bass.
Burns, James MacGregor. 1963. *The deadlock of democracy*. Englewood Cliffs, NJ: Prentice-Hall.
Burns, James MacGregor. 1978. *Leadership*. New York: Harper & Row.
Burrough, Bryan, and John Helyar. 1990. *Barbarians at the gate*. New York: Harper & Row.
Comte, Auguste. 1975. In *Auguste Comte and Positivism*, 185–54. System of positive polity. Translated by J. H. Bridges, edited by Gertrud Lenzer. New York: Harper & Row.
Conger, Jay A., and Rabindra N. Kanungo. 1988. Behavioral dimensions of charismatic leadership. In *Charismatic leadership*, edited by Jay A. Conger, Rabindra N. Kanungo, and Associates. San Francisco: Jossey-Bass.
Cunliffe, Marcus. 1982. *George Washington: Man and monument*. New York: New American Library.
Cyert, Richard M., and James G. March. 1963. *A behavioral theory of the firm*. Englewood Cliffs, NJ: Prentice-Hall.
Daft, Richard L. 1986. *Organization theory and design*, 2d ed. St. Paul, MN: West.
Dahl, Robert A. 1956. *A preface to democratic theory*. Chicago: University of Chicago Press.
Fayol, Henri. 1949. *General and industrial management*. Translated by Constance Storrs. London: Pitman. (Original, 1916).
Flexner, James Thomas. 1967. *George Washington in the American Revolution*. Boston: Little, Brown.
Freeman, R. Edward, and Daniel R. Gilbert, Jr. 1988. *Corporate strategy and the search for ethics*. Englewood Cliffs, NJ: Prentice-Hall.
Gardner, John W. 1990. *On leadership*. New York: Free Press.
Georgiou, Petro. 1973. The goal paradigm and notes towards a counter paradigm. *Administrative Science Quarterly* 18: 291–310.
Goodsell, Charles T. 1983. *The case for bureaucracy*. Chatham, NJ: Chatham House.
Grenier, Guillermo J. 1988. *Inhuman relations*. Philadelphia: Temple University Press.
Hall, Richard H. 1977. *Organizations*, 2d ed. Englewood Cliffs, NJ: Prentice-Hall.
Herzberg, Frederick. 1966. *Work and the nature of man*. New York: Crowell.
Howell, Jane M., and Bruce J. Avolio. 1992. The ethics of charismatic leadership: Submission or liberation? *Academy of Management Executive* 6: 43–54.
Kanungo, Rabindra N. 1992. Alienation and empowerment: Some ethical imperatives in business. *Journal of Business Ethics* 11: 413–22.
Keeley, Michael. 1980. Organizational analogy: A comparison of organismic and social contract models. *Administrative Science Quarterly* 25:337–62.
Keeley, Michael. 1988. *A social-contract theory of organizations*. South Bend, IN: University of Notre Dame Press.
Lindblom, Charles E. 1965. *The intelligence of democracy*. New York: Free Press.
Madison, James. 1961. *Federalist* No. 10; *Federalist* No. 49; *Federalist* No. 51. In *The Federalist Papers*, edited by Clinton Rossiter. New York: Mentor.
Mashaw, Jerry L. 1983. *Bureaucratic justice*. New Haven, CT: Yale University Press.
Mayhew, David R. 1991. *Divided we govern*. New Haven, CT: Yale University Press.

Mintzberg, Henry. 1983. *Power in and around organizations*. Englewood Cliffs, NJ: Prentice-Hall.

Morison, Samuel Eliot. 1965. *The Oxford history of the American people*. New York: Oxford University Press.

Padover, Saul K. Ed. 1953. *The complete Madison*. New York: Harper & Brothers.

Pfeffer, Jeffrey, and Gerald R. Salancik. 1978. *The external control of organizations*. New York: Harper & Row.

Plato. 1974. *The Republic*. 2d ed. Translated by Desmond Lee. Harmondsworth, England: Penguin.

Roberts, Nancy C., and Raymond Trevor Bradley. 1988. Limits of charisma. In *Charismatic Leadership*, edited by Jay A. Conger, Rabindra N. Kanungo, and Associates. San Francisco: Jossey-Bass.

Rost, Joseph C. 1991. *Leadership for the twenty-first century*. Westport, CT: Praeger.

Saint-Simon, Claude-Henri de. 1976. *On the industrial system*. In *The political thought of Saint- Simon*, edited by Ghita Ionescu. London: Oxford University Press. (Original, 1821)

Schein, Edgar H. 1980. *Organizational psychology*, 3d ed. Englewood Cliffs, NJ: Prentice-Hall.

Selznick, Philip. 1957. *Leadership in administration*. Evanston, IL: Row, Peterson.

Silverman, David. 1970. *The theory of organizations*. London: Heinemann.

Steers, Richard M. and Lyman W. Porter, eds. 1987. *Motivation and work behavior*, 4th ed. New York: McGraw-Hill.

Sundquist, James L. 1986. *Constitutional reform and effective government*. Washington, DC: Brookings Institution.

Weick, Karl E. 1985. Sources of order in underorganized systems: Themes in recent organizational theory. In *Organizational theory and inquiry*, edited by Yvonna S. Lincoln. Beverly Hills, CA: Sage.

Wilson, James Q. 1989. *Bureaucracy*. New York: Basic Books.

Yukl, Gary A. 1989. *Leadership in organizations*, 2d ed. Englewood Cliffs, NJ: Prentice-Hall.

Zaleznik, Abraham. 1989. *The managerial mystique*. New York: Harper & Row.

9

Ethics, Character, and Authentic Transformational Leadership Behavior

Bernard M. Bass and Paul Steidlmeier

Are Bill Gates and Lou Gerstner transformational leaders? What about "Chainsaw Al" Dunlap? For many moral analysts, leadership is a many-headed hydra that alternately shows the faces of Saddam Hussein and Pol Pot as well as those of Nelson Mandela and Mother Teresa. The stories that recount the accomplishments of such leaders raise moral questions concerning both the character of the leaders and the legitimacy of their programs. In this chapter, we attempt to differentiate such leaders (as Pol Pot and Saddam Hussein) from authentic charismatic and transformational leaders in terms of ethical discussions of character and authenticity, as well as the major themes of the modern Western ethical agenda: liberty, utility, and (distributive) justice.

The ethics of leadership rests upon three pillars: (a) the moral character of the leader; (b) the ethical legitimacy of the values embedded in the leader's vision, articulation, and program which followers either embrace or reject; and (c) the morality of the processes of social ethical choice and action that leaders and followers engage in and collectively pursue. Such ethical characteristics of leadership have been widely acknowledged (Wren, 1998; Kouzes & Posner, 1993; Greenleaf, 1977; Conger & Kanungo, 1998). Transformational leaders set examples to be emulated by their followers. And as suggested by Burns (1978) and demonstrated by Dukerich, Nichols, and associates (1990), when leaders are morally mature, those they lead display higher moral reasoning. But not all leadership fits the same pattern and ethical analysis shifts with varying leadership modalities. Two forms of leadership behavior, transactional and transformational, and their components are analyzed here in terms of moral issues.

TRANSACTIONAL AND TRANSFORMATIONAL LEADERSHIP

Transactional leadership involves *contingent reinforcement*. Followers are motivated by the leaders' promises, praise, and rewards; or they are corrected by negative feedback, reproof, threats, and disciplinary actions. The leaders react to whether the followers carry out what the leaders and followers have "transacted" to do. In *contingent rewarding* behavior, leaders either make assignments or consult with followers about what is to be done in exchange for implicit or explicit rewards and the desired allocation of resources. When leaders engage in *active management-by-exception*, they monitor follower performance and correct followers' mistakes. When leaders engage in *passive management-by-exception*, they wait passively for followers' mistakes to be called to their attention before taking corrective action with negative feedback or reprimands. *Laissez-faire* leaders avoid leading.

Transformational leadership contains four components: *charisma* or *idealized influence* (attributed or behavioral), *inspirational motivation*, *intellectual stimulation*, and *individualized consideration* (Bass, 1985, 1998; Bass & Avolio, 1993). Followers identify with the charismatic leaders' aspirations and want to emulate the leaders. Shamir, House, and Arthur (1993), Conger and Kanungo (1988, 1998), and Kanungo and Mendonca (1996) conceive of the same components as all falling under the category of charismatic leadership.

For the purposes of discussion, we will speak of transformational and transactional leaders when, in fact, most leaders have a profile of the full range of leadership that includes both transformational and transactional factors. However, those whom we call transformational do much more of the transformational than the transactional. In their defining moments, they are transformational. Those whom we label as transactional leaders display much more transactional leadership behavior. They are more likely to have attitudes, beliefs, and values more consistent with transactional leadership, but they still may be likely to be transformational at times.

ETHICAL ISSUES IN TRANSACTIONAL AND TRANSFORMATIONAL LEADERSHIP

Each component of either transactional or transformational leadership has an ethical dimension. It is the behavior of leaders—including their moral character, values, and programs—that is authentic or in-authentic. Most leaders are likely to display a mixed moral profile, so when we speak of authentic transformational leaders or authentic transactional leaders, we are labeling leaders who generally are more authentic than inauthentic.

Both styles of leadership, transformational and transactional, have strong philosophical underpinnings and ethical components (Table 9-1). In individualist philosophies, where leaders and followers each rationally pursue their own self-interests, it is generally thought that leaders should be transactional. A *free contract* is often assumed as a model of transacting between leaders and followers. A contract has to have moral legitimacy (Donaldson & Dunfee, 1994). The moral legitimacy of transactional leadership is demanding in many ways. It depends on granting the same liberty and opportunity to others that one claims for oneself, on telling the truth, keeping promises, distributing to each what is due, and employing valid incentives or sanctions. It recognizes pluralism of values and diversity of motivations (Rawls, 1971).

Transactional leadership models are grounded in a world view of self-interest. But the exclusive pursuit of self-interest is found wanting by most ethicists (Gini, 1995, 1996; Rosenthal & Buchholz, 1995). Authentic transformational leadership provides a more reasonable and realistic concept of self—a self that is connected to friends, family, and community whose welfare may be more important to oneself than one's own. One's moral obligations to them are grounded in a broader conception of individuals within community and related social norms and cultural beliefs. Although there is plenty of transactional leadership in punishments for transgressions, authentic transformational leadership is more consistent than transactional leadership with Judaic-Christian philosophical traditions and discourses on the leadership of the moral sage that presuppose a trusting community as the central life context. Nonetheless, it is a matter of modern Western moral concern that ideals not be imposed, that behavior not be coerced, and that the search for truth not be stifled. Ethical norms and behavioral ideals should not be imposed but freely embraced. Motivation should not be reduced to coercion but grow out of authentic inner commitment. Questioning and creativity should be encouraged. Followers should not be mere means to self-satisfying ends for the leader, but should be treated as ends in themselves. We label as inauthentic or "pseudo" that kind of transformational leadership that tramples upon those concerns.

Burns (1978) discussed leadership as *transforming,* and, on occasion, as *transformational.* Both the leader and the led are transformed—sharply changed in performance and outlook. But transforming others is just one of the *effects* of the leadership. We also need to examine the

TABLE 9-1. Leading Moral Components of Transactional and Transformational Leadership

Leadership Dynamic	Ethical Concern
	Transactional Leadership
Task	Whether what is being done (the end) and the means employed to do it are morally legitimate
Reward system	Whether sanctions or incentives impair effective freedom and respect conscience
Intentions	Truth telling
Trust	Promise keeping
Consequences	Egoism vs. altruism—whether the legitimate moral standing and interests of all those affected are respected
Due process	Impartial process of settling conflicts and claims
	Transformational Leadership
Idealized influence	Whether "puffery" and egoism on part of the leader predominate and whether he or she is manipulative
Inspirational motivation	Whether or not he or she provides for true empowerment and self-actualization of followers
Intellectual stimulation	Whether the leader's program is open to dynamic transcendence and spirituality or is closed propaganda and a "line" to follow
Individualized consideration	Whether followers are treated as ends or means, whether or not their unique dignity and interests are respected

behaviors of authentic transformational leadership and the *attributions* given to transformational leadership on a moral basis; that is, the processes of vision articulation and choice are matters of moral concern, not just the consequences. It is the presence or absence of such a moral foundation of the leader as a moral agent that grounds the distinction between *authentic* versus *pseudo*-transformational leadership.

Burns (1978), Bass (1985), and Howell and Avolio (1992), among others, have examined the morality of transformational leadership. For Burns, to be transformational, the leader had to be morally uplifting. For Bass, in his early work, transformational leaders could be virtuous or villainous, depending on their values. Howell and Avolio felt that only socialized leaders concerned for the common good could be truly transformational leaders. Personalized leaders, primarily concerned with their own self-interests, could not be truly transformational leaders. Publicly, however, and at a distance, they could act as if they were truly transformational, although privately they were more concerned about themselves. O'Connor, Mumford, and colleagues (1995) showed how such inauthenticity in transformational world-class leaders could result in destructive outcomes.

Critics attribute manipulative, deceptive, and other such devious behaviors to so-called transformational leaders. Martin and Sims (1956) and Bailey (1988) hold that to succeed, *all* leaders must be manipulative. But, in fact, it is *pseudo-transformational* leaders who are deceptive and manipulative. Authentic transformational leaders may have to be manipulative at times for what they judge to be the common good, but manipulation is a frequent practice of pseudo-transformational leaders and an infrequent practice of authentic transformational leaders. We contrast authentic and pseudo-transformational leadership in terms of the four components of transformational leadership already mentioned: idealized influence (or charisma), inspirational motivation, intellectual stimulation, and individualized consideration.

IDEALIZED INFLUENCE

If the leadership is transformational, its charisma or *idealized influence* is envisioning and confident, and sets high standards for emulation. Recent literature underscores the spiritual dimensions of such influence (Fairholm, 1998, part V; Kanungo & Mendonca, 1996, pp. 87ff.), as well as the moral dimensions of the influence process itself (Kanungo & Mendonca, 1996, pp. 52–56).

A first difference between authentic transformational leadership and pseudo-transformational leadership lies in the values for which they are idealized. For instance, the authentic leader calls for universal brotherhood; the pseudo-transformational leader highlights fictitious "we-they" differences in values and argues that "we" have inherently good values and "they" do not. Bass (1985, pp. 182–85) summed up the importance of the values held by a transformational leader in determining his or her actions. The observed behavior might seem the same, but according to Burns (1978), only if the underlying values were morally uplifting, could the leader be considered transforming. Bass originally argued that transformational leaders could wear the black hats of villains or the white hats of heroes depending on their values. This is mistaken; only those who wear white hats are seen as truly transformational. Those in black hats are now seen as *pseudo-transformational*. That is, while they may be transformational, they are inauthentic as transformational leaders. They are the false messiahs and tyrants of history.

Pseudo-transformational idealized leaders seek power and position even at the expense of their followers' achievements. They indulge in fantasies of power and success. They may argue that they are doing so for the good of the organization. Like charismatics, in general, they feel that they honestly know the right answers to problems that need to be sold through effective impression management. Sometimes, they even deceive themselves about their competencies. They exhort their followers to "Trust me!"—but they cannot be trusted. They engage in more self-displays to get more attention from their followers. Their visions are grandiose. They do not have the same sense of responsibility as do authentic charismatic-inspirational leaders.

Pseudo-transformational idealized leaders may see themselves as honest and straightforward and supportive of their organization's mission, but their behavior is inconsistent and unreliable. They have an outer shell of authenticity but an inner self that is false to the organization's purposes. They profess strong attachment to their organization and its people but privately are ready to sacrifice them. Inauthentic CEOs downsize their organization, increase their own compensation, and weep crocodile tears for the employees who have lost their jobs.

In addition to what has already been said, Howell and Avolio (1992) point to the need of authentic transformational leaders to promote ethical policies, procedures, and processes within their organizations. They need to be committed to a clearly stated, continually enforced code of ethical conduct that helps establish acceptable standards. They need to foster an organizational culture with high ethical standards by appropriate recruitment, training, and rewards to eventuate in the internalization in all the organization's members of shared moral standards.

INSPIRATIONAL MOTIVATION

The *inspirational motivation* of transformational leadership provides followers with challenges and meaning for engaging in shared goals and undertakings. The inspirational appeals of the authentic transformational leader tend to focus on the best in people—on harmony, charity, and good works; the inspirational appeals of the pseudo-transformational leader tend to focus on the worst in people—on demonic plots, conspiracies, unreal dangers, excuses, and insecurities. Kanungo and Mendonca (1996, pp. 61ff) have linked this to an *empowerment process*. For them, empowerment is more than broadening the scope of participation by followers. It is motivational and enabling, highlighting a new realization and transformation of the person.

Idealized, inspirational leaders, who are pseudo-transformational, may mislead, deceive, and prevaricate. They can be subtle and speak with a forked tongue, for instance, offering followers empowerment, yet continuing to treat them as dependent children (Sankowsky, 1995). They talk about empowerment but actually continue to seek control (Conger & Kanungo, 1998). Previously, Bass (1985) mistakenly argued that, although the dynamics might be the same if the leaders had virtuous or evil ends, the moral differences were a matter of their aims and values, not the dynamics involved in their influence. But the dynamics and means-to-ends as well as the ends are different for authentic and inauthentic transformational leaders. The authentic are inwardly and outwardly concerned about the good that can be achieved for the group, organization, or society for which they feel responsible. The inauthentic and pseudo-transformational may publicly give the same impression and be idealized by their followers for it, but privately be concerned about the good they can achieve for themselves. They are captains who sail under false colors. They are spiritual leaders who are false prophets.

INTELLECTUAL STIMULATION

The intellectual stimulation of transformational leadership incorporates an open architecture dynamic into processes of situation evaluation, vision formulation, and patterns of implementation. Such openness has a transcendent and spiritual dimension and helps followers to question assumptions and to generate more creative solutions to problems. It is especially suited to the normative side of ethics, where human probing of the ground of being is both fathomless and endless. To the point, this dynamic breaks the bonds of organizational and leadership cultures that ignore fundamental questions such as altruism (Kanungo and Mendonca, 1996, pp. 79ff).

The intellectual stimulation of pseudo-transformational leaders manifests a logic containing false assumptions to slay the dragons of uncertainty. Pseudo-transformational leaders overweight authority and underweight reason. They take credit for others' ideas but make them scapegoats for failure (Sankowsky, 1995). They substitute anecdotes for hard evidence. They feed on the ignorance of their followers so that their followers will accept more ambiguities and inconsistencies, opening the opportunities for the self-enhancement of charlatans:

> People like Rush Limbaugh and Louis Farrakhan live well off ignorance.
> . . . They are smart, ambitious men with great charisma, who look like
> giants to people of minor intellect. They are snake oil salesmen. They are

confidence men who exploit. . . ignorant, scared, angry, frustrated people for personal gain in the name of doing good for the entire nation or race. (Lockman, 1995, p. 9a)

Authentic transformational leaders persuade others on the merits of the issues. Pseudo-transformational leaders set and control agenda to manipulate the values of importance to followers often at the expense of others or even harm to them. Authentic transformational leaders openly bring about changes in followers' values by the merit and relevancy of the leader's ideas and mission to their followers' ultimate benefit and satisfaction (Howell, 1988). Pseudo-transformational leaders may create the impression that they are doing the right things, but will secretly fail to do so when doing the right things conflicts with their own narcissistic interests. They are less likely to listen to conflicting views and more likely to be intolerant of the differences of opinion between their followers and themselves (Howell & Avolio, 1992). They substitute emotional argumentation for rational discourse.

INDIVIDUALIZED CONSIDERATION

The individualized consideration component of transformational leadership underscores the necessity of altruism if leadership is to be anything more than authoritarian control (Kanungo & Mendonca, 1996, pp. 85ff). The transformational leader treats each follower as an individual and provides coaching, mentoring and growth opportunities (Bass, 1985). While true transformational leaders are concerned about developing their followers into leaders, pseudo-transformational leaders are more concerned about maintaining the dependence of their followers. They exploit the feelings of their followers to maintain deference from them (Sankowsky, 1995). Pseudo-transformational leaders will welcome and expect blind obedience. They will attempt to enhance their personal status by maintaining the personal distance between themselves and their followers. They encourage fantasy and magic in their vision of the attractive future while true transformational leaders promote attainable shared goals. Narcissistic pseudo-transformational leaders manipulate arguments about political choices with a "twist that achieves the desired responses" (Bass, 1989, p. 45). Their style of individualized consideration foments favoritism and competition among followers in the guise of being helpful. While the authentic individually considerate leader is concerned about helping followers to become more competent to provide for a more successful succession, the inauthentic counterpart seeks to maintain a parent-child relationship.

Another difference between authentic and pseudo-transformational leadership is that authentic transformational leaders, who may have just as much need for power as pseudo-transformational leaders, channel the need in socially constructive ways into the service of others. Pseudo-transformational leaders use power primarily for self-aggrandizement and are actually contemptuous privately of those they are supposed to be serving as leaders (Howell & Avolio, 1992). Although this may not be expressed publicly, privately pseudo-transformational leaders are concerned about their power and gaining more of it. Insiders who work closely with them know them to be deceptive, domineering, egotistical demagogues, while their public image may be that of saviors. Pseudo-transformational leaders are predisposed toward self-serving biases. They claim they are right and good; others are wrong and bad. They are the reason things go well; other persons are the reason for things going badly. They wear different masks for different occasions, believe themselves to be high in self-monitoring, but are betrayed by their nonverbal contradictory behavior.

THE MORAL SPECTRUM OF TRANSFORMATIONAL LEADERSHIP

Transformational leadership traces out a complicated moral spectrum, in which most leaders combine both authentic and inauthentic behavior. For example, many leaders, particularly political leaders who cannot move too far in front of their followers, walk a fine line of moral probity. In their efforts to accent the positive, to make inspiring appeals, to maintain the enthusiasm and morale of followers, they are inauthentic in transformational leadership. They withhold the release of information. Or they time its release for when it will do the most good. They give the appearance of confidence even when they are unsure about what they are doing and what they are telling followers to do. They initiate projects that they personally oppose and delay implementing them so that the projects are never completed. They publicly support but privately oppose proposals. They openly compromise but privately divert the implementation of the compromise (Martin & Sims, 1956; Bass, 1968). They may have the public image of a saint but privately are deceptive devils. They may appear to their followers to behave as a transformational leader, but the appearance is deceptive, for inwardly they remain more interested in themselves than their followers. They knowingly focus their followers, on fantasies instead of attainable visions. They engage in shams and pretense. They don't practice what they preach. And these masquerades are at the expense of their followers. They are *pseudo-transformational*. They are Freud's (1913) totemic leaders who satisfy the fantasies of their followers, although they appear to direct their followers toward transcendental purposes, but in fact tend to cater to the self-delusionary interests of their followers.

In short, while authentic and inauthentic transformational leaders may fail to exhibit any one of the four components—idealized influence, inspirational motivation, intellectual stimulation, or individualized consideration—the component that ordinarily is missing in the personalized leadership of the pseudo-transformational leader is individualized consideration. Thus, many intellectually stimulating, inspirational leaders such as Hyman Rickover, who transformed the U.S. Navy into the nuclear age, were known for their self-aggrandizing, inconsiderate, abusive, and abrasive behavior (Polmar & Allen, 1982). Furthermore, instead of earning idealized influence from their followers, pseudo-transformational leaders seek to become the idols (rather than the ideals) of their followers (Howell & Avolio, 1992). The ethics of transformational leadership are subverted by the pseudo-transformational leader's contempt for self and others, by learning to rationalize and justify their deceptions, and by their feelings of superiority. They see themselves as having an unconventional but higher morality (Goldberg, 1995). Nevertheless, they are mistaken. O'Connor, Mumford, and associates (1995) contrasted the biographies of eighty-two world-class personalized and socialized charismatic leaders. The socialized charismatics were rated more highly in their morality than were the personalized, especially as they behaved during their rise to power.

For example, in an election campaign, authentic transformational leaders point the public to the societal problems they truly believe need solving. Inauthentic transformational leaders point to the same issues but are personally uninterested in doing something about them. In an election campaign, authentic transactional leaders make promises they think they can keep, if elected. But they may be overly optimistic and be unable to keep the promises. Inauthentic transactional leaders know they making promises they cannot keep, if elected.

If transformational leadership is *authentic* and true to self and others, it is characterized by high moral and ethical standards in each of the dimensions discussed previously. At the same time, it aims to develop the leader as a moral person and creates a moral environment for the organization. In Fairholm's terms (1998), it is at once a type of leadership grounded in values, based in trust and rooted in spirituality. As an *ideal moral type,* authentic transformational leadership contrasts sharply with what we term its pseudo or unethical manifestations, as well as with conventional transactional leadership.

The best of leadership is both transformational and transactional. Transformational leadership augments the effectiveness of transactional leadership; it does not replace transactional leadership. (Waldman, Bass, & Yammarino, 1990; Kanungo & Mendonca, 1996, pp.

53ff.). Take the example of Abraham Lincoln. He made many trans-actional executive decisions based on his own sense of timing and political expediency such as delaying the Emancipation Proclamation until after the first Union victory at Antietam in 1862. Even then, to hold the slave states of Delaware, Maryland, Kentucky and Missouri in the Union, the Proclamation prohibited slavery only in those eleven states that had seceded. As an authentic transformational leader, his sense of duty and what he personally thought was right, good, and proper propelled him into executive decisions unapproved by Congress and unsupported by public opinion. He suspended habeas corpus in 1862 when Washington, D.C., was almost surrounded by rebel troops. Nevertheless, by his second inauguration in 1864, he was espousing a generous, forgiving peace settlement "with malice towards none."

While transactional leadership manages outcomes and aims for behavioral compliance independent of the ideals a follower may happen to have, transformational leadership is predicated upon the inner dynamics of a freely embraced change of heart in the realm of core values and motivation, upon open-ended intellectual stimulation and a commitment to treating people as ends not mere means. To bring about change, authentic transformational leadership fosters the modal values of honesty, loyalty, and fairness, as well as the end values of justice, equality, and human rights. But pseudo-transformational leadership endorses perverse modal values such as favoritism, victimization, and special interests and end values such as racial superiority, submission, and social Darwinism (Carey, 1992; Solomon, 1996). It can invent fictitious obstacles, imaginary enemies, and visions that are chimeras.

Transactional leadership is moral when the truth is told, promises are kept, negotiations are fair, and choices are free (Hollander, 1995). It is immoral when information harmful to followers is deliberately concealed from them, when bribes are proffered, when nepotism is practiced, and when authority is abused.

CHARACTER AND TRANSFORMATIONAL LEADERSHIP

In leadership, character matters. This is not to deny that evil people can bring about good things or that good people can lead the way to moral ruin. Rather, leadership provides a moral compass and, over the long term, both personal development and the common good are best served by a moral compass that reads true. In this section we draw some lessons from the traditions of the *moral sage* and *social prophet* that have enjoyed prominence in a wide variety of cultures. Whether visionary or ascetic, the sage and prophet have also widely been perceived as agents of change, as well as people to be emulated and as leaders of others, not followers. To be sure, moral leadership is not to be confused with occupying official positions of authority. In fact, the sage and prophet often held no official office and inveighed against the moral corruption of the "principalities and powers."

An approach to ethics based upon moral character and virtue enjoys an extraordinarily broad cross-cultural base in terms of the "framing narratives" that guide ethical discourse in cultural settings as diverse as Western and Confucian traditions. From Plato's "philosopher king" to the virtuous Confucian minister of the state, the "moral sage" and the "superior person" are portrayed as both a font of wisdom and the embodiment of virtue, whose very presence and being bring about personal and social transformations.

Both Socrates and Confucius have come to epitomize leaders with authentic *idealized influence.* There is no doubt that over the centuries they have taken on heroic dimensions. Their framing narratives underscore a fundamental dynamic of leadership. Each proposed to his followers the highest ethical standards that they themselves implemented in their own lives. More important, in terms of authenticity, each was recognized as a sage and leader by others, not by self-proclamation.

Historically, the central focus of ethical concern in Chinese traditions manifests a right ordering of personal relationships. Epitomized in Confucius' "five relations" (Taylor & Arbuckle, 1995; Tu, 1985, ch. 3), Chinese ethics emphasizes personal virtue and specifies proper conduct in family, kinship, and friendship relations, as well as among social equals and between superiors and subordinates in sociopolitical organizations and institutions. The social and political order has always been seen as a moral issue, and it plays a critical role in realizing humanity's ethical destiny (Schwartz, 1985, p. 52; deBary, 1991a). The virtues of *ren* (human heartedness, benevolence, love) and the virtue of *yi* (righteousness) are the grounding virtues of the moral life. They express the way (*dao*) that one existentially embraces. *Ren* is the lodestar that permeates every action of the superior person.

The moral person in each tradition would sacrifice anything for the sake of virtue. For example, the Confucian moral tradition is strikingly clear about the relation of profits to moral virtue. From the *Analects* one reads:

> Wealth and honor are what every person desires. But if they have been obtained in violation of moral principles, they must not be kept. Poverty and humble station are what every person dislikes. But if they can be avoided only in violation of moral principles, they must not be avoided.

> If a superior person departs from humanity (ren), how can s/he fulfill that name? A superior person never abandons ren, even for the lapse of a single meal. In moments of haste, one acts according to it. In times of difficulty or confusion, one acts according to it. (Analects, 4.5)

In Socratic terms, one finds a striking similarity: the moral person does not "put money or anything else before virtue" (*Apology*, 42A).

Both Socrates and Confucius base their approach upon authentic *inspirational motivation*. Each proposes a transcendent vision of fulfillment, justice, and peace based upon the right ordering of relationships. Each is transcendent and grasps the "beyond in our midst," a better future. Each transforms by invitation, not by coercion. Each manifests consistency between word and deed.

The inspiration is simple: virtue is its own reward. The basic scenario of the moral sage in each tradition emphasizes virtue and moral character. In the days leading up to his condemnation to death, Socrates was taken up with a single question: *how to be excellent at being human?* He sharply criticized the pseudo-transformational sophists—the purveyors of false wisdom—because they did not know themselves; even worse, they abandoned fidelity to the way of truth. While pretending to be wise, they were foolish. The Socratic enterprise is grounded in a relentless pursuit of the truth, in the development of wisdom, and in the cultivation of virtue. Indeed, Socrates himself transformed others precisely because of his fearless commitment to virtue.

For Confucius, the moral sage (*shengren*) is the key person in bringing about personal righteousness and social justice. A superior person (*jyundz*) is a moral person who walks the moral way and attempts to practice virtue through self-cultivation. Both the sage and the superior person live under the restraint of virtue and aim to transform society accordingly. A superior person is perforce a moral leader (*Analects*, 17:3). The common, inferior, or small person (*xiaoren*) either does not know or does not follow the way and is not a positive moral force.

Even though written texts idealize both Confucius and Socrates, the commitment to authentic *intellectual stimulation* of their disciples is notable in each. Both are memorable for their "ways of proceeding" (methodologies) that were based upon relentless questioning. For each, moral wisdom was the highest prize. It was for his spirit of inquiry and transformative vision that Socrates was put to death for according to his words in Plato's *Apology*:

> ... it is the greatest good for a man every day to discuss virtue and the other things about which you hear me talking and examining myself and everybody else ... the unexamined life is not worth living for a man. (Plato, prior to 387 B.C.E./1969, 36c)

In today's world, Socrates and Confucius seem almost hopelessly naive, offering a vision based on the premise that through personal cultivation guided by moral leaders people will develop strong moral character and embrace virtue above all other things and, in so doing, will transform themselves and society. Personal virtue and moral wisdom of the leader provide the checks and balances upon power and self-aggrandizement! From this simple framework of *truth-wisdom-virtue* a vision of the transforming power of the moral sage has flowed down through the ages. The heart of the moral enterprise is the development of good character, which is defined by commitment to virtue in all circumstances. This framework was integrated into Judeo-Christian traditions through personages such as Augustine, Aquinas, and Maimonides. In Judeo-Christian traditions, the *moral sage* (saint, holy person) exercises a transforming influence upon all those whom he or she contacts. The moral sage is a leader.

From the literature on transformational leadership, it is clear that there are many points of congruence between the "authentic moral sage" and the "authentic transformational leader." Being a moral leader is more a creative art than science. Its hallmark is existential practice, where one engenders virtue in self, others. and society through example and virtuous conduct. The "superior person" transforms relations between people in society to reflect the "way" of the "mandate of heaven." What emerges is that a moral person is a superior person precisely by his or her embrace of the way of virtue. The process of growth in virtue is one of creative transformation of self (Tu, 1985; deBary, 1991a; 1991b). But this is no individualist project; it occurs both within and for a fiduciary community. A person becomes virtuous within a community. A person becomes virtuous for the community to "give all people security and peace" (Confucius, first century C.E./1994, *Analects*, 14, 42). The true transformational leader is to be, in Confucian terms, a "superior person." We examine this further in light of how a leader deals with impression management.

SOPHISTRY, PRETENSE, AND IMPRESSION MANAGEMENT

Impression management is the regulation of information about a vision, the organization, and the self. The authentic transformational leader may remain ethical in using impression management to provide followers with "identity images" of trustworthiness, credibility, moral worth, innovativeness, esteem, and power (Gardner & Avolio, 1998, p. 40). Conversely, impression management may be the sophistry and pretense of the pseudo-transformational leader providing self-glorification, "spin" on events, excuses, and the big lie. The criticism of its immorality reads as if it were directly taken from the *Analects* and from the *Apology*!

To foster their influence and esteem among their followers, "transformational" persons, particularly those leaders who want to bolster their charismatic and inspirational image, engage in impression management (Gronn, 1995). Gardner and Avolio (1998) note that many charismatic leaders orchestrate their presentations to frame, script, and stage their performance. The presentations can be moral, amoral, or immoral. For example, to maintain morale in the face of uncertainties, without sacrificing their virtuousness, competent leaders may send out messages to rally support. Evidence may be provided projecting an image of strength and decisiveness. On the other hand, morality will be tested when incompetent leaders focus all the attention on their strengths rather than their weaknesses, appeal to the fantasies of their followers, adopt the values they feel fit the implicit theories that followers have about ideal leadership, paint a vision of the future that is more fantasy than reality, and exaggerate the meaningfulness of the followers' efforts. They are, in short, the "sophists" and "small persons" whom Socrates and Confucius condemned. The most telling difference between them and true moral leaders is that their puffery and self-aggrandizement emanates from them and their handlers, rather than from acclamation by the people who might choose to emulate them.

When self-promotion and hype are excessive, they can create the impression of being manipulative, untrustworthy, overzealous, and conceited (Gardner & Avolio, 1998). The relentless moral inquiry advocated by both Socrates and Confucius, as well as much religious tradition, easily punctures such balloons.

THE MODERN ETHICAL AGENDA OF INDIVIDUAL LIBERTY, UTILITY, AND JUSTICE

To guide moral actions, modern Western ethics marks a change in Western tradition in its articulation of ethical criteria. While recognizing the moral heritage based upon faith, modern Western ethics was inspired to large degree by reason and by science. It has placed emphasis upon rules or principles to be followed in concrete situations; as a social ethic it has emphasized procedural justice. At one extreme, this new ethical agenda has assigned the highest value to individual liberty and the right of the individual both to determine his or her interests and to pursue them. When a leader appears to arbitrarily or surreptitiously influence the values of followers or to interfere with individual determination and pursuit of interests, it is judged morally objectionable. This issue goes to the heart of the dimensions that we ascribe to an authentic transformational leader. It questions whether it is possible to have "idealized influence" and "inspirational motivation" without controlling, dominating, and otherwise diminishing the liberty of conscience, free choice, and self-determination of followers. It questions whether leadership that asks for the dedicated commitment of followers can, in the same breath, truly provide for individualized consideration of a follower's interests.

Libertarians such as Robert Nozick (1974) and Ayn Rand (1964) view any form of leadership that dominates followers as antithetical to core values. They see the exercise of liberty and free choice by the individual as the heart of the moral enterprise and the thwarting of such liberty by others as the major moral evil. For Nozick and Rand, life is inherently social, in the sense that one pursues happiness while rubbing up against others doing the same. However, their view of society is atomistic: Society is an aggregate of self-contracting individuals who go about life both determining what is their happiness and how to pursue it. Based upon such a dynamic of liberty, social moral obligations derive only from free valid contracts and the truthfulness and promises they entail. Transactional leadership is valid to the extent that it is consistent with a morally legitimate contract between affected individuals. In this view, transformational leadership can be viewed only with suspicion as a covert exercise at control and domination. Everyone should be his or her own transforming leader.

There is little moral role for leaders in such a context, except to enhance individual liberty, rights, and self-determination. Unfortunately, a good deal of the leadership literature is predicated upon the "leader–single follower" model and neglects the dynamics of "leader–diverse stakeholders." There are certainly grounds for such a focus: A leader may be a catalytic agent of a follower's personal development. The leader may be inspirational, may set an example to emulate, enhance liberty and choice, and facilitate the pursuits of one's interests. However, the moral analysis of leadership is severely deficient if it is limited to such considerations. The leader is more than an "enhancer" of individual self-determination and is also more than the most effective calculator of the "greatest happiness of the greatest number."

The Human Relations Movement is at the other extreme of the libertarian ethical position. It espouses shared values, equality, power sharing, consensus, and participative decision making. It sometimes equates individual leadership with dominant behavior, the power of authority, the giving of directions, the arbitrary making of decisions, and neglect of followers' interests (Rost, 1991). We argue that such a notion of leadership is truncated and neglects the inspirational side of leadership and the legitimate needs for the power of position, authoritative initiatives, and leader and follower responsibilities. In community affairs, the Human Relations Movement takes the form of "grass-roots" democracy. In organizations, it is seen in much of the theory and practices of organizational development (OD). It is also seen in sensitivity training that features the spontaneous emergence of the different roles of leadership in initially ambiguous situations. Learning how to give and receive feedback provides the means for the group to progress. For organizations to improve themselves, the seeds of reform reside in the values, interests, and capabilities of their members. Organizations could improve if the members were empowered to try out their ideas and learn from feedback (Bass, 1968). The follower-leader distinction should wither away (Burns, 1998; Rost, 1991).

POWER, PERSUASION, CHECKS AND BALANCES, AND THE MODERN ETHICAL AGENDA

We have presented authentic transformational leadership as an ideal type. Transformational leadership, particularly pseudo-transformational leadership, may lend itself to the unchecked abuses of power. It is power abuses that concern us here (Tsou, 1995). Keeley (1995) faults transformational leadership for lacking the checks and balances of transactional leadership. Much of the checks-and-balances argument refers to macrosocial legislative, administrative, and judicial checks and balances upon political power, rather than checks and balances upon power within organizations. The latter does exist, in theory at least, in terms of (ideally) independent boards of directors, stakeholder proxies, labor unions, the free choice of suppliers, and consumer sovereignty. Indeed, competitive market theory presupposes that power is held in check and that oligopolistic or monopolistic forms of power should be regulated if not eliminated. Furthermore, in complex markets and enterprises where the managers lead the firm as agents of the principals' interests, checks and balances are a problem precisely when markets are dominated by power groups and agents feel they can ignore the principals' interests. They may be aided and abetted by the lack of appropriate auditing and disclosures of revenues and expenses. Exploitative and abusive bosses remain with us. How can they be controlled or dislodged, particularly if they are also pseudo-transformational? Boards of directors, government regulators, and union officials provide possible checks. Boards may force resignations; regulators may fine; unions may strike. All may sue.

The bigger question is about what protects minority opposition in organizations and communities when the majority succumbs to the appeals of the transformational leader. Keeley (1995) looked to James Madison's contention in the *Federalists Papers* that a constitutional government required contending interests to be heard so that after rational debate, among the contending factions, optimal decisions could be made. Otherwise, the many factions of society could be controlled by those in power and would abandon their own best interests if they were coerced into sharing the same interests. According to Keeley (1995), interpreting Madison, an unhealthy concentration of power, and dictatorship by the majority at the expense of the minority, results from transformational leadership that succeeds in convincing people with truly diverse interests that they share common goals, even if they truly don't. For Keeley the rules of governance must require the separation of powers of the executive, the assembly, and the judiciary. Outcomes must depend on negotiation and the give-and-take of transactional leadership. If only the interests of the strongest faction dominate, more factional conflict will emerge with less tolerance for minority views. Rival and opposing interests are best controlled if purpose and power are separated and transactional negotiations, trade-offs, and exchanges produce compromises acceptable to all concerned. This is in contrast to the emphasis of transformational leadership on the sharing in a common vision and a common purpose.

The all-or-none argument of Keeley misses the point. Madison himself embraced the overriding importance of the common good and espoused the need to sacrifice private opinion and private interests to the public good (Wren, 1998). In the politics of checks and balances, particularly when it comes to marginal moral standards, transactional negotiations are likely to see much bluffing, withholding information, manipulating facts, making political alliances and trade-offs, settling past obligations, delaying implementations, openly compromising but covertly diverting plans, and timing the release of news. Power is used to weaken opposition and strengthen support. When authentic transformational leaders see themselves in a win-lose negotiation, they try to convert it into a win-win joint problem-solving situation, or, if this fails, they become effective transactional negotiators trying wherever possible to use persuasion rather than power.

For Thomas Jefferson, checks and balances would not be needed if the country shared common interests. His transformational vision was that of a nation of small, independent farmers and mechanics with common interests who could reach the right decisions after rational debate. Public education to create an informed citizenry was required for this to happen. In this vein, John Stuart Mill argued strongly for encouraging free speech to provide the marketplace for ideas in which the best arguments buttressed by the most compelling evidence and reasoning would prevail (Higgenbottom, 1996).

SUMMARY AND CONCLUSIONS

Critics argue that transformational leadership is unethical. They contend that its rhetoric may appeal to emotions rather than to reason. They contend that it lacks the checks and balances of democratic discourse and power distribution. They contend that it violates the principles of the OD movement and that it manipulates followers into ignoring the followers' own best interests.

The critics fail to consider the positive aspects of inspirational leadership. They ignore the shortcomings of democratic processes and OD. They fail to distinguish between transformational and pseudo-transformational leadership. We agree with Gill Hickman (1993) that rather than being unethical, true transformational leaders identify the core values and unifying purposes of the organization and its members, liberate their human potential, and foster pluralistic leadership and effective, satisfied followers.

Rather than being immoral, transformational leadership has become a necessity in the postindustrial world of work. As Cascio (1995) has pointed out, the traditional manufacturing or service job, a fixed bundle of tasks performed by an individual worker, has been replaced by a manufacturing or service process, completed by a flexible team with diverse skills, interests, and attitudes. As a consequence, self-aggrandizing, fantasizing, pseudo-transformational leaders can be branded as immoral. But authentic transformational leaders, as moral agents, expand the domain of effective freedom, the horizon of conscience, and the scope for altruistic intention. Their actions aim toward noble ends, legitimate means, and fair consequences. Engaged as they are in the moral uplifting of their followers, in the sharing of mutually rewarding visions of success, and in enabling and empowering them to convert the visions into realities, they should be applauded, not chastised.

ACKNOWLEDGMENTS

The authors wish to express their appreciation to two anonymous reviewers and to Professor Joanne Ciulla of the Jepson School of Leadership, University of Richmond, for her insightful suggestions.

REFERENCES

Bailey, F. G. 1988. *Humbuggery and manipulation: The art of leadership.* Ithaca: Cornell University Press.

Bass, B. M. 1968. How to succeed in business according to business students and managers. *Journal of Applied Psychology,* 52: 254–62.

Bass, B. M. 1985. *Leadership and performance beyond expectations.* New York: Free Press.

Bass, B. M. 1989. The two faces of charisma. *Leaders 12 (4):* 440–45.

Bass, B. M. 1998. *Transformational leadership: Industrial, military, and educational impact.* Mahwah, NJ: Lawrence Erlbaum Associates.

Bass, B. M., and B. J. Avolio. 1993. Transformational leadership: A response to critiques. *Leadership theory and research: Perspectives and directions,* edited by M.M. Chemers and R. Ayman. New York: Free Press.

Burns, J. M. 1978. *Leadership.* New York: Harper & Row.

Burns, J. M. 1998. Empowerment for change. In *Kellogg Leadership Studies Project: Rethinking leadership, 1994-1997,* edited by B. Adams & S. W. Webster. College Park: Center for Political Leadership and Participation, University of Maryland.

Carey, M. R. 1992. Transformational leadership and the fundamental option for self-transcendence. *Leadership Quarterly 3:* 217–36.

Cascio, W. 1995. Whither industrial and organizational psychology in a changing world of work? *American Psychologist 50:* 928–39.

Confucius. 1994. *Analects of Confucius—with modern Chinese and English translations,* edited by G. Xin. Beijing: Foreign Languages Press. (Original work composed during the lifetime of Confucius [circa 551 BCE-479 B.C.E.] and his disciples; the standard version of this piece used today emerged in the first century C.E.)

Conger, J., and R. N. Kanungo, eds. 1988. *Charismatic leadership: The elusive factor in organizational effectiveness.* San Francisco: Jossey-Bass.

Conger, J., and R. N. Kanungo. 1998. *Charismatic leadership in organizations.* Thousand Oaks, CA: Sage Publications.

de Bary, W. T. 1991a. *Learning for one's self. Essays on the individual in Neo-Confucian thought.* New York: Columbia University Press.

de Bary, W. T. 1991b. *The trouble with Confucianism.* Cambridge, MA: Harvard University Press.

Donaldson, T., and Dunfee T. W. 1999. *The ties that bind: A social contracts approach to various ethics.* Boston: Harvard Business School Press.

Dukerich, J. M., M. L. Nicholas, D. R. Elm, 1990. Moral reasoning in groups. *Human relations* v. 43 (May 1990) pp. 473–93.

Fairholm, G. W. 1998. *Perspectives on leadership: From the science of management to its spiritual heart.* Westport, CT: Quorum Books.

Freud, S. 1913. *Totem and taboo.* New York: Vintage Books.

Gardner, W. L., and B. J. Avolio. 1998. The charismatic relationship: A dramaturgical perspective. *Academy of Management Review 23:* 32–58.

Gini, A. 1995. Too much to say about something. *Business Ethics Quarterly 5:* 143–55.

Gini, A. 1996. Moral leadership and business ethics. In *Kellogg Leadership Studies Project: Ethics and leadership, working papers,* edited by B. Adams and S. W. Webster. College Park: Center for Political Leadership and Participation, University of Maryland.

Goldberg, C. October 1995. Psychologist posits the origins of evil. *Monitor.* Washington, DC: American Psychological Association.

Greenleaf, R. 1977. *Servant leadership.* New York: Paulist Press.

Gronn, P. C. 1995. Greatness revisited: The current obsession with transformational leadership. *Leading & Managing 1:* 14–27.

Hickman, G. 1993. *Toward transformistic organizations: A conceptual framework.* Washington, DC: Unpublished paper, American Political Science Association.

Higginbottom, G. 1996. Public broadcasting is good for the public. *Binghamton Press*, Binghamton, NY, 23 July, p. A-6.

Hollander, E. 1995. Ethical challenges in the leader-follower relationship. *Business Ethics Quarterly 5:* 54–65.

Howell, J. M. 1988. The two faces of charisma: Socialized and personalized leadership in organizations. In *Charismatic leadership: The illusive factor in organizational effectiveness*, edited by J. Conger and R. Kanungo. San Francisco: Jossey-Bass.

Howell, J. M., and B. J. Avolio. 1992. The ethics of charismatic leadership: Submission or liberation? *Academy of Management Executive 6 (2):* 43–54.

Kanungo, R. N., and M. Mendonca. 1996. *Ethical dimensions in leadership.* Beverly Hills, CA: Sage Publications.

Keeley, M. 1995. The trouble with transformational leadership: Toward a federalist ethic for organizations. *Business Ethics Quarterly 5:* 67–95.

Kouzes, J. M., and B. Z. Posner. 1993. *Credibility: How leaders gain and lose it and why people demand it.* San Francisco: Jossey-Bass.

Lockman, N. (19 December, 1995). American ignorance, American hate. *Press & Sun-Bulletin*, Binghamton, NY, p. 9A

Martin, N. H., and J. H. Sims. 1956. Thinking ahead: Power tactics. *Harvard Business Review 6 (6):* 25–36, 140.

Nozick, R. 1974. *Anarchy and utopia.* Cambridge, MA: Harvard University Press.

O'Connor, J. O., M. D. Mumford, T. C. Clifton, T. L. Gessner, and M. S. Connelly. 1995. Charismatic leaders and destructiveness: An historiometric study. *Leadership Quarterly 6:* 529–55.

Plato. 1969. *The apology of Plato.* Translated by H. Tredennick. New York: Penguin Books. (Original work written prior to 387 B.C.E.)

Polmar, N., and T. B. Allen. 1982. *Rickover.* New York: Simon & Schuster.

Pye, L. W. 1995. Factions and politics of *guanxi:* Paradoxes in Chinese administrative and political behavior. *The China Journal 34:* 35–54.

Rand, A. 1964. *The virtue of selfishness.* New York: New American Library.

Rosenthal, S. B., and R. A. Buchholz. 1995. Leadership: Toward new philosophical foundations. *Business and Professional Ethics Journal 14:* 25–41.

Rawls, J. 1999. *A theory of justice.* Cambridge, MA: Belknap Press.

Rost, J. C. 1991. *Leadership for the 21st century.* Westport, CT: Praeger.

Sankowsky, D. 1995. The charismatic leader as narcissist: Understanding the abuse of power. *Organizational Dynamics 23:* 57–71.

Schwartz, B. I. 1985. *The world of thought in ancient China.* Cambridge, MA: Belknap Press of Harvard University Press.

Shamir, B., R. J. House, and M. B. Arthur. 1993. The motivational effects of charismatic leaders: A self-concept based theory. *Organizational Science 4:* 577–94.

Solomon, R. 1996. Ethical leadership, emotions and trust: Beyond "charisma." In *Kellogg Leadership Studies Project: Ethics and leadership, working papers*, edited by B. Adams and S. W. Webster. College Park: Center for Political Leadership and Participation, University of Maryland.

Taylor, R. L., and G. Arbuckle. 1995. Confucianism. *The Journal of Asian Studies 54:* 347–53.

Tsou, T. 1995. Chinese politics at the top: Factionalism or informal politics? Balance-of-power politics or a game to win all? *The China Journal 34:* 95–456.

Tu, W. 1985. *Confucian thought: Selfhood as creative transformation.* Albany: State University of New York Press.

Waldman, D. A., B. M. Bass, and F. J. Yammarino. 1990. Adding to contingent-reward behavior: The augmenting effect of charismatic leadership. *Group & Organizational Studies* 15: 381–94.

Wren, J. T. 1998. James Madison and the ethics of transformational leadership. In *Ethics, the heart of leadership,* edited by J. Ciulla. Westport, CT: Praeger.

Index

About the Editor and the Contributors

BRUCE J. AVOLIO is the Donald and Shirley Clifton Chair in Leadership at the University of Nebraska in the College of Business Administration. He is the Director of the Gallup Leadership Institute and is a Gallup Senior Scientist. Avolio has an international reputation as a researcher in leadership, having published more than 80 articles and 5 books. His last two published books were entitled *Full Leadership Development: Building the Vital Forces in Organizations*, and *Developing Potential Across a Full Range of Leadership: Cases on Transactional and Transformational Leadership*.

DR. BERNARD M. BASS is a distinguished professor emeritus of management at Binghamton University. Since 1946, he has published more than 300 journal articles and 21 books, concentrating on leadership and organizational behavior. He has consulted and conducted training for many of the Fortune 500 firms and run workshops in more than 40 countries. For the past 25 years, he has focused on research and applications to management development of transformational leadership and has in recent years completed several essays on the ethics of leadership.

JAMES MACGREGOR BURNS is Senior Fellow at the Jepson School of Leadership Studies and Woodrow Wilson Professor of Government,

Emeritus at Williams College. He is also a Fellow of the American Academy of Arts and Sciences. Burns is the author of *Leadership* and a number of biographies and books on government, politics, and democracy. He won the Pulitzer Prize for his biography of Franklin Roosevelt, *The Lion and the Fox*. His most recent book is *Transforming Leadership: The Pursuit of Happiness*.

JOANNE B. CIULLA is Professor and Coston Family Chair in Leadership and Ethics at the Jepson School of Leadership Studies, University of Richmond. She is one of the founding faculty members of the school. Ciulla has also held the UNESCO Chair in Leadership Studies at the United Nations University's Leadership Academy. She is the author of numerous articles, and books including *The Working Life: The Promise and Betrayal of Modern Work, The Ethics of Leadership,* and the forthcoming *Honest Work: A Business Ethics Reader* with Robert C. Solomon and Clancy Martin.

AL GINI is professor of philosophy at Loyola University, Chicago, and co-founder and associate editor of the *Business Ethics Quarterly*. He is also a regular commentator on Chicago's NPR affiliate WBEZ. His most recent books include *My Job Myself: Work and the Creation of the Modern Individual* and *The Importance of Being Lazy: In Praise of Play, Leisure, and Vacations*.

EDWIN P. HOLLANDER is University Distinguished Professor in the Industrial/Organizational Psychology graduate programs at CUNY's Baruch College and Graduate Center. He was Provost of Social Sciences and Administration at SUNY Buffalo, and Director of the Social/Organizational Psychology Department there. His books include *Leaders, Groups, and Influence,* and *Leadership Dynamics*. He has taught at Carnegie-Mellon, Washington University and American University, with visiting appointments at Wisconsin, Harvard, Oxford, Istanbul (Fulbright), and London's Tavistock Institute (NIMH Senior Fellow).

MICHAEL KEELEY was professor of management at Loyola University of Chicago prior to his retirement. He has degrees in engineering and business, and a Ph.D. in organization behavior from Northwestern University. He is the author of *A Social-Contract Theory of Organizations, Labor Supply and Public Policy,* and *Population, Public Policy, and Economic Development* as well as numerous articles in management and applied philosophy journals.

EDWIN E. LOCKE is Dean's Professor of Leadership and Motivation Emeritus at the R.H. Smith School of Business at the University of

Maryland, College Park. He is internationally known for his research and writings on work motivation, leadership, and related topics, including the application of objectivism to psychology and management. He is a senior writer for the Ayn Rand Institute.

TERRY L. PRICE is associate professor of leadership studies at the University of Richmond's Jepson School of Leadership Studies. He is co-editor of *The International Library of Leadership*, forthcoming from Edward Elgar Press, and author of *Understanding Ethical Failures in Leadership: The Moral Psychology of Exception Making*, forthcoming from Cambridge University Press.

ROBERT C. SOLOMON is Quincy Lee Centennial Professor of business and philosophy and distinguished teaching professor at the University of Texas at Austin. He is the author of more than 37 books including *Above the Bottom Line*, *It's Good Business*, *Ethics and Excellence*, and *New World of Business*, as well as *The Passions*, *In the Sprit of Hegel*, *About Love*, *A Passion for Justice*, *Up the University*, *A Short History of Philosophy*, *The Joy of Philosophy*, and *Building Trust* with Chilean Senator Fernando Flores.

PAUL STEIDLMEIER is associate professor of management in the School of Management of Binghamton University (SUNY). He is a specialist in international economic development strategy and in business and society relations. His publications include *People and Profits: The Ethics of Capitalism* and articles on business ethics in China and developing countries.